The Insider-Outsider of Early 20th-Century German Industry

The Insider-Outsider of Early 20th-Century German Industry

Günter Henle and the Klöckner Steel Conglomerate, 1899–1955

Volker R. Berghahn

BLOOMSBURY ACADEMIC

LONDON • NEW YORK • OXFORD • NEW DELHI • SYDNEY

BLOOMSBURY ACADEMIC
Bloomsbury Publishing Plc
50 Bedford Square, London, WC1B 3DP, UK
1385 Broadway, New York, NY 10018, USA
29 Earlsfort Terrace, Dublin 2, Ireland

BLOOMSBURY, BLOOMSBURY ACADEMIC and the Diana logo are trademarks of
Bloomsbury Publishing Plc

First published in Great Britain 2024

ISBN: HB: 978-1-3504-4844-5
ePDF: 978-1-3504-4845-2
eBook: 978-1-3504-4846-9

Typeset by Newgen KnowledgeWorks Pvt. Ltd., Chennai, India

To find out more about our authors and books visit www.bloomsbury.com
and sign up for our newsletters.

Contents

Acknowledgments   vi
List of Abbreviations   viii

Introduction   1
1   The First Decades from Hohenzollern Monarchy and Weimar
    Republic through the End of the Nazi Dictatorship   9
2   British Occupation Policies, 1945–6   41
3   Decartelization, Dismantling, and Deconcentration   63
4   The United States and the Completion of the Reshaping of West
    German Industry   87
5   The Origins and Creation of the European Coal and Steel Community 111
6   Some Concluding Topics for Future Research   139
Conclusion   159

Notes   161
Select Bibliography   187
Index   189

Acknowledgments

As happens to most authors whose books are based on years of scholarly research in archives and libraries, the books could not have been written without the exchange of ideas and the advice of friends and colleagues.

Among them I would like to mention first of all Bernd Weisbrod. After he had read my biography of Hans-Günther Sohl and his close professional and cultural relationship with Günter Henle, we discussed my idea of writing a study of Henle's life and work. There were considerable collections of documents relating to the Klöckner corporation that Henle had rebuilt after 1945. I had also read Henle's memoirs, but only to find that they were quite sparse on his family background. Henle had passed away in 1979, and I was wondering if there were members of his family who would be able to help me with my plans. Bernd Weisbrod happened to know from his years in the History Department of Bochum University his daughter-in-law, Susanne Henle. I wrote to her, and over the next few years I was grateful not only for the advice he shared with me based on his deep knowledge of German industrial history and of iron and steel in particular but also for facilitating my contact with her and her family.

She and her husband Peter together with their two sons, Clemens and Felix, became indispensable sources for my quest to retrieve Günter Henle's background and especially his life and work before 1945. Clemens Henle, who is himself researching the history of the Klöckner and Henle families with regard to both their European and American branches up to the 20th century, generously gave me access to the Familien-Archiv that he also curates. His brother Felix also joined in several most helpful meetings I had with the two of them in Düsseldorf.

While I therefore consider myself very fortunate to have met them and their parents and would like to thank them most sincerely, I also received excellent advice and many critical comments from trusted friends and colleagues who read different chapters of this book. In particular, I would like to express my gratitude to Manfred Rasch, Edzard Reuter, Gustav Schmidt, Ingrid Sommerkorn, Peter Soergel, Jonathan Wiesen, Jay Winter, and Fiona Jayatilaka.

Finally, there is Marion, my wife and gentle critic of virtually all my work. The discussions I had with her after she had read my chapters greatly helped me, as I was wrestling with Günter Henle's biography and how to define him as an

Insider-Outsider; how to interpret his silences, and his role as an anti-Nazi and member of the German-Jewish community whose life was threatened by Hitler's anti-Semitic policies, on the one hand, and, on the other, as a businessman who in the Second World War directed Klöckner & Co. and traveled around Europe as a steel merchant in the early 1940s. To her and our children I dedicate this book.

Abbreviations

AFL	American Federation of Labor
AKU	Allgemene Kunstzijde Unie N.V.
ATH	August-Thyssen-Hütte
BASF	Badische Anilin und Soda-Fabriken
BdA	Bundesvereinigung deutscher Arbeitgeberverbände
BDI	Bundesverband der Deutschen Industrie
BICO	Bipartite Control Office
BVG	Betriebsverfassungsgesetz
CDU	Christlich-Demokratische Union
CEO	Chief Executive Officer
CIO	Congress of Industrial Organization
CNPF	Conseil National du Patronat Francais
CSU	Christlich-Soziale Union
DGAP	Deutsche Gesellschaft fuer Auswärtige Politik
DGB	Deutscher Gewerkschaftsbund
DIHT	Deutscher Industrie- und Handelstag
DKBL	Deutsche Kohlenbergbau-Leitung
DKV	Deutscher Kohlenverkauf
DNVP	Deutschnationale Volkspartei
ECSC	European Coal and Steel Community
EEC	European Economic Community
EFTA	European Free Trade Association
ERP	European Recovery Program (Marshall Plan)
FDP	Freie Demokratische Partei
GEORG	Gemeinschaftsorganisation Ruhrkohle
GHH	Gutehoffnungshütte
HICOG	High Commission for Germany
ICI	Imperial Chemical Industries
IG	Industriegewerkschaft
IRA	International Ruhr Authority
IRC	International Raw Steel Cartel
ISEC	International Steel Export Cartel

JCS	Joint Chiefs of Staff
KHD	Klöckner-Humboldt-Deutz Corporation
NAM	National Association of Manufacturers
NATO	North Atlantic Treaty Organization
NGCC	North German Coal Control
NGISC	North German Iron and Steel Control
NSBO	Nationalsozialistische Betriebszellen-Organization
OMGUS	Office of Military Government US
RWHG	Reichswerke Hermann Göring
SA	Sturmabteilung
SPD	Sozialdemokratische Partei Deutsdchlands
SS	Schutzstaffel
TrHV	Treuhand-Verwaltung
TrV	Treuhand-Vereinigung
VDEh	Verein Deutscher Eisenhüttenleute
VfW	Verwaltung für Wirtschaft
VSt.	Vereinigte Stahlwerke
WSJ	*Wall Street Journal*
WVESI	Wirtschaftsvereinigung der Eisen- und Stahlindustrie

Introduction

Among Germany's big manufacturing engineering corporations of the postwar decades it was not just Daimler or Maschinenfabrik Augsburg-Nürnberg (MAN) but also Klöckner-Humboldt-Deutz and Magirus that were internationally known as makers of tractor-trailers and buses for commuters and long-distance railroad transportation. When it comes to steel-making, Klöckner is again among the major names, though it was not quite as big and widely recognized as Krupp and Thyssen or American, Japanese, and South Korean competitors. Locals will be familiar with the corporation's "Georgsmarienhütte," near Osnabrück in Westphalia, or the Troisdorf Steelworks, close to Bonn on the Rhine River. Still, these companies were part of Klöckner Werke Aktiengesellschaft (A.G.), a diversified heavy-industrial conglomerate with its trading arm of Klöckner & Company (Co.) operating in many parts of the world. Klöckner's expansion started after the First World War and continued after the defeat of the Nazi dictatorship in the Second World War. While Peter Klöckner, the founder of the conglomerate, had wide name recognition, Günter Henle, his son-in-law, may be less well-known, but, born in 1899, he became the driving force behind Klöckner's postwar reconstruction, first as its "Generaldirektor" and then as a member of the supervisory board. He died in 1979.

If we consider his position and influence in the powerful steel industry of the Ruhr region, Henle was no doubt an insider among the owners and managers of the big steel and mining corporations of the post-1945 decades. But what makes his life and work so intriguing and in need of closer study is that he was at the same time an outsider among his colleagues who formed something like the industrial establishment of West Germany's reconstructed heavy industry. To begin with, he was not a Bergassessor a.D., that is, a graduate of one of the mining academies who had served with one of the regional mining authorities before taking a position in one of the big coal and steel corporations. Unlike

many of his colleagues, Henle did not gain an expert knowledge of mining and iron as well as steel-making. Instead he had studied law at the universities of Würzburg and Marburg after the First World War and had joined the Foreign Office of the Weimar Republic where he served loyally in The Netherlands,

Argentina, and ultimately in the early 1930s under Leopold von Hoesch at the German embassy in London. His self-identity was that of a German patriot who, as a very young recruit, had fought in several of the horrific battles on the Western Front in 1917–18.

But what made him an outsider during the subsequent years under Nazism and the Hitler dictatorship was that his paternal grandfather hailed from a Jewish family. His great-grandparents remained Jewish but baptized his grandfather as a child, who then married into the landed Bavarian nobility. Günter's father, Julius, served in the bureaucracy of the Bavarian monarchy until 1918 during which he was elevated into the service nobility to become Julius von Henle and ultimately rose to the top position of Regierungspräsident (regional administrator) of Lower Franconia. No less significant, he continued to serve in this position during the Weimar Republic and the difficult years of political and economic upheaval in the 1920s until he reached retirement age in 1929. Having been subjected to popular anti-Semitism in Bavaria even before 1929, he spoke up against it.

His son first experienced anti-Semitic discrimination soon after the Nazi seizure of power in 1933, when his Würzburg fraternity humiliated him by revoking his membership because of his Jewish family background. It did not matter to his "brothers" that he was a decorated veteran of the First World War and could look back on a distinguished diplomatic career. Although he also fell under the discriminatory laws and decrees with which the Nazis began to oust German-Jewish civil servants and academics, his superiors at the London embassy protected him until the death of Hoesch in 1936. At that point, Joachim von Ribbentrop was sent to Britain to negotiate an alliance with Germany, and it was unacceptable for Günter Henle, by now classified as "quarter Jewish" under the Nazi Nuremberg Laws, to stay in the diplomatic service and asked to be retired. He was not jobless for long. In 1933, he had fallen in love and subsequently married the stepdaughter of Peter Klöckner, the steel industrialist, and in 1936 he joined this prosperous family enterprise.

When Peter Klöckner passed away in October 1940, and the family inherited the conglomerate, it was Hermann Göring who, with his appetite to enlarge his Reichswerke steel empire, came along with the local Gauleiter to expropriate the Klöckner heirs. The family survived economically because Günter Henle's friends and colleagues, most notably among them Karl Jarres, the former mayor of Duisburg where Klöckner was headquartered, negotiated a deal with the Reich economics ministry whereby the family was allowed to keep Klöckner's trading arm, Klöckner & Co. This enabled Günter Henle to travel in Germany, but also to The Netherlands and Switzerland, to trade steel products, indirectly contributing to Hitler's wars. However, he will also have realized that having been marked as "Jewish" under Nazi terminology that he, an anti-Nazi, was endangered at a time when the regime began to deport and murder Europe's Jewish populations. After all, by 1942–3 the Reich Führer SS Heinrich Himmler and his ilk began to target the male spouses of so-called mixed marriages. It seems that Henle was protected by his "Aryan" friends in the Ruhr industries—a story for which I will be providing more detail in Chapter 1.

The point to be made here is that, except for his autobiography dating from 1968 and studies on his musical legacy, the music publishing house G. Henle Verlag, there is no biography of Henle's industrial and political life and work. One reason for this lacuna is that professional historians of German business and industry have for many years been wedded to other genres of historical writing. Until the beginning of the current century they tended to be more interested in comprehensive analyses of the role of industry in the national economy and its connections with the international economy. They studied the growth of large corporations with a focus on quantitative performance, backed by tables and graphs.

It is only more recently that research began to shift toward an examination of the less tangible and more qualitative aspects of big business. Books appeared on management cultures or the complex relations with trade unions and employees of all stripes. Structures and organizations were at the center of earlier historical scholarship. The men who ran these corporations did not appear as individuals with complex biographies.

This book takes a different approach to the history of German heavy industry by dealing with the life and work of an individual, Günter Henle. It must be stressed that it is not a full "cradle-to-grave" biography, as such an enterprise would have obliged me to write a book of some five hundred or more pages. Instead, I decided to adopt a narrower focus by examining in more detail the two crucial lessons that Henle took away from his experience in Hitler's Third Reich and that he helped implement and practice in both his corporation and West Germany's steel industry during the postwar decades: the far-reaching reorganization of labor relations under the banner of codetermination. While the first chapters will examine him within the context of his larger economic and political activities, I shall also examine his second quest, that is, West Germany's reconciliation with her neighbors who had suffered under the Nazi occupation and European integration outside the Soviet Bloc from the 1950s onward. This also implies Henle's acceptance of the leading role of the United States as the postwar hegemonic power of the West and Washington's plans to create an Open Door world economy, based on economic competition and without protectionist territorial blocs and cartels in the European and particularly German tradition.

Henle's life and work after 1945 was not plain sailing. In 1945, after encouraging him to rebuild his corporation in the summer of 1945, the British occupation authorities suddenly interned him on December 1 under an Allied automatic arrest decree. Released in September 1946, he resumed his directorship of the badly damaged Klöckner Werke A.G., parts of which the British occupation authorities had begun to dismantle and to deconcentrate. But with the beginning of the Cold War, the top decision makers in the White House and in Congress began to reverse the initial punitive course of the Morgenthau Plan against West German industry and banking and promoted reconstruction. Henle was now able to rebuild Klöckner Werke into an international conglomerate that included the Klöckner-Humboldt-Deutz machine engineering corporation in Cologne. As before, Klöckner & Co., the relatively smaller family firm, acted as the global trading arm of the larger conglomerate.

Henle, the former Weimar diplomat, had, after moving to Klöckner, never been one of those notoriously autocratic steel bosses of the Ruhr region. Hailing from a Bavarian family of civil servants, he was not only a highly educated person who had a deep knowledge of European culture but was also an accomplished pianist. On one occasion, while serving at the German embassy in Buenos Aires in the 1920s, Henle played the solo part of Beethoven's choral phantasy for piano, choir, and orchestra. After 1945, he expanded these interests and established the G. Henle Music Publishing House that still enjoys a very high reputation around the world for editing and publishing original scores of a wide range of classical compositions.

However, the focus of this book is not on this publishing house nor on the growth of the Klöckner A.G. and its subsidiaries during the 1960s and 1970s. I hope that an economic historian will write the latter's larger business history on the basis of massive archival documentation that this scholar will have at their disposal. At the center of this more limited study is Henle's role in the reorganization of labor relations in the postwar steel industry and the introduction of parity codetermination, which put equal representation of the two sides of industry on the supervisory boards of the large steel companies as well as a worker director with equal rights on the management board. The other political achievement of Henle in the early postwar period to be discussed in more detail in subsequent chapters is his role in the integration of Western Europe.

This very compressed summary of Henle's early life and work provides, I hope, a few hints as to why I wanted to undertake a more focused study of a life that, in so many ways, was quite extraordinary and certainly different from that of the other members of the Ruhr industrial establishment. After publishing biographies of two other prominent West German businessmen— Otto A. Friedrich of the Phoenix tire manufacturer in Hamburg-Harburg and powerful CEO of Thyssen Steel, Hans-Günther Sohl—it is now for the third time that I am venturing to write a study of yet another industrialist who lived through the Nazi ordeal and played an important role in the reconstruction of West Germany after 1945. I do so again with some hesitation. To my mind, biography is the most difficult genre of historical writing, and certainly more difficult than telling the organizational history of a political party, or of a cultural or economic association, all of which tend to be quite *menschenleer* (devoid of human beings). Moreover, the biographer is under a special obligation to immerse themselves as deeply as possible in a human life and to deal with its complexities, with its twists and turns, and its ups and downs, while also bearing in mind the larger socioeconomic, political, and cultural environment in which an individual lived and acted. This applies especially to Germans of Henle's generation who survived the Hitler dictatorship and, occupying influential positions in the economy after 1945, were faced in the 1930s and early 1940s with often agonizing moral choices between collaboration and resistance. The earlier studies of Friedrich and Sohl examine how they confronted these choices.[1] But Henle's biography presents an even more complex picture when it comes to the Nazi period as well as the early postwar decades.

There is a final aspect that also motivated me to write this book. As I assembled the Henle family's history, I learned that Peter Henle, Günter's son, was married to Susanne, whose father Berthold Beitz, together with his wife, is honored at Yad Vashem in Israel as a "Righteous Among the Nations." As Yad Vashem's comprehensive investigations confirmed, both of them rescued many Jews when they were sent to Borislav in Galicia during the Second World War where Berthold Beitz managed an oil company and witnessed the brutal treatment of Jews by the SS.[2] In a further twist of history, Beitz started his postwar career with an insurance company in Hamburg, but then joined Alfried Krupp in Essen. The latter had been tried at Nuremberg and imprisoned as a war criminal, until he was pardoned by John McCloy, the US High Commissioner in West Germany. Berthold Beitz now became Alfried Krupp's right-hand person who helped him to rebuild the Krupp empire in the 1950s and 1960s.[3] This means that Beitz, like Henle, was both an outsider and insider, first as a rescuer of persecuted Jews when many of his colleagues collaborated with the Nazis, and again after 1945 as Krupp's top manager, which he joined without the title of Bergassessor a.D. and without being familiar with mining and steel-making. That the Henle and Beitz families should intermarry is surely another remarkable reflection of the drama of German history in the 20th century that is worth mentioning.

If these were, in rough outline, the problems I was facing when I began to read about Günter Henle, the genre of biography offers one advantage: its organizing principle is more straightforward than that of political or economic historians or social scientists who tend to take a "structuralist" approach to their research. By contrast, in Chapter 1, I will be primarily concerned with the unfolding of Günter Henle's life and work from his childhood and socialization into the world in which he was born at the turn of the 20th century. The most plausible approach to take is therefore a quite strictly chronological one, even if it is also necessary to provide context and to introduce various other topics synchronically to cover parallel events and experiences. Accordingly, the main chapters that follow deal first with Henle's upbringing and education up to his early professional life as a foreign service officer in the 1920s and 1930s as well as his experiences as an endangered businessman during the "Third Reich" up to the end of the Second World War.

This chapter relies rather heavily on the memoirs that Henle published in 1968 and therefore raises questions of gaps and silences.[4] However, I was fortunate in that the Henle family gave me access to a number of documents, such as the long questionnaire (Fragebogen) that Günter Henle had to fill in as part of the denazification procedure that most adult Germans had to submit after 1945. Yet, in the absence of more detailed primary sources, it seemed legitimate to extract from his book's early chapters information that give an impression of who Henle was and what had shaped him in the first decades of his life and work. This chapter is also focused on Henle's situation during and several months beyond the end of the war until November 1945 when he struggled to rebuild the corporation that the Nazi regime had taken away from him. There are also the anxieties that Nazi persecution created for men like Henle who was married to a Christian so that this chapter will say something about the increasingly precarious predicament of families with a Jewish background. It is my attempt to reveal both the continuities and discontinuities across the divide of the defeat of Nazism and the reconstruction of West Germany.

Chapter 2 then examines how the British occupation authorities suddenly implemented an automatic arrest decree in the autumn of 1945 under which dozens of managers were forced to abandon their early rebuilding efforts.

Günter Henle, too, was sent to Bad Nenndorf near Hannover in Lower Saxony where he was harshly interrogated. Subsequently, he was put into an internment camp at Eselheide near Paderborn in Westphalia until the autumn of 1946 when he returned to Duisburg to lead his badly ruined enterprise after he had been "denazified."

Chapter 3 covers Henle's campaigns against British attempts to split up the Klöckner conglomerate. Partially successful, he continued Peter Klöckner's policy of rebuilding a complex steel-making and manufacturing engineering empire during the years of economic boom and prosperity in the 1950s. This was also the time when, as discussed in Chapter 4, he helped put the system of codetermination in coal and steel on the statute book that created a new socioeconomic partnership between owners and managers of the heavy industries in the Ruhr region, on the one hand, and the employees and trade unions, on the other. As a firm believer in the need to integrate Western Europe, Henle then played an important role in the creation of the European Coal and Steel Community (ECSC) of 1951, examined in Chapter 5 also in terms of its impact on the Allied program of deconcentration of the country's big conglomerates in the Ruhr region, but also in chemicals and electrical engineering.

If, apart from his fighting in the First World War, the 1930s and early 1940s under Nazism, as well as the two postwar decades were the truly dramatic years in Henle's life, Chapter 6 discusses a number of topics that touch upon Henle's life as an industrialist during the 1960s and 1970s and that will have to be more fully researched in a separate business history of the Klöckner conglomerate in the 20th century. The conclusion returns to the underlying issue of Henle as an insider-outsider and the unusual history of his family at a time of momentous socioeconomic, political, and cultural change in Central Europe.

The First Decades from Hohenzollern Monarchy and Weimar Republic through the End of the Nazi Dictatorship

Early Years in Bavaria in War and Peace, 1899–1922

When Günter Henle was born on February 3, 1899, his father Julius was employed as a higher civil servant in the region of Lower Franconia within the Kingdom of Bavaria.[1] Julius was born in 1864 and had completed his law degree in 1888 before he opted for his civil service career. Having obtained a couple of promotions, he worked in the Bavarian Ministry of the Interior where he gained a reputation as one of its most promising administrators. No less significant, Julius came from a large, prominent Jewish family that included the pioneering anatomist Jacob Henle. Jacob, a teacher of the microbiologist Robert Koch, had been baptized as a child as the family converted to Catholicism. Due to anti-Semitic laws that denied residency to more than one heir for each Jewish family in Bavaria, Julius' paternal grandparents, even though they refused to convert to Christianity, gradually baptized all their children. One of them, Julius's father Otto, a pharmacist in Regensburg, had married Eleonore Edle von Widmann, who hailed from the Franconian landed nobility. Julius's parents did everything to hide its Jewish family history. As it happened, Henle was a common surname among Catholic Swabians, and this coincidence seems to have given them some protection against a popular anti-Semitism that was on the rise in the later 19th century. After all, the bishop of Regensburg and Passau, Anton von Henle, could easily be mistaken as a distant relative. With his aristocratic mother being a staunch Catholic, Julius had all the social credentials, and these were more important than Otto's ancestry.

Continuing his rise in the Bavarian civil service, Julius was promoted ministerial counsellor (Ministerialrat) in 1908 and ministerial director (Ministerialdirektor) four years later. In 1913, the king of Bavaria recognized his services and achievements, for example, in the fields of health insurance and poverty relief, by elevating him to the service nobility. Henceforth his name was Julius Ritter von

Henle, though the title was not hereditary so that his children carried the name without the noble prefix. In the meantime, he had married Lida whose mother had Anglo-Saxon roots in the United States and had been raised in the Protestant faith. The Catholic Church in Rome and in Bavaria expected children to be raised in the Catholic faith, but Lida, the Protestant, insisted that she was responsible for the education of the von Henle children. Her influence prevailed, so that her son Günter, when filling in the questionnaire that the Allies required most adult Germans to complete after 1945 as part of their denazification policy, did not mention his Jewish family background and merely stated that he was Lutheran.

At the outbreak of the First World War, the fifty-year-old Julius von Henle signed up as a volunteer with the Bavarian Landwehr where he rose to the rank of major and was awarded the Iron Cross First and Second Class. Discharged in 1917, he was appointed regional president (Regierungspräsident) for Lower Franconia, which lay in the northern part of the Bavarian kingdom, with the ancient city of Würzburg as its capital. As before, Julius proved to be a skillful and circumspect administrator who was able to navigate his region through Germany's military defeat by the Western Allies, the collapse of the monarchy in November 1918, and the revolutionary upheavals of 1919. After the establishment of the parliamentary-democratic Weimar Republic, Julius stayed on as regional president and steered Franconia through the years of instability during the early 1920s. In 1923, followed the catastrophe of the hyperinflation, the collapse of the economy, and the abortive attempt by Adolf Hitler and former General Erich Ludendorff in November to overthrow the Weimar Republic. Between 1924 and 1929 the political system and the economy restabilized and von Henle continued his work as unelected regional president, paying particular attention to health care and local agriculture. He took retirement on August 1, 1929, just before the onset of the Great Depression. Having received further honors from the City of Würzburg, he returned to Munich where he and Lida resided in a very upscale apartment at Prinzregentenplatz in the center of the city.

Julius von Henle had received significant honors for his services as regional president. Among them was an honorary doctorate from the University of Würzburg in 1922 at which point he also became an honorary member of its academic senate. The city named a street after him, and in the nearby spa town of Bad Kissingen one of the walks for guests taking a cure was known as the Von Henle path. Julius was also a highly cultured person. Although he did not play an instrument, he was a lover of classical music and a supporter of the city's professional musicians and the arts more generally. In short, both as a civil servant and as a private citizen Julius tried to live up to the constitutional standards of the Bavarian monarchy before 1918 and of the Weimar Republic in the 1920s. In this, he was supported by his wife Lida who had a daughter Ilse, a year before Günter, with both children growing up in a sheltered upper-class environment.

Lida had an unusual family background. After her forbears had emigrated to North America on the Mayflower in the 17th century, her great-grandfather settled in Cuba where he had built a sugar plantation that was worked by slaves imported from Africa. When her grandfather died, her grandmother and her mother Georgiana moved from Cuba to New York where she married William

Albert, the owner of a toy store. However, the 1870s were years of economic depression and Albert's overextended business folded. It was at this point that he turned to his German relatives who had stayed behind in Frankfurt. They put him in touch with a British private bank with investments in railways. Ultimately, he was fortunate enough to be offered the directorship of the Metropolitan Railways Company's office in Constantinople in 1875. Eventually his wife and daughters joined him there. As Albert's new job was not particularly onerous, he had time to involve himself in the local German diaspora. He became the president of the "Teutonia Club" and also managed to garner a position as honorary consul and diplomatic representative of the United States. In his various jobs Albert accumulated enough wealth to take his family vacations on the Bosporus and to travel with his daughters to Germany for summer vacations. It was possibly on one of these trips to Munich that Lida met the young Julius.

Unfortunately, we know little about Julius's and Lida's life and their experiences and attitudes under National Socialism after their retirement. For decades they had seen themselves as Christian Germans, only to find that the Nazis denied them their identity and turned them into a discriminated "un-German" minority. They will naturally have been aware of the dramatic political changes around them and must have been greatly worried about the Hitler movement, even before 1933, as the Nazis and the SA (Stormtroopers) were very visible in their Munich neighborhood, with Hitler's headquarters not far away. There is at least one tangible piece of evidence of Julius's attitude: The May 1930 issue of the *Abwehrblätter*, the monthly journal of the *Verein zur Abwehr des Antisemitismus*, published an article entitled "Bayerische Stimmen gegen Judenhass" in which von Henle and a number of other well-known public figures, such as Professor Lujo Brentano, Jacobus von Hauck, the arch bishop of Bamberg, and Dr. Wilhelm Hoegner, submitted a statement. Julius wrote that "anti-Semitism is a cultural disgrace (*Kulturschande)* fighting against which is the task of every thoughtful (*einsichtigen*) friend of the Fatherland." It was a statement that the Nazis apparently remembered when they seized power in 1933. Von Henle became a target of their rabid anti-Semitism, with the new Franconian government eventually changing the name of the street in Würzburg that its Republican predecessors had named in his honor. When the Hitler regime promulgated the Nuremberg Laws in 1935 in which "non-Aryans" were registered by their Jewish ancestry, Julius von Henle became categorized as "half-Jewish."

It would be interesting to have at least some reliable information about the couple's reactions to the escalating discrimination against Jewish families, friends, and neighbors around them between 1933 and the outbreak of war, particularly, for example, to the 1938 pogrom. Nor do we know how endangered Julius von Henle felt when the Nazis began to deport the Jewish husbands in so-called mixed marriages—a topic that we shall have to come back to in the context of his son Günter's life and work, since he, too, was married to a Protestant wife. Apparently, Julius remained physically unharmed by the regime, possibly protected by influential former colleagues and friends. He died peacefully on February 16, 1944. He was buried in the city's Waldfriedhof, with his family seeing to it that his grave was regularly planted with flowers well into the postwar period.

Julius's and Lida's son Günter, born in February 1899, grew up in Munich where he attended primary school from 1905 and the local Realgymnasium thereafter. Encouraged by his parents, he also took lessons with the well-known pianist Walter Lampe as well as the violinist Herma Studeny. He was in his final two high school years when the First World War broke out in August 1914. Too young to be immediately mobilized, he was, as so many of his generation, a patriotic teenager who, having just turned seventeen after his school graduation in 1916, signed up for a royal field artillery regiment in Munich. He was transferred to the 11th Bavarian field artillery regiment at Würzburg whence he was deployed to the Western Front. In early 1918 he was attached to one of the still embryonic flying corps but was then sent into action in the trenches of the Western Front and participated in some of the harrowing battles. Eventually he earned the Iron Cross Second and later First Class, as well as the Bavarian War Service medal Fourth Class with swords, plus a Front Soldier Cross, certifying that he had seen frontline action. Unfortunately, his memoirs contain little information on his wartime experiences, but he certainly came back politicized.

By the summer 1918 it had dawned on the young Henle that the Kaiser's spring offensive was grinding to a halt after the arrival of fresh American troops deployed to roll back the German advance in France. In November, the imperial government of Prince Max von Baden was forced to sign an armistice. Wilhelm II fled into his Dutch exile, while Henle returned to his home base in Würzburg, refusing to feel dejected by the end of the fighting. After radical left-wing revolts that broke out in Berlin, Munich, and the Ruhr industrial region, although largely sparing Würzburg, Henle volunteered as a Lieutenant of the Reserve to serve in government units that defeated the leftist uprisings in Munich and Plauen. Subsequently, he registered at Würzburg University and for a semester also at the University of Marburg to lay the foundations for a professional career. Veterans like him were given preferential treatment, and so he was able to pass his first law exams in the summer of 1920 and thereafter qualified for a "Dr. jur. et rer. pol.," although it should be added that it was possible to obtain a law school doctorate by submitting a relatively short analysis of some legal case so that it did not take him years of research in archives as was expected in the humanities. Henle later admitted that he was surprised to be awarded a summa cum laude for his work—though he also wrote that he appeared for the oral examination before a committee of professors not only in the requisite coat tails but also with his military decorations on his chest. Clearly, this was bound to put his committee in the mood to treat him generously.

However, Henle did not spend all his time preparing for his exams in a hurry. When the right-wing Kapp-Putsch broke out to topple the Weimar government in March 1920 and the trade unions proclaimed a general strike, the insurgents were quickly defeated. After this, it was for the extreme left to stage several uprisings, and Henle joined voluntary units that were deployed in their suppression. In the spring of 1921, Max Hoelz led a left-wing coup in the Mansfeld region west of Halle, and again Henle fought with troops that were brought in to stop Hoelz. It is also telling of Henle's political views at this time that he became a member of two student fraternities in Würzburg and Marburg that practiced ritualized duels with sharp-edged sabers. The deep scars inflicted on him by an opponent from another fraternity remained visible on his left cheek and forehead for the rest of his life. They were visible marks of his bourgeois background, while his distant Jewish family roots were swept under the carpet. It was only the anti-Semitic policies of the Nazis and their right-wing allies after 1933 that confronted Henle with this family background, as will be seen when we discuss his career during the "Third Reich" and the humiliating treatment he received by his fraternity "brothers."

Life as a Diplomat in Weimar Germany and the "Third Reich," 1923–36

With his doctoral examinations behind him, Günter Henle faced the question of what to do professionally. There was the possibility of following in his father's footsteps and of becoming a civil servant. With the encouragement of his parents, he had also become an accomplished pianist. Apart from studying under Lampe, he had also taken lessons with such famous teachers as the renowned Beethoven interpreter Frederick Lamond. Years later, as noted in the introduction, Henle was still accomplished enough to play the solo part of Beethoven's choral phantasy for piano, choir, and orchestra. A third option was the diplomatic service, and when he made inquiries with the German Foreign Ministry and received an encouraging response, Henle opted for a career that, after passing the requisite tests, put him inside the time-honored office building of the Bismarckian era in Berlin's Wilhelmstrasse for his initial training.[2] It seems that his politics had become more centrist and pro-Republican. In his memoirs, Henle respectfully remembered foreign ministers Walther Rathenau, Joseph Wirth, Friedrich Rosen, and Gustav Stresemann under whom he served and who he observed closely as shapers of German foreign relations in difficult times during the 1920s. During this time, he prepared for another major Foreign Ministry examination in May 1923 for which he wrote a preparatory research paper on the postwar rebuilding of Germany's commercial fleet and passed with a grade of "good."

Having crossed this hurdle, Henle received his first diplomatic posting to the consulate general in Amsterdam at the end of 1923. And just as he had used his stay in Berlin to enjoy the musical life of the German capital, he now attended the orchestral concerts that were performed in Amsterdam's Concertgebouw. After meeting the Baroness van Tyll van Serooskerken, who was an "outstanding violinist," he repeatedly accompanied her on the piano. On Sundays, he would visit the renowned Rijks-Museum where he discovered his love for the masters of 17th-century Dutch painting.

Keen to get to know South America, Henle applied for a transfer and in May 1925 was sent to the German embassy in Buenos Aires. Soon after this arrival he learned of the political-ideological conflicts within the local German community that made dealing with its members just about the "most difficult [assignment] abroad." However, he was happy to attend events at the German-Argentinian Society and to meet visitors, such as the wartime British prime minister David Lloyd George and Reich chancellor Hans Luther. Luther had facilitated the ratification of the Locarno treaty that Stresemann and Aristide Briand had signed in 1925 and which came to be celebrated as a major breakthrough in Franco-German relations. Henle also used his time to travel to Brazil, Paraguay, and Chile, but as before in Europe he always came back to his love of music. Among the famous artists with whom he established a close friendship was the Austrian conductor Erich Kleiber whose dress rehearsals he frequently attended. Kleiber met his wife through Henle who became the godfather of young Carlos Kleiber. Later Carlos followed his father as a conductor and was arguably even more famous.

Henle's rich formative years in South America during which he perfected his Spanish and Portuguese ended in 1929 when he was called back to Berlin, initially hoping to be given the traditional six-month leave. He was instead told that his experience was urgently required without a break. In the autumn of 1929 the stock market had crashed and several international agreements had to be negotiated. After Stresemann's death and the steep rise in German unemployment, Europe became the focus of German diplomacy. In 1931, Henle was assigned to the embassy in London. His first boss was Konstantin von Neurath who was called back to Berlin in the summer of 1932 to become foreign minister in the cabinet of Reich chancellor Franz von Papen. Neurath was replaced in London by Leopold von Hoesch, who, as ambassador in Paris, had worked hard to improve Franco-German relations. Both von Hoesch and Henle now quickly gained the confidence of the British political establishment at a time when, following the Nazi seizure of power in January 1933, Anglo-German relations were encountering increasing difficulties. Was Hitler to be trusted when he offered a peace-pipe to Britain by talking about an Anglo-German alliance and negotiating the 1935 Naval Agreement while simultaneously introducing universal military service in breach of the Versailles Treaty? Was it the "Führer's" hope to cut a deal with the British government whereby he would not challenge Britain's overseas Empire, provided the appeasers in the London cabinet allowed him to acquire "living space" in Eastern Europe? What did Hitler mean when, after the sudden death of von Hoesch in 1936, he appointed Joachim von Ribbentrop, his trusted foreign policy "expert," as the new ambassador to the Court of St. James, sending him off with the mandate that he should bring him "the alliance with England"?

During his five years in London, Henle took the opportunity of informing himself about both official and popular British public opinion. He joined local social associations such as the St. James Club and the Queens Club while also witnessing the evolution of Anglo-German relations under Hitler with growing unease. Like other colleagues critical of Nazi foreign policy, he inevitably began to appear in the crosshairs of the new architects of German diplomacy in Berlin. With anti-Semitic policies assuming ever more dogmatic forms, Henle also became a target of Hitler's racism. Although he never mentioned it in his memoirs, his father Julius von Henle had in Nazi terminology become a "half-Jew." It did not matter to the regime that Henle's grandfather had converted to Christianity long ago as a child, that Julius had been baptized, and that Julius's father Otto, Julius himself, and his son Günter had all married Christian women. Under the Nuremberg Laws Julius was "half-Jewish," and it did not matter that Günter's self-definition, like that of his father, was that they were above all patriotic Germans. The Nazis also took no account of the fact that he had fought in the First World War and that, as a highly decorated veteran, his "Germanness" was part of his identity. Instead Jews were now deemed part of an "un-German race." However, as a Legationsrat at the German embassy in London he was a civil servant to whom the Civil Service Law that the Nazis had introduced in 1933 applied. While Jewish professors and other civil servants had their rights of lifetime tenure cancelled and were dismissed, the purge did not immediately affect Foreign Ministry personnel, and it may well be that von Hoesch, a conservative, held his protective hand over Henle.

When standing trial as a war criminal at Nuremberg in 1946, Ribbentrop, whom Hitler had appointed foreign minister after the failure of the 1936 London ambassadorial mission, claimed not to have been an anti-Semite and there is evidence that he kept a German-Jewish diplomat in his ministry as late as 1944. But this did not prevent Ribbentrop's entourage at the embassy from eyeing Henle with suspicion. After all, there was the Civil Service Law that in principle also applied to him. This may explain why soon after Hoesch's death he was recalled to Berlin where he was told that his services were no longer required and that he should ask for his (at first provisional and later definitive) retirement—on the grounds, as he put it in his postwar Allied denazification questionnaire—because one of his grandfathers had been Jewish-born. That he never tried to join the Nazi Party may also have been a factor that put his career under a cloud. Nor did he become a member of Nazi affiliates, though he remained with the Deutsche Jägerschaft and may have joined the Reichsluftschutzbund. However, in his questionnaire he listed this latter membership merely as a possibility, as he was uncertain about it and may have confused it with his wife's. Since the Foreign Ministry granted him retirement status, he probably received a small pension.

Working for Klöckner and Surviving Rising Nazi Anti-Semitism, 1937–45

Günter Henle was not without a job for long. In 1932, he had repeatedly been invited to social evenings by Robert Lehr, then mayor of Düsseldorf, and on one of these occasions he met Anne-Liese, the step-daughter of the well-known industrialist Peter Klöckner.[3] They fell in love and got married in the summer of 1933. With their three children who were born in 1934, 1937, and 1938, the young couple enjoyed the social and cultural life of London, even if his job at the German embassy became more and more stressful. After he was forced to leave the Foreign Ministry, it was his father-in-law who rescued him. Born in the Rhineland in 1863, Peter Klöckner had at first specialized in the iron trade but was able to move into steel-making when he saved the "Hasper Eisenwerk" in Hagen in the southern part of the Ruhr region from bankruptcy in the 1890s. In 1903, he joined the supervisory board of the "Aumetz-Friede" steelworks in Lorraine that also required restructuring. Having converted the enterprise into a shareholding company, the Klöckner A.G., Peter built it up into one of the most modern heavy-industrial enterprises in Western Europe. By 1911, he had added two coalmines at Castorp-Rauxel in the eastern Ruhr region northwest of Dortmund, thus practicing Verbundwirtschaft, that is, the close integration of coal and steel.

Peter Klöckner always saw his growing, trans-regional conglomerate also as a trading house and therefore founded Klöckner & Co. jointly with his brother Florian in Duisburg in 1906 to act as a bridge between the steel-making, manufacturing, engineering, and sales. Having lost the works in Lorraine after the First World War, his Klöckner Werke A.G. went even more determinedly into steel-processing. He expanded the Haspe complex by another one at Georgsmarienhütte south of Osnabrück in Westphalia. In Osnabrück itself, he continued the casting of wheels for locomotives and wagons, added another mill at Troisdorf near Siegburg east of Bonn, and a third one at Quint near the ancient Roman city of Trier on the Moselle river. Finally, in the 1920s, he moved into machine manufacturing when he integrated the gas-engine factories at Deutz just east of Cologne with another engine factory further south at Oberursel, northwest of Frankfurt. In short, the industrialist now was the co-owner of Klöckner & Co. and a major shareholder in Klöckner A.G., the whole comprising a systematically diversified steel trust, one of the largest conglomerates in Germany.

The Great Depression of the early 1930s hit the conglomerate hard. But in January 1933, after the Nazi's seizure of power Hitler, having promised to pull the country out of its economic hole and to solve the problem of mass unemployment, adopted a policy of what has been called "military Keynesianism" by placing large state orders with heavy industry. What differentiated Hitler's economic policy from that of Franklin D. Roosevelt's New Deal in the United States was that it was designed to rearm the country in preparation for the eventual acquisition of "living space" in a war of expansion and uninhibited looting. Whatever his long-term aims, Hitler's "military Keynesianism" was a great boost to the steel and manufacturing engineering industries. For example, Krupp received orders from the army for military vehicles that, in light of the restrictions of the Versailles treaty, were camouflaged as trucks and agricultural tractors. The Klöckner Werke A.G. also benefited from this rearmament program and the resulting expansion of the economy. By February 1934, Georgsmarienhütte was able to resume continuous production. By 1935, its rolling mill capacities had been reinforced, and three years later a third blast furnace had been added. Klöckner's diversification strategy also evolved successfully when in 1936 the company took a stake in the Magirus Works at Ulm in South Germany, a leader in the manufacturing of trucks, buses, and fire engines. Thus, even if Peter Klöckner had reservations about the Nazi regime, never joined the party, and was on the Gestapo's watch list, this did not stop his firm from exploiting the opportunities that Hitler's rearmament program presented.

Having turned seventy-three in 1936, Peter Klöckner had been hoping that his son Waldemar would eventually take over from him. But shortly before his 23rd birthday Waldemar was killed in a car accident on December 21, 1936. His father and the family were devastated. There were no other children so that Peter Klöckner began to consider his son-in-law as a successor after Henle had lost his Foreign Ministry job. It was but a small step for him to join the corporation and he did so on January 2, 1937. Having had no commercial training, he first immersed himself in the trading side of Klöckner & Co., acquiring the necessary business expertise before learning about the complexities of iron- and steel-making, also by taking evening courses at Berlin's Technical University. He joined the executive boards of the works of the Klöckner Werke A.G. and also became a junior partner in Klöckner & Co. with its headquarters in Duisburg on the Rhine.

Although busy in his new jobs, Henle did not feel overburdened as long as his father-in-law was alive. One of the tasks he took on in 1938 and 1939 was to represent Klöckner in the Steel Works Association (Stahlwerksverband), a lobby that had closed ranks at the end of 1938, probably in response to Göring's and his sidekick Paul Pleiger's attempts to establish the predominance of their state-owned steel-making empire, the Reichswerke Hermann Göring (RWHG). This Nazi juggernaut had been founded in the context of Hitler's 1936 Four-Year Plan, This stipulated, in a secret appendix, that Germany's rearmament program on land must be completed by 1940. While planning to launch his long envisaged conquest of "living space" in the East and the exploitation of the defeated Soviet Union by the early 1940s, preparations had begun in 1938–9 to create a formidable air force with long-range bombers, capable of hitting New York, and a navy with super battleships and aircraft carriers for future transcontinental warfare against the United States and the British Empire and Commonwealth. The Steel Works Association, chaired by Ernst Poensgen, the CEO of the mighty Vereinigte Stahlwerke (VSt.), was meant to act as a counterweight to the Reichswerke. With its byelaws approved in October 1938, it quickly succeeded in December 1938 in lifting a temporary ban on orders (Auftragssperre), probably imposed by their RWHG competitor.[4]

However, tensions soon also arose between the members of the association over production allocations and prices charged. As one of the smaller enterprises, Klöckner felt sidelined by the larger corporations, and in December 1939 Henle was sent to try to persuade Walter Schwede of VSt. to end the association's discriminatory policies.[5] The latter expressed sympathy but then strung Klöckner along. Henle tried again in July 1940.[6] These negotiations indicated that the traditional German cartel system to regulate quotas and prices was not a cushy horizontal agreement between independent companies but a source of friction, which provides one reason why—as will be seen in later chapters—the Americans wanted to destroy cartels after 1945.[7] According to the Henle Papers disagreements also arose over how to deal with pensions and who to nominate as successor to chairs when the holders decided to retire.[8] There was also the problem in June 1941 of what to do, in advance of the invasion of the Soviet Union, with a proposed "Ukraine Committee." This had presumably been established for the exploitation of the Stalinist empire's southern region, rich in coal, iron ore, and manganese deposits expected to fall into German hands after another short lightning war, this time against the Soviet Union.[9]

It is striking that Henle dutifully notified the association and other groups, such as the Bochumer Verband, when he was unable to attend one of their meetings. It is not clear from the available evidence whether he genuinely had other, more important, engagements or whether he wanted to distance himself from these lobbies, especially after the death of Peter Klöckner in October 1940, whereafter Henle increasingly came under pressure because of his Jewish ancestry. The change in the political climate and the growing influence of the Nazi regime upon industry is also reflected in the changes of the greetings at the end of letters to be found in the Henle Papers. In 1938–9 letters were still signed with the traditional "freundlichen Glückauf!"[10] The next step was to sign with "Glückauf und Heil Hitler!," until the obligatory "Heil Hitler!" appeared at the bottom of most correspondences.[11]

Peter Klöckner's death left his widow, Henle, and the family with a huge responsibility of the conglomerate with its thousands of employees. There was of course also the old question of how to deal with the Hitler dictatorship and in particular with Göring, the regional Gauleiter, and the growing pressures to produce coal, steel, machinery, and other war materials at a time when the Wehrmacht, having defeated Poland in 1939, had conquered France and the rest of Western Europe as well as Denmark and Norway in 1940.[12] Only Sweden had been exempted from occupation, based on the calculation that, by accepting Swedish neutrality, it would be possible to obtain large quantities of high-quality iron ore on a barter basis. Having occupied Norway and gained

Stockholm's cooperation, the Nazis refrained from conquering this particular Nordic kingdom, as this would merely have exposed the long railroad routes from Kiruna and other mines in the far North to Swedish resistance groups, the more so after the sea lanes from Narvik along the Norwegian coast to the port of Emden in Germany were being increasingly blocked by the Royal Navy.

However, by the winter of 1940–1, Henle's dilemma became more acute as to whether to collaborate or shift to the type of covert economic opposition that other steel trusts, such as VSt., entertained at this time.[13] The Nazi conquest of "living space" and the invasion of the Soviet Union had been on the cards since Peter Klöckner's passing in the autumn of 1940, when Anne-Liese Henle as the official heir of the conglomerate (since 1937 organized as the Peter-Klöckner-Familienstiftung) and her husband as the overall partner and executive director were confronted with the quandary of what to do. The issue was resolved for them by Göring's voracious appetite to gain more direct control of the big steel corporations.

For Klöckner Werke A.G. the hour of truth came when in 1941 Henle was summoned before Duisburg's Nazi mayor Hermann Freytag who explained to him in the presence of the local party leader that Gauleiter Josef Terboven had decreed Henle's removal from all positions in the corporation.[14] Terboven, already a trustee of the Thyssen conglomerate, was not the only regional party leader who had been setting his sights on local firms, though it should be noted that these maneuvers were also motivated by the fact that, in the eyes of the NS regime, the Henles had a non-Aryan grandfather. Jakob Sprenger, the Gauleiter of Hesse, had attempted a similar power grab with respect to the Opel Works in Rüsselsheim that General Motors of Detroit had acquired in the early 1930s.[15] What happened next in Duisburg was similar to the fate of Opel Cars. Concerned about this producer of passenger cars and importantly also of trucks, the Wehrmacht's Armaments Procurement office under General Georg Thomas appeared on the scene, anxious to keep Opel out of Sprenger's clutches. As far as the future of Klöckner A.G. and Terboven's ambitions were concerned, it was probably even more significant that Hermann Göring who had been pursuing the centralization of the steel industry ever since 1936–7 and the founding of the RWHG had learned of Terboven's ambitions.

Henle and Florian Klöckner, the chair of the Klöckner Werke A.G. and Klöckner-Humboldt-Deutz (KHD) supervisory boards, may have known about rivalries between Göring and Terboven. No less anxious than General Motors had been to preserve at least some influence over their properties, the Henle/Klöckners, like the Opels in Hesse, found allies in the Rhineland and Berlin. In this case, they relied on Karl Jarres, a friend of Peter Klöckner's, who had been the mayor of Duisburg up to 1933, and also on Ernst Poensgen of VSt., with whom Henle had earlier been in touch in the context of the Steel Works Association's politics.[16] Jarres, who had served as Reich Minister of the Interior and vice-chancellor of Germany between 1923 and 1924 and was runner-up in the first presidential election of 1925, now traveled to Berlin as the chief executive of the Familienstiftung to enter into talks that apparently exploited the irritation that Terboven's maneuvers had caused in the capital's bureaucracy. The emissary could not stop a takeover of Klöckner Werke A.G. but succeeded in salvaging Klöckner & Co., the trading arm in Duisburg, for the family and thus prevented this firm from falling—as Henle later put it—into "brown" hands. Wilhelm Marotzke, a reliable retired Ministerialdirektor, was appointed to lead the Klöckner Werke A.G. and its many works through the next difficult years. The banker Robert Pferdmenges continued on the supervisory board, until, himself no friend of the Nazis, was put under house arrest in 1944. Henle's and his wife's names were not mentioned in a slim book that Volkmar Muthesius, a well-known journalist of German heavy industry, published in 1941 entitled *Peter Klöckner und sein Werk.*[17] Clearly, this was not the time for Henle's name to appear anywhere.

Having been taken out of the firing line, Henle pursued his job as a steel trader quietly, while the Nazi regime continued relentlessly to centralize the armaments economy, aided by Albert Speer, the Minister for Armaments, and by Walter Rohland, from 1943 the chairman of the VSt. board and, like Speer, another slave driver in the Nazi economy. Klöckner & Co.'s low-key operations as a commercial company enabled Henle cautiously to continue as a partner. In 1942, he undertook business trips to The Netherlands, France, and Switzerland, negotiating deals that provided a livelihood for the firm and hence for its employees as well as his own family. In 1942, Klöckner & Co. yielded a surplus of some 349,000 marks, reduced in 1943 due to the course of the war to 248,000 marks. The family lived in a house in Duisburg at Wilhelmshöhe No. 10 with a floor space of just under 2,000 square meters. They were also sufficiently well off to afford vacations in Austria and Italy. Nor did Günter Henle give up his interest in music, and on one of his business trips to Southern Germany he resumed contact with his former piano teacher Walter Lampe. He also held on to leases of forests and a hunting lodge near Herschbach north of Koblenz that Peter Klöckner had first obtained.

In the meantime, the Nazi regime continued to step up its persecution of those of Germany's Jews who had not left the country before or after the Pogrom of November 1938. But, as before, Henle's postwar memoirs do not contain any information about his views on the deportations of Jews even though from 1943 these began to include men who were married to Christian women. Nor do we have Henle's retrospective comment on the evolving military situation, except for a few critical remarks about Allied operations and preparations for the conquest of southern and Western Europe.

This raises the most difficult question of this chapter: We have no clear comments from Henle on his political or personal situation during the wartime period or from the period after 1945 when the Nazi nightmare was finally over. Nevertheless, this is the point to explore his situation during those perilous years and to try to explain, on the basis of very incomplete evidence, why he kept silent in his memoirs about Nazi anti-Semitism and persecution and how these dictated his business activities for Klöckner & Co. Lacking tangible evidence it is possible only to put forward a few arguments and hypotheses for future investigation.

As to Nazi anti-Semitism, he was very personally confronted with discrimination for the first time soon after 1933 when the fraternities at German universities introduced an "Aryan paragraph" and later integrated themselves, not always happily, into the Nazi movement. Accordingly, Henle and his brother-in-law Heinz Eyrich were forced to leave the Corps Moenania and had to return their shoulder band and hat.[18] To complete the humiliation, he was also struck off the Corps Teutonia in Marburg where he had studied briefly in the early 1920s. Even if Henle never talked about it in public, these measures must have been very embittering for him when, after his years as a loyal *Corpsbruder* and his record as a highly decorated front soldier of the First World War, his self-identity as a patriotic German suddenly no longer mattered. After 1945, he refused to set foot again in the fraternity house in Würzburg. The nation-wide Pogrom of November 1938 cannot have escaped him. Then, beginning in 1939–40 began the murder and ghettoization of Jews in the wake of the defeat and brutal occupation of Poland, with worse to come after the invasion of the Soviet Union in 1941. He will also have feared for Julius von Henle's life since his father was more endangered until he passed away in February 1944, probably protected by friends and former colleagues. The Gestapo did not knock on his door, even if knowledge of deportations of Jewish families was widespread.

Günter Henle's fate and continued business activities were also in jeopardy in those years. But, unlike members of many German-Jewish families, he was not arrested. What seems to have saved him was that he was married to Peter Klöckner's "Aryan" step-daughter Anne-Liese. Henle was also able to continue to manage Klöckner & Co., the steel trading arm that had not been taken away by the regime. Still, in the most radical terms of Nazi terminology, they lived in a "mixed marriage," a category that the regime defined incoherently and contradictorily and that has recently been examined most carefully and comprehensively by Beate Meyer.[19] As Hitler's anti-Semitic policies escalated at the beginning of the Second World War. After the atrocities committed by the SS, but also by Wehrmacht units in Poland, Himmler's and Heydrich's Reichssicherheitshauptamt in Berlin organized the mass murder of Jewish men, women, and children in the cities and villages of Eastern Europe and from June 1941 in the Soviet Union, followed by the merciless deportations of Jews from all over Europe and also from Germany to Auschwitz and other death camps that began in 1942. At the same time, "mixed marriages" came increasingly under bureaucratic pressure. "Aryan" wives were urged to divorce their husbands, thereby earmarking the latter for deportation. But when Goebbels, as Gauleiter of Berlin, launched a wave of arrests of Jewish men in "mixed marriages" and temporarily housed them in a building in Rosenstrasse, their "Aryan" wives rallied and conducted a long and persistent protest outside the detention center, whereupon Goebbels, presumably with Hitler's approval, suddenly released the detainees.[20]

There is, however, considerable scholarly disagreement over the meaning of this release. Some historians, such as Wolf Gruner, have played down the significance of the successful Rosenstrasse protests, seeing them as a mere blip on the screen of Nazi persecution and mass murder.[21] Nor do the skeptics view the climbdown as evidence of a greater flexibility in Hitler's policy toward the Jews. Instead, they argued that it was merely a postponement in anticipation of Germany's ultimate victory that would have enabled the regime to wipe out all Jews in Europe, as Hitler and his henchmen had repeatedly been threatening. On the other hand, Nathan Stoltzfus and others view the Rosenstrasse events as evidence that the Nazis were capable of a "pragmatic" handling of such crises to avoid undermining the all-important popular support of the war effort.[22] Whatever the case, as a result some 11,000 Jewish partners in "mixed marriages" survived, whilst others who were deported, worked as forced laborers, with many of them perishing due to exhaustion and undernourishment.[23] The debate among historians becomes even murkier when a further Nazi measure is considered: the division into "ordinary" German Jews and "privileged" ones.[24] Since Henle never elucidated his experiences and thoughts under the threat of Nazi persecution, we are, in the absence of statements by him, dependent on cautious guesses. It is probably safe to assume that, if not officially, he was at least informally "privileged," as influential connections in the Ruhr steel industry would have worked to stop his arrest. In the last months of the war, Henle disappeared and later never discussed with his family where he had gone. It is well possible that he was arrested by the Gestapo as some neighbors claimed. After the war, according to family recollection, Henle was so traumatized by what could have happened to him and his family that he just did not want to talk about it and never even once mentioned his non-Aryan ancestry in his memoirs.[25]

If Henle's silence about the discrimination as a "non-Aryan" since 1933 seems plausible, his refusal to discuss his work at Klöckner between 1937 and 1941 leads to another difficult but more general question of the behavior of Germany's economic elites during the "Third Reich." I do not wish to promote conspiracy theories, but is it possible that there was an at least unspoken agreement among those steel managers who met in the internment camp at Eselheide near Paderborn after 1945 that it was better to remain mum. After all, even the most opaque public statement would have triggered further questioning by journalists and others that, in an open society, simply could not be stopped. It was only after the war that everybody had the benefit of hindsight and one of his colleagues on the Klöckner executive board would remind him later that Hitler's invasion of Poland in September 1939 was then deemed to be the beginning of a catastrophic end.[26]

Whatever Henle's inklings about a coming war, it was easier to pursue his work for Klöckner and to remain silent at the time as well as later when the lethal Nazi dictatorship was at last over. After all, he and his family had survived. To protect his wife and children, he moved them to a not-spacious hunting lodge at Herschbach, where local Nazis terrorized the "mixed blood" family in a building that quickly filled up with bombed-out refugees. When the US army advanced toward the Rhineland, Henle took them to Garmisch-Partenkirchen in Upper Bavaria. All the while he looked after Klöckner & Co. in Duisburg, as Allied aircraft bombed the installations of Klöckner Werke A.G. that Göring had confiscated. During one of his visits to his family, Henle learned that his house in Duisburg had been largely destroyed in one of the air raids. He now moved to Haus Hartenfels, the residence that his parents-in-law had built long ago outside Duisburg. It was no doubt a safer place than the city of Duisburg itself with its obvious targets of steel forges and rolling mills. But in early January 1945 an anti-aircraft battery was put up in Hartenfels garden whose gunners were billeted in the villa under the command of an Austrian master sergeant.

Henle's memoirs are also silent about his professional activities in the chaotic autumn and winter of 1944–5. He merely described a trip that he undertook by car to Berlin at the beginning of January 1945. He mentions that he saw Karl Kimmich, from 1933 to 1942 a member of the management board of Deutsche Bank, on whose counsels he had relied in previous years.[27] It was a dangerous journey. Whatever its purpose and results, Henle was not the only Ruhr industrialist who, with defeat imminent, discreetly tried to organize his business interests—in this case—in Klöckner & Co. in preparation for the period after the war. The many covert maneuvers at this time can be followed very directly in the minutes of the management board of VSt. It continued to hold meetings as late as March 1945 at which members discussed operational questions, as if the struggle would continue for months.[28]

With Hitler having ordered that the Reich be defended to the last bullet, many managers upheld a façade of obedience, as they nervously witnessed how the regime stepped up the arrests of people from all walks of life who were suspected of defeatism or sabotage. Terroristic practices were openly used not only against soldiers who had lost their units and were wandering aimlessly in the rear areas or had decided to quit fighting. If a soldier could not produce valid papers when stopped by one of the flying squadrons that were roaming the countryside, he was executed on the spot. Other soldiers were put before military judges who handed down ever more draconian verdicts. During the final phases of the war, these courts ordered the execution of some 20,000 combatants, and by the end of 1944 death sentences were also being imposed on the upper echelons of managerial personnel in the Ruhr region.

Working for the regime in whatever capacity, directly or indirectly, high or low, had become life-threatening—not just in the desperate defensive battles at the front but also in the board rooms of industry on the home front. Hans Reuter, the CEO of the Demag Corporation, was condemned to death, but escaped execution. Hans-Günther Sohl, the deputy chair of the VSt. management board, was denounced by a high-ranking SS officer with whom he had had an angry exchange in the summer of 1944 about Sohl's alleged hoarding of raw materials. Accusing him of sabotage, the officer wrote a letter to Heinrich Himmler, urging him to punish Sohl. When the Reichsführer SS showed this letter to armaments minister Albert Speer, the latter asked him to ignore the denunciation.[29] It was within this precarious political climate and in the eerie twilight of military collapse that Henle maneuvered and undertook his trips, apparently in the hope that some of the assets of Klöckner & Co. would remain intact and could be mobilized for reconstruction once Hitler had been defeated.

The Ruhr Industries at the End of the Second World War

Just how haphazard things had become also emerges from Henle's account of his life during the final weeks under the Nazi dictatorship. On March 24, 1945,

American troops crossed the Rhine at Remagen, a few miles south of Bonn. Düsseldorf surrendered without resistance on April 13. On the day before, a group of Americans suddenly emerged in their Jeep from an adjacent forest next to Haus Hartenfels.[30] They inspected the building and took a special interest in Henle's collection of hunting rifles. On the following day, the same American sergeant appeared again in the damaged Klöckner office building in Duisburg after the Wehrmacht had retreated further east without a fight. Even stranger than this encounter was Sohl's experience when the Americans moved into Düsseldorf where he had retreated to the Park Hotel, expecting to be taken into custody for questioning. But the officers showed no interest in him and instead were looking for Gauleiter Karl Friedrich Florian and other top Nazis. They also requisitioned the hotel so that Sohl and his colleague Wolfgang Pohle of the Mannesmann steel corporation had to find private accommodation in a hurry.[31]

When British and American troops conquered the rest of the Ruhr industrial region, with Montgomery's armies subsequently advancing north-east toward Westphalia, the Klöckner Werke A.G. steel mills and factories from the lower Rhine region all the way to Osnabrück were liberated. Although transportation was poor and travel permits issued by the occupation authorities were difficult to come by, Henle lost no time to travel to the corporation's dispersed properties, inspecting them in the hope of regaining the ownership rights that the Nazis had taken from him. He succeeded in obtaining permits for only limited production until the Allied authorities, anxious to get production going, issued more definitive regulations.[32] Although the Klöckner Works and also the offices in Duisburg had been badly damaged, he found that Georgsmarienhütte, located at some distance from the Ruhr region to the south of Osnabrück, had suffered relatively little damage. While the city itself had been heavily bombed, the local steel works were also in fairly good condition so that their directors and workers began to clear the rubble only three days after the city had been occupied by the British. At the same time, the stone quarries at nearby Piesberg were taken over by a British major. Back in the Rhineland, Henle resumed his position as chair of the Klöckner Werke A.G. board and also continued to direct Klöckner & Co. Looking for office space outside Duisburg, he found something in a largely undamaged building in Bad Godesberg near Bonn, some 50 miles from Duisburg further south along the Rhine.

Like many other businessmen and corporate executives, Henle will have had some difficulty in making sense of British occupation policies after London took control of the Ruhr region from the Americans. Many Germans had heard of the plan that US treasury secretary Henry Morgenthau had drawn up in 1944. Its alleged aims had been ruthlessly exploited by Goebbels's propaganda as an illustration of the terrible fate that awaited Germany's civilian population. The Morgenthau Plan was submitted to US president Franklin D. Roosevelt and British prime minister Winston Churchill at the Quebec Conference in September 1944. While it advocated a harsh treatment of the Germans, recent research has shown that it was not about re-agrarianization and a complete destruction of the country's industries that Goebbels had been highlighting.[33] Instead the basic idea was to destroy the war-making capacity of German industry, and of the heavy industries of the Ruhr region in particular, by dismantling factories and seizing heavy machinery as material reparations to be delivered to the Allies, including the Soviet Union and Belgium. However, vigorous opposition to Morgenthau by the War and State Departments had resulted in the shelving of the plan's more radical proposals, even if some of its elements found their way into the Joint Chiefs of Staff (JCS) directive 1067 that the American Military Government received in the early months after the signing of the Unconditional Surrender document by the Wehrmacht leadership in May 1945.

However, as Lucius D. Clay, the US military governor, traveled around the Western zones of occupation, he was struck by the destruction that air warfare had wrought. Having grown up in the American South, these images reminded him of what he had learned in school about the aftermath of the Civil War. He also knew that if you occupy an enemy country under the rules of international law, you "own" it, that is, you are responsible not only for restoring and maintaining law and order but also for the feeding of the local population. Given the densely populated Ruhr region, this meant that millions of men, women, and children and also former slave workers and returning German soldiers had to be cared for. With Britain no less exhausted by the war effort than Germany, members of the recently elected Labour Government in London under prime minister Clement Attlee did not have the resources needed to feed the population in their zone. On the other hand, the United States did have plenty of grain and other foodstuffs that could be shipped to Germany, even if it took some time to organize these relief programs. Worse from the British point of view, US president Harry Truman had stopped the credit facilities that Washington had extended to Britain under the 1942 Lend-Lease Agreement, in itself not a particularly generous aid package that nevertheless had kept Britain in the war.

Reorganizing the Ruhr Steel Industry, May–November 1945

In these circumstances, it was not surprising that the military authorities in the British zone of occupation tried to get production going without delay. It was not just a humanitarian obligation, but also a necessity to lure a skilled and willing population back to work and thus to prevent massive protests and riots by desperate people who had lost their jobs, food supplies, and homes. With electricity generation also desperately needed, efforts were made to get coal-fired power stations going and also to recruit young men from other regions who were prepared to work in the mines. This is the larger context of a peculiar twilight period that began in the late spring of 1945 until November of that year when the British occupation authorities actively encouraged German industrialists and workers to start rebuilding. Surveying the chaos and destitution in the cities of the Ruhr region, prominent corporate managers went to see the British occupation authorities to express their willingness to make their contribution to economic reconstruction.

Accordingly, it took the management board of VSt. just one day after the signing of the Wehrmacht surrender document in early May 1945 to hold their first meeting at which members discussed the next steps to be taken.[34] With board chair Walther Rohland opening the meeting, they agreed to answer all questions of the British authorities honestly and openly. As stockpiles of iron ore, and other raw materials, had been quietly set aside months before the end of the war and some foundries did not need major repairs, Eduard Houdremont of Krupp announced during the same month that steel production could resume, if raw materials and workers could be made available. In Düsseldorf, other managers formed a circle for informal discussions on how to initiate the rebuilding process. Responding to these activities, British officers gave permission on May 31, 1945, for the clearing of rubble and for repairing production facilities without delay.

Karl Jarres, until his dismissal by the Nazis in 1933 as mayor of Duisburg, composed a memorandum that he submitted to the British on July 12, 1945.[35] It contained a frank admission of the crimes that had been committed. He mentioned the 1938 Pogrom, the existence of concentration camps, and the unleashing of a war of aggression by Nazi Germany before pleading with the occupation authorities to treat the defeated country mildly.

He then made proposals for the training of apprentices and the need to recognize pension rights. Similarly, Ernst Poensgen, until 1943 chairman of the VSt. management board, had begun even before Jarres to write down his experiences during the Nazi period by drafting a book that he entitled "Hitler and the Ruhr Industry." Given his own prominent role in the Nazi economy, it may not be surprising that Rohland was not keen on discussing the past. When he saw Poensgen's manuscript, he tried to correct various statements and passages. His concern was, of course, to look after his own future and that of VSt. While Jarres was putting the finishing touches to his memorandum, Henle was among those who, trying not to dwell on traumatic Nazi years, began to think not merely about the training of young workers and jumpstarting production but also about the future of labor relations.

On July 12, 1945, Henle made an appointment with the long-standing Klöckner family friend Robert Lehr. Lehr, the former mayor of Düsseldorf with a creditable anti-Nazi record, had been put in charge by the British of internal affairs within the regional Oberpräsidium in Düsseldorf and had called a meeting between employer and employee representatives that Henle attended.[36] The spokesperson for labor across the table had apparently only just been identified as the representative for the Düsseldorf district, with trade unions, whose founding the British authorities were anxious to promote, still being in the process of electing their leaders. Some of them had just returned from exile or from Nazi concentration camps. There was unanimity at the meeting that unitary trade unions should be created. Another topic was as to whether employees should be included in the emerging chambers of commerce. Finally, there was the question of a revival of works councils that had been created by law during the Weimar Republic until the Nazis had replaced them with the Nationalsozialistische Betriebszellen-Organization (NSBO). When the question of the treatment of former Nazis came up, the trade union side merely insisted on the removal of known activists but took a more lenient view of those who had been mere followers. Finally, there was a consensus at the meeting that the military authorities be persuaded to forward denunciations submitted by Germans to a tribunal before launching their own Allied investigations. Lehr agreed to discuss this proposal not just for Düsseldorf but for the region at large. After this meeting, Henle was asked to stay behind together with Niels von Bülow, the president of the Chamber of Commerce, Sohl and two others, apparently to discuss more specific issues relating to Klöckner and VSt.

While Henle spent the following weeks trying to rebuild Klöckner A.G., he was thrust into the limelight at the end of August when Rohland decided to call a membership meeting of the once powerful Northwest (District) Group of the Wirtschaftsvereinigung Eisen- und Stahl-Industrie (WVESI).[37] The meeting had originally been suggested by the two provincial governments of North-Rhine and Westphalia to which the membership firms responded immediately. Although the meeting had been called at short notice and getting to Düsseldorf was still onerous, more than half the invitees had turned up, representing around 95 percent of the iron and steel producers in the two provinces. Still acting as the group's chair, Rohland began the discussion with the announcement that the 21st Army Group had decreed the suspension of economic associations such as the Nordwest Group but that its commander had subsequently given special permission to hold the current meeting. In his introductory speech, Rohland then reviewed what he believed were the considerable achievements of the group since he had assumed its chairmanship in 1942 and also thanked its administrators for their commitment in difficult times. Next he announced that the Economic Department of the Oberpräsidium had received a letter from Brigadier Berthier, the director of the "Ruhr Economic Planning Subcommittee," who had ordered the resumption of the work of more specialized economic associations but had also demanded their reorganization. As the Economic Department of the Oberpräsidium added, members were asked to declare their renewed support for the Nordwest Group in compliance "with the basic principles of a genuine democracy." Henle thereupon announced that the Klöckner A.G. had accepted this requirement but that a final decision could only be made once new bylaws had been ratified, of which the meeting had merely seen a draft.

After some discussion of this draft, Rohland proceeded to the election of the association's board and its chair. He mentioned that according to Directive 49 of the Military Government he was expected to resign from his position. He then added that "for various [other] reasons" he himself did not think it "advisable" to continue as chairman. He insisted that his retreat was not to be misunderstood as a desertion. However, he had become convinced that "the present time required" a person who, "in all respects," would be adequate to "current conditions" and hence in a better position than he to represent the association's concerns. What seems to have been behind this opaque statement was that the British authorities had in the meantime gained a fuller picture of the key role that Rohland had played in the Nazi economy not only as the chair of the VSt. management board but also at the highest level in the mobilization of arms production in cooperation with Albert Speer. Accordingly, "Panzer-Rohland," as he was widely known during the war, was no longer acceptable to the British as a spokesperson of the steel industry. In fact, the Allies arrested him a few weeks later and interrogated him, although he was not put on trial at Nuremberg.[38] Fortunately, Rohland had already found a successor who was a perfect candidate under "current conditions": Günter Henle was a person who both his colleagues and the British authorities found acceptable.

Rohland's proposal to make Henle the new chairman of the Nordwest Group was approved by the meeting and forwarded to the British authorities for ratification. Henle now took the chair and conducted the remaining debate on the future mission and program of the group in a studiously non-autocratic way. He thanked Rohland for his work as his predecessor and added, probably more facetiously than self-effacingly, that the ex-chair had not picked a lucky number in the selection of his successor. Still, he wanted to thank Rohland once more for his past services—a statement after which the minutes recorded the "strong applause of the assembled." Having thanked the members for the confidence they had shown in him, Henle opened the floor for a discussion on the future direction of the association. One of the speakers was Georg Lübsen, a member of the management board of Gutehoffnungshütte (GHH). At the time this steel trust was chaired by Hermann Reusch, whose father Paul had been a major figure in the heavy industry of the Ruhr region. When, after years of disagreements with the Nazis, Paul Reusch resigned in 1942, his son also left GHH in a huff and took a job as a mining inspector in occupied Yugoslavia. When Hermann Reusch returned to the Ruhr region in 1945, his stand against the Nazis was an asset, but, like his father, he continued to run the GHH as a patriarch. His colleague Lübsen evidently reflected this tradition when he urged that WVESI should go back to its pre-1933 tasks that the group had fulfilled so successfully ever since its founding in 1874. Krupp's Eduard Houdremont, on the other hand, while inclined to agree with the previous speaker's pride in past achievements, insisted that "autocracy" had to stop. As the association had just gotten rid of external (Nazi) compulsion, it was even more important that future tasks be approached in a spirit of "inner preparedness" and solidarity.

Henle tended to agree with these remarks in principle, but then added, evidently critical of Lübsen's nostalgia, that new paths had to be taken forward. The quest was now to create an economic system in which industry and individual entrepreneurs would be able to act more freely, though within the limits that were imposed by British Military Government and its rulings and decrees. At the same time, he continued, the group would also have to be guided by the need to bear in mind the commonweal of German society. This meant that the group's tasks would "naturally" be different from those of its predecessor. As the new bylaws stipulated, its mission was not only the promotion of its common economic and specialized interests but also to serve the economy as whole and mindful of the interests of all Germans. His colleagues should remember, Henle added, that the period of centralized planning and direction by the government was over. At the same time, he accepted that there was the need for planning by individual members within their company. The goal would be to limit such planning tasks to what was unavoidable and to confine them, as far as possible, to a minimum in terms of issues and timeframes. To Henle, this also meant that the group would, as a matter of course, support the local administration and the British Military Government with advice in every way and with all its capacities. After all, he was convinced that the authorities could not find a better supporting organization than the group in its new incarnation. Relying on more than seventy years of expertise, WVESI was, Henle concluded, in a position to do justice to the tasks that it was being asked to assume. In this sense, he hoped that it would be possible for the association to look forward to a "satisfying future."

Finally, he pleaded for the group's executive to be kept small, before he nominated Carl Lipp of Hoesch and—rather surprisingly perhaps—also Rohland. His nomination seems to have been a reflection of the aura that had surrounded "Panzer-Rohland" not only from the war years but also following the armistice when he continued as chairman of the VSt. management board. If the British authorities, perhaps at first not quite aware of his role in the Nazi economy, were initially inclined to keep him on, by the fall of 1945 they had changed their mind. In October Rohland was interned at Kransberg near Frankfurt where he was interrogated and treated as a possible witness in the war crimes trials at Nuremberg against Speer and other top brass Nazis and possibly also in the subsequent separate trials of industrialists such as Alfried Krupp, Friedrich Flick, and Hermann Röchling.

Henle and his colleagues moved ahead briskly with their reconstruction efforts. Evidently in an effort to keep these centralized, a "Social-Economic Working Circle of the [Ruhr] Trusts" was invited to a meeting held in the conference room of the "Verein der Deutschen Eisenhüttenleute" (VDEh) in Düsseldorf with the idea of forming an employers' association to counterbalance the impending reestablishment of trade unions.[39] The reappearance of a representation of the workers also made it desirable to add a department for social questions to the group. This was supposed to work on issues of concern to employers and was modeled on the old Arbeitnordwest Group that had looked after the Nordwest's ordinary members in the past. However, given the size of this membership, the meeting decided not to pursue this plan, as the newly constituted Nordwest Group was smaller and deemed to be more effective. It was merely agreed to use the negotiations as an opportunity to propose the founding of a more comprehensive employers' federation that would cover the iron, metal, and electrical engineering industries within Rhineland-Westphalia. This arrangement was supposed to provide a new framework, within which agreements on wages and benefits would be negotiated with both the Allies and the unions in conjunction with the administrative centers whose reach would be a combination of industrial branches that corresponded with the organizational structures adopted by the unions.

While his chairmanship of the group no doubt kept Henle very busy in subsequent weeks, the question of labor relations demanded an urgent resolution. On September 14, 1945, he sent a letter to the Economic Department of the North-Rhine Oberpräsidium with copy to its Westphalian counterpart.[40] In the letter, he reported that all those present at a Nordwest meeting on August 31 had meanwhile signaled that they wanted to continue their membership. He reiterated what he had said to his colleagues at the first meeting when he spoke about the group's democratic principles and the desire to provide advice as well as relevant paperwork to the German administration and especially also to the Military Government. Henle also mentioned various contacts that had been set in place to increase cooperation with other industrial organizations. Finally, he requested that the regional administrations facilitate the creation of economic associations to act as industrial lobbies next to the employers organizations. In October and November, he had further exchanges and meetings relating to the regulation of labor and the role of workers' representatives. Thereupon, on November 8, 1945, the Labor Department of the North-Rhine Oberpräsidium issued a memorandum concerning the proposed codification, purification, and simplification of labor laws to the Düsseldorf headquarters of the British Military Government.[41] It was followed two days later by another very detailed letter by the same department to the Düsseldorf headquarters of the regional administration relating to a "future labor constitution."

What was on Henle's mind in the autumn of 1945 also emerged from a letter he sent to Robert Lehr who (as mentioned) had been appointed Oberpräsident of the North-Rhine province by the British. He attached a memorandum containing his thoughts on how to grapple with the Nazi past and its postwar fallout.[42] It had been at Lehr's home that he had met Peter Klöckner's step-daughter Anne-Liese, his future wife, in 1932. The two men had kept in touch in the "Third Reich" after Lehr, who, born in 1883 and the son of a Prussian officer, had been a member of the German Nationalist People's Party (DNVP) during the Weimar years. But after Alfred Hugenberg, the DNVP chairman, had concluded his infamous pact with Hitler in early January 1933 (that paved the way for Hitler's chancellorship at the end of that month) Lehr had openly opposed the Nazis.

When the latter came to power, Lehr was ousted from his long-held job as mayor and briefly incarcerated. In 1935, he joined a local anti-Nazi resistance group of conservatives and, having survived the regime, he, with his extensive knowledge and experience of the Rhineland and its industries, was appointed by the British Military Government. In his memorandum, Henle mentioned that he had lost his job at the German embassy in London in 1936. He also had no doubt that the Nazis had to be made accountable for their crimes. But there were limits. While many people demanded a thorough purge, merely to have been a member of a Nazi organization was, in his view, not a justification for dismissal. Highlighting the intellectual and cultural achievements of the German nation, he pointed out that the Nazis had proletarianized the population, which is why he felt that there now existed a real danger that people would become radicalized. In his letter Henle finally added that, if necessary, he would provide a translation of his memo, apparently thinking that it might be useful to Lehr in his negotiations with the British authorities.

A few weeks later, Henle wrote to Lehr again on a more specific matter of importance to the Ruhr industries: Heinrich Dinkelbach, who, as late as the spring of 1945, had still served on the management board of VSt., had drawn up a plan for a restructuring of the Ruhr steel corporations that he had sent to Henle via the Duisburg Chamber of Commerce with the request for comment from Lehr. To obtain more information on this initiative, Henle had made an appointment with Dinkelbach for November 26, 1945. He was accompanied by Niels von Bülow, the president of the Düsseldorf Chamber of Industry and Commerce. Having obtained more information on Dinkelbach's plan, Henle now informed Lehr.[43] Addressing him in familiar "Du" terms, Henle stressed the importance of this matter and therefore felt obliged to inform him of the "considerable qualms" that he and his colleagues had about Dinkelbach's proposals. To explain all this to Lehr, Henle asked to see him for a personal discussion in Düsseldorf. He added, there was also the Mannesmann Corporation that had opposed the proposals "very emphatically."

Although the Klöckner Werke A.G. was also affected by Dinkelbach's plan, his own conglomerate had kept Henle very busy with many other matters over the summer. As he wrote in his memoirs, in 1945 he had had to deal with many "difficulties and obstacles."[44] Above all, there were the "constant meetings" to restart production that was "our main worry." Much of July was also spent with trying to get a dispensation from Military Government Law 52 that had decreed the automatic seizure of his personal assets. There was also the need to find new managers. In August, he was elected to the supervisory board of KHD which meant that he had to travel to southwest Germany and Frankfurt in order to be able to hire a person who had been identified for a top position on the KHD management board. Similarly, he had frequent meetings with the military authorities in Cologne where he was also in touch with Robert Pferdmenges, the well-connected private banker in Cologne and member of the Klöckner supervisory board. A close friend of Konrad Adenauer, Pferdmenges had been nominated president of the Cologne Chamber of Commerce. In short, he was a very influential man of whom more will be heard in subsequent chapters.

While Henle was constantly on the road trying to rebuild both his own enterprises and organizing the industrial interest groups of the Rhineland, it was during the night of November 30 that he was in for a disturbing surprise that will be examined at the beginning of Chapter 2.

British Occupation Policies, 1945–6

Internment in Bad Nenndorf and Eselheide

Henle's arrest in the early hours of December 1, 1945 had the appearance of a night-and-fog operation. According to his memoirs, Henle had attended a committee meeting of the "provisional [Duisburg] city parliament" earlier that day and had gone back to his town apartment at Ludgeris-Strasse in the evening that was closer to the Klöckner headquarters than his family residence in Wilhelmshöhe.[1] A local radio station reported in the morning of December 1 that a British sergeant and two soldiers had knocked on Henle's door just after midnight to arrest him. The other families in the building had been ordered to stay at home and not to use their telephones. To make certain that the whole operation remained secret, the membranes of their telephones had been removed. With a few other colleagues who had also been rounded up, Henle spent the rest of the night in the caretaker apartment of his house in Wilhelmshöhe. They were then carted to Iserlohn near Hagen at the eastern end of the Ruhr industrial region where they were put in dark solitary confinement for the next three days. After this they were shackled and put on a truck that took them to the main British interrogation center at Bad Nenndorf, a spa town a few miles west of Hannover. It seems that the British had not coordinated this move too well with their other departments. For on December 14, 1945, the Klöckner Steel Works in Osnabrück received a permit to produce, as they had done in the past, locomotive wheels and other steel cast products while Henle was interrogated in Bad Nenndorf.

Conditions there have been analyzed in Heiner Wember's scholarly study in which he describes the brutal treatment of internees, especially of former SS officers.[2] But life for the industrialists was also very harsh, as described by Henle's colleague Hans-Günther Sohl in his *Notizen*.[3] The latter learned during his interrogations that he was not suspected of any particular crimes, as was the case with the SS men. Rather he had come under an "automatic arrest" warrant for businessmen who had spent the first months since the end of the war to repair and revive their enterprises with the approval of the British occupation authorities. But then, somewhat belatedly, the latter had received orders from the Labour government in London to arrest coal and steel managers and to destroy or dismantle industrial installations. At first the dismantling occurred jointly with Soviet engineering teams who took away the large rolling mill of the Vereinigte Stahlwerke at Dinslaken, to be reassembled in the Soviet Union. With the onset of the Cold War, the Soviet teams were stopped by the Americans and thereafter limited their operations to their zone of occupation in the East, while British engineers continued until 1949 with the removal and dynamiting of installations in their zone.

Henle spent the next six months at Bad Nenndorf in "highly primitive accommodation with insufficient food and drink" as well as "severe penitentiary conditions and rough treatment by the guards."[4] If this was not humiliating enough, especially for him who the Nazis had expropriated and discriminated against, although he was also protected by his marriage to Peter Klöckner's stepdaughter Anne-Liese and presumably also by colleagues in the Ruhr steel industry. However, his wife and children suffered hardly less. Her assets had been confiscated together with her husband's, and she did not know what had happened to Günter. Anne-Liese now moved heaven and earth to obtain news of her husband's whereabouts. Thus, on January 2, 1946, she wrote to Annelis Sohl, the wife of Hans-Günther, who had also been arrested on November 30, after she had heard from an unnamed source in Düsseldorf that Sohl and Walter Schwede were in Bad Nenndorf. Did she know if Henle was also there? Annelis, somehow better informed, confirmed her own husband's location and tried to reassure Anne-Liese. In her subsequent increasingly desperate attempts to make contact with her husband, she found herself in a bureaucratic maze. When at last she got confirmation that her husband was alive and well, though not in Bad Nenndorf, but in Eselheide, she began to collect affidavits from people who knew him, including Klöckner workers and trade unionists, and to plead with the British that in light of his anti-Nazi record he should be set free without delay. Among her advocates was Michael Thomas, a German-Jewish refugee based in Hamburg, where he was charged with the rebuilding of the German press. He pleaded, though unsuccessfully, with the British authorities that Henle be released early like the banker Hermann Joseph Abs. He had met Henle and Sohl in Bad Nenndorf and was freed as early as Easter 1946, evidently thanks to his many professional and international contacts that he had. Knowing the right people in high places thus continued to be important, and this—as will be seen—was true also of Henle.

In the late spring, interrogations at Bad Nenndorf came to an end. He and his colleagues were now trucked further west to Eselheide, an internment camp near Paderborn in Westphalia. Compared with what they all had experienced before, Eselheide was an oasis. Interrogations were less harsh, and the inmates had plenty of time to organize their own social and cultural life. While Henle gives few details relating to his time at Eselheide, we know of conditions through the letters that fellow-inmate Sohl sent to his wife.[5] Censorship prevented him from commenting on the political and economic discussions that these men had about current developments and about reconstruction plans for the future. In fact, it is somewhat ironic that the British authorities allowed them to interact so freely. After all, many of them had begun with the rebuilding of their companies before their arrest and with British encouragement. Now they no doubt also talked about what they wanted to do once they were released. However, they also organized cultural events, such as readings of literature, drama performances, and music evenings. No less important, they all realized that English would be a major language of the future, and so Henle and the former Demag director Hans Reuter who also had a good knowledge of the language, gave their colleagues invaluable tutorials.

In the meantime, the British authorities had gained a more detailed knowledge of Henle's family background and his life under Nazism. There was a growing sense that his internment was arguably the most unjust in comparison to the rest of the group of former steel managers interned in Eselheide whose corporations had more decisively contributed to the Nazi war effort. No less important, apart from his wife's tireless efforts to get her husband's release, there was Robert Lehr, a friend from the interwar years, who, with his anti-Nazi record, had been made administrative president (Oberpräsident) of the North-Rhine region.[6] This put him in a position in the fall of 1946 to see to it that Henle, a former member of Duisburg's provisional government of 1945, was nominated to the provincial council in Düsseldorf that, with the piecemeal emergence of German political representation under Western Allied license, was due to hold its opening meeting in December 1946. To facilitate Henle's attendance, he was given a "parliamentary leave" from Eselheide.[7] Apparently he was not the only one who wondered why he had been locked up in the first place. As Henle put it in his memoirs, even to "our strict supervisors" it had become less and less clear for "what concrete reason" he was still kept in this camp. As had probably been the intention from the start, Henle's "parliamentary leave" was converted into a permanent discharge so that he got home on September 9, 1946.[8] After this he, like millions of other adult Germans, had to fill in a denazification questionnaire and, after submitting additional affidavits from Konrad Adenauer, Robert Pferdmendes, and Klöckner employees, was classified as "entlastet" (exornerated). While some of his colleagues, including Sohl, had to wait for another nine months before they were sent home one by one, Henle was allowed, after a delay to deal with the bureaucratic issues, to resume the reconstruction work that he had begun in the summer of 1945 before his arrest.

Karl Jarres and the Attempts to Forge a New Relationship with Workers and Trade Unions

Before turning to Henle's post-internment activities, this is the place to examine the fate of the Klöckner conglomerate, while he was in Bad Nenndorf and Eselheide. As has been mentioned in Chapter 1, Karl Jarres, the former mayor of Duisburg who had been ousted by the Nazis, had gone to Berlin in 1942 to negotiate a deal for Henle after the Nazi seizure of what Peter Klöckner had built up before his death in 1940.[9] All Anne-Liese and the family were allowed to keep was control of Klöckner & Co., the trading arm. Once the Hitler dictatorship had at last been defeated, Henle was able to take charge of Klöckner Werke A.G., pending further decisions on property rights by the Western Allies. As chair of its supervisory board, he worked very hard to refloat the two enterprises over the summer months while also chairing the Nordwest Group of the Wirtschaftsvereinigung, following Walter Rohland's resignation. Henle's arrest by the British on December 1 was a severe blow, the more so since the Labour government in London was still thinking of nationalizing the Ruhr coal and steel industries, a measure that would expropriate the family as the majority owners, together with the other Klöckner Werke A.G. shareholders. But as long as this step had not been taken by the new Attlee government, Günter Henle was still in charge. This also applied to his role in the large and diversified Klöckner-Humbolt-Deutz (KHD) truck and locomotive manufacturing company in which he had assumed the chair of the supervisory board in August 1945. On November 24, a mere week before his arrest, he had written to Lehr to voice his opposition to the above-mentioned plan that Heinrich Dinkelbach had developed for the reorganization of the steel industry, although Dinkelbach did not touch upon the ownership question.[10]

After being sent to Bad Nenndorf and Eselheide, Henle was again fortunate: Jarres agreed to step into the breach by agreeing to become the chairman of the Klöckner Werke A.G. supervisory board, while the team that Henle had appointed to the management board, continued with its efforts to keep the firm afloat. There was also the encouragement that the Cologne banker Robert Pferdmenges, with his many connections to the Ruhr steel industries, gave at the end of December 1945 to German politicians whom the British had put in charge of the embryonic Land (provincial) governments in their zone of occupation. As he put it:[11]

> Let us not be discouraged; the world needs us. This is the British zone of occupation. I have myself lived in London for many years; they were the best years of my life. Let us loyally cooperate with the occupation authorities and not allow ourselves to be disorientated, even if we are convinced that this or that decision is unjust. We'll be helped again sooner or later. We'll again be able to work and reconstruct.

However, it was not just a matter of organizing the Ruhr industries and their lobbies. Trade union leaders who had survived the Nazi period or had returned from exile as well as the rank-and-file workforces were reappearing on the scene. The final surrender document had not even been signed when, on May 4, 1945, Bruno Fugmann, the director of the Friedrich-Alfred-Hütte, had a meeting with workers' representatives at Krupp-Stahlbau in Essen.[12] He learned that the latter wanted to create works councils along the lines of the works council law of the Weimar years, although that law's continued validity was unclear. There is also a report of July 24, 1945, that worker representatives in Duisburg had been given permission by the British military authorities to establish a unitary trade union, founded to overcome the former Weimar divisions between Social Democrat, Communist, and Catholic unions.[13] In other words, by the autumn 1945, the Ruhr steel companies also had to find answers to the question of whether to treat representations of their workforces as partners or as them-versus-us opponents.

It is against this background that Jarres's efforts have to be seen. They led him to contact Carl Severing whom he knew, albeit vaguely, from the Weimar years. The latter, a lifelong Social Democrat, had been Reich minister of the Interior in the Cabinet of Otto Braun from 1928 to 1930 and then Prussian minister of the Interior until the illegal "coup" that Reich chancellor Franz von Papen staged against the democratically elected Social Democrat Prussian government in July 1932.[14] Hated by the Nazis, Severing had gone into inner emigration in 1933. Having survived the Hitler regime, he now lived in Bielefeld, not far from Herford, his place of birth. Four days after Henle's arrest, Jarres wrote to Severing in the hope that he would be able to mediate contacts with influential trade unionists in the Rhineland.[15] He began his letter by apologizing for being uncertain how to address the former minister and therefore merely greeted him as a person whom he remembered "fondly" from his Weimar years as mayor of Duisburg. He added the hope that Severing was well in these "terrible days that we are living through today." After a brief reference to the esteem that the addressee continued to enjoy among the German working class and mentioning his own forced removal by the Nazis, Jarres introduced himself as the acting chair of the Klöckner Werke A.G. and the Demag A.G. The arrest of Henle and other industrialists, he continued, had had a paralyzing effect on the steel industry. Apparently thinking of Henle's fate and that of the former head of Demag, who had survived a death sentence imposed by the Hitler regime, he told Severing that many who had been arrested on December 1, 1945, by the British had been "completely without reproach (einwandfrei)" and had suffered severely under Hitler. As an example, Jarres mentioned Henle's removal from Klöckner Werke A.G. in 1942, thereby also alluding to Henle's Jewish family background. He added that Henle had in the summer of 1945 established a good rapport with the British as well as the trade unions. His arrest on December 1 had therefore been "incomprehensible."

Severing replied on December 12, writing that he had been glad to hear from Jarres and had earlier on tried to discover his whereabouts but had not been able to obtain reliable information on him.[16] At the same time he was not only rather pessimistic about the future but also uncertain if he could be of much help with the British authorities or the emerging trade unions. Jarres did not give up, and on January 2, 1946, asked him for a meeting, at Severing's convenience, either in Düsseldorf or Bielefeld.[17] The latter replied a week later, and a meeting was indeed arranged for January 12 when they met for two hours at the offices of an old friend of Severing's and now the burgomaster of Oelde, a small town between Hamm and Gütersloh in Westphalia.

In the meantime, Jarres had gained more information on the aims of the newly formed Klöckner works councils and local trade unionists after meeting three of their representatives on December 31, 1945.[18] They told him that their organizations were determined actively to involve themselves in the governance of the steel companies. It was even more worrisome to Jarres that the three men had mentioned that they hoped to place a trusted representative on steel management boards. Trying to get a fuller picture, Jarres subsequently met with other representatives of the Klöckner works council movement at which more detailed demands had been put forward.[19] Thus, a worker and a social worker were to be added to the management boards, nominated by the workforce and supervised by the trade union. All works were also supposed to have an office looking after social welfare matters. Most far-reaching of all, there was to be parity between worker representatives and those of the shareholders on the supervisory boards. Invoking the Allied Potsdam Agreement of August 1945, Jarres's interlocutors claimed to speak for the "true forces of reconstruction" and their desire to be involved in the governance of the Klöckner A.G. Although everything was said to be provisional, it was Paul Harig, a Communist, who offered a justification for their demands.

According to his file note, Jarres replied that the council's proposals went far beyond what was acceptable. He added that during a preliminary meeting he had mentioned, as his personal view, three possibilities, namely, the nomination of one worker trustee to the management board as well as one or more such representatives to the supervisory board and its main committee, and thirdly the participation of one trustee to look after questions of social welfare and personnel. After the lunch break, Harig and his comrades reiterated their claim that a worker representative and social trustee be put on the management board. They also insisted on parity representation on the supervisory board, at least until a law implementing this model had been ratified and the supervisory board had worked out a modus operandi. After this, Jarres felt that all he could do was to promise that these proposals be submitted to the next meeting of the Klöckner Werke A.G. supervisory board on January 17, 1946.

Armed with this information, Jarres was understandably anxious to see if Severing could be helpful to him when they met in Oelde on January 12, 1946. According to the file note that Jarres wrote after the meeting, their exchange of views was very friendly and mainly concerned with future labor relations and the reconstitution of unions. Jarres told Severing about his recent contacts with trade union leaders and the questions that the three representatives of local workers organizations had raised at a meeting with him on January 9 relating to worker participation in the enterprise.[20] Severing who had risen in the metal workers union before 1914 regretted the current state of uncertainty that he thought would continue for some time. The conversation then turned to the problem of the revival of a works council law of the Weimar days that had given industrial workers a representation in large corporations. As Jarres put it, there was no doubt that workers can and would demand stronger representation in the postwar economy and in the governance of companies. It seems that he, while not opposed to this idea, insisted that any new arrangement must not lead to workers having the exclusive right to make decisions. Entrepreneurial leadership and "the co-determination … by capital" that had been invested in the corporation should not be "excluded." Rather it was a matter of the "smart cooperation" of managers, investors and workforces, that is, of a form of "economic democracy" that Severing—Jarres asserted—had always advocated.

More specifically, the Social Democrat ex-minister believed that putting an "experienced and energetic" member of the workforce on the management board and two employee representatives on the supervisory board would be "the best solution." To him it was a matter of course that the worker on the management board must be a person who is up to the task and would have to serve for a longer period. Nor should it be a representative who could be recalled at the constituent workers' whim. He had to be capable of resisting such pressures, if the workforce made "unreasonable and impossible" demands. In the end, Severing nevertheless remained reluctant to participate in negotiations between the two sides of industry. He also thought that the French and the Soviets would frown on his assuming any such role. Even the British military authorities would prefer for him to remain in the background.

On January 17, 1946, Jarres chaired a meeting of the Klöckner supervisory board at which—as he had mentioned to the three works council representatives on January 9—he reported on the demands for parity representation that Harig and his colleagues had been advancing during their earlier discussions.[21] The board members made a few general points that a "responsible participation of those workers who were prepared to contribute to the reconstruction of larger enterprises" was desirable. If a law regulating these relations could not be put on the statute book in the foreseeable future for the whole of industry, the board deemed it useful if negotiations on the basis of mutual trust between the trade union leadership and employer representatives took place within the Klöckner Werke A.G. with the "aim of [reaching] a voluntary understanding." Should such an understanding come about, the board was willing to take the necessary decisions. Accordingly, the board's main committee was to prepare these decisions and, if necessary, even to take them on its own, if it proved difficult to call another meeting of the full supervisory board. Travel in the region was after all still difficult. While all this sounded very reasonable, the board nevertheless passed a resolution that put up a high wall against forging a consensus between the two sides: it bluntly rejected, at least for now, the "wishes" that representatives of the works councils had put forward.

Inevitably perhaps, the board's resolution and the demands of the works councils made the rounds among the other steel corporations. Thus the "Iron

Circle" of WVESI came together on the day after the Klöckner meeting.[22] Its members first discussed prices for iron products, before Hermann Reusch (again installed at Gutehoffnungshütte, this time as his father Paul's successor) spoke up to point out that the impending works council law had raised the question of the cooperation between the two sides of industry. Pressures of time necessitated close contact between suitable representatives from "the two camps," now that the works councils and trade unions of some of the big corporations had put forward "concrete demands" and had become involved in "practical" ways. Similar claims had also been made with respect to the mining industry. For Reusch, the question was therefore what sort of proposals might be formulated that would enhance cooperation with the unions.

Jarres was then asked to give a report on the situation in Duisburg in which he repeated what he had learned from the Klöckner worker representatives and Harig about their quest for parity on the supervisory board and the appointment of workers to the management board. He added that the board had rejected these ideas at its meeting on January 17. Jarres mentioned furthermore that questions had been raised with regard to the political past and acceptability of two of the Klöckner Works executive managers. The earlier negative resolution of the board notwithstanding, Jarres, unwilling to give up, repeated his view that it was desirable in principle for employees who wished to support the reconstruction effort to participate in the governance of the steel corporations in a responsible manner. He concluded that these innovations ultimately required ratification at the "Reich" level [!, reichsgesetzliche Regelung] or at least a regional ruling for Rhineland and Westphalia. However, for the time being, Jarres added, the Klöckner supervisory board had agreed to enter into voluntary agreements with the trade unions, in case a legislative settlement at a higher level experienced delays. And whoever the worker representatives might be, they had of course to be sufficiently qualified. Finally, he appealed to his colleagues not to do anything that would inflame the situation. Referring to his meeting with Severing, the latter—Jarres concluded—had also favored discussions in a small circle "von Mensch zu Mensch." This is why he now hoped to meet with key unionists, such as Hans Böckler.

It was at this point of the meeting that Heinrich Dinkelbach revealed that the VSt. works councils had been holding a conference on January 9, at the end of which a motion had been passed to place VSt. into public ownership. After various observations by other members, Jarres again insisted on the need for cooperation, although it must not be allowed to degenerate into horse trading ("Kuhhandel") nor be treated in a dilatory fashion. After that there were contributions from other members of the circle that included a mention of the "rubbery" character of some of the draft regulations relating to codetermination. When they were received with consternation ("Befremden"), Reusch, having reiterated Jarres's appeal for interactions with the unions at a personal level, pleaded for direct negotiations so as to prevent the adoption of works council rules that would be even more disadvantageous to the employers. He proposed that a committee be set up consisting of Jarres, Kost, and "Becker-Remscheid," the owner of a tool manufacturing company, as a representative of the steel-processing companies. Their mandate was to approach Lehr with the request to become a mediator between the two sides of industry and to rely on the counsels of Julius Scheuble, the president of the regional labor office. In pursuit of these resolutions, discussions subsequently took place, as the employers were anxious to develop some kind of legal framework with the trade unions. Moreover, the British occupation authorities also wanted to know what was going on so as to be able to assess the situation.

As he had promised to the Klöckner works council representatives, Jarres called them together again on January 21 to report on the negative resolution of the supervisory board that he thought was "calmly" received.[23] Harig (Hagen-Haspe) and Franz Lenz (Osnabrück) announced that they would inform the respective workforces at impending meetings. They asked for a copy of the resolution which Jarres refused to provide. When he offered excerpts instead, and this offer was accepted, Jarres learned something that probably helped him design his subsequent approach to the whole question of worker participation. Harig and his comrades had held a meeting among themselves prior to the discussion with Jarres at which "sharp differences of opinion" had erupted among the representatives after Harig had apparently tabled a motion, proposing that the deconcentration of the big corporations be implemented that the Allies had proclaimed at the Potsdam Conference in August 1945. This indicated to Jarres that "the Communist wing of the council representatives, comprising eleven members of a total of thirteen, had seceded from the base-line drawn by the trade unions." According to a declaration they had issued, this majority wanted to take over individual firms themselves irrespective of their ties "to other parts of the Klöckner Corporation and their profitability or impact of their actions on the economy at large." Jarres had also learned that the Osnabrück representatives had joined Harig although only four of the twenty-one works council members in this group were Communists. However, the delegates from Düsseldorf and Troisdorf as well as Strohmenger of the Düsseldorf Main Office had so vigorously opposed Harig's proposal that a vote on it was never taken.

The meeting of January 21 also discussed the demand that directors who were politically compromised by their former Nazi Party membership should be dismissed. Again Jarres spoke against such a move, arguing that qualified leaders were badly needed and that there must be no "schematic denazification" and dismissals because of a former passive party membership. After this, Jarres must have come to realize that any agreement between the two sides of the steel industry could be forged only if the employers rallied and reached a consensus with the top union leadership that would overrule the squabbling works councils at the local level.

The Klöckner management board then took a small first step within the corporation, possibly at Jarres's behest, by establishing an office for social and personnel questions to coordinate social policies. Strohmenger was put in charge of this operation.[24] Perhaps, more importantly, Jarres encouraged the calling of a meeting between the employers and trade unionists that Werner Hansen, the head of the trade union secretariat of the British zone, had begun to organize, to be held on January 25, 1946. It was also known that the British occupation authorities were by now taking a stronger interest in German efforts to stabilize labor relations.[25] Accordingly, this latest exchange of views was introduced by Agar of the Industrial Relations Department that the British had established, though he made clear that he had not come to monitor the discussions among the German participants but to be a mediator and facilitator. His remarks, he said, would be brief, after which he would leave the meeting. Based on the minutes, Agar's words were indeed conciliatory and designed to encourage German participation not only with regard to codetermination but also a host of other issues, such as housing, the provision of raw materials, and the closing down of some enterprises. Agar concluded his remarks by announcing that subsequent meetings were already being planned at which Jean Lenzen, the chair of employers located on the left bank of the Rhine, assisted by Georg Gleitsmann, the association's secretary general, would take turns in the chair with Böckler, assisted by his colleague Werner Hansen.

Hans Böckler and the Quest for Parity Codetermination

After Agar's departure, chairman Lenzen raised a number of related issues before giving the floor to Böckler. The trade union leader appealed to his audience to conduct these conversations in "absolute honesty." He stressed this because the unions had frequently introduced topics that the employers did not like or that even were anathema to them. It was necessary, he continued, to look for solutions that served the economy as a whole. After all, there were many Germans whose views were quite simple, while those of others were more farsighted. Yet all of them were making a connection between the pre-1945 economic system and the Nazi regime, its war, and the repercussions it had had on the postwar situation. The pre-1945 economic system, Böckler continued, had failed completely and had pushed the country into misery. The task at hand was therefore to find new forms of running an industrial economy.

If the entrepreneurs in his audience had expected Böckler to demand parity codetermination, they were probably surprised by his moderate tone. He merely urged participants to connect with the Economic Department of the Oberpräsidium. Referring to the occupation authorities, he advised that the British should be brought in only if it looked that no progress could be made without them. Reaching the end of his remarks, Böckler thought that cooperation was also important in cases when, on Allied orders, works were threatened with closure. Like Jarres, he ended his remarks by stressing the need for the two sides to "create, from the start, a solid foundation for our work." Confident that this could be achieved, he merely wanted the meeting to ponder how to do this most effectively. Would those present perhaps have a proposal for a realization of these goals? In the end, participants did agree to develop an overall plan. What their endeavor should aim to demonstrate was that the two sides were "seriously" committed to rebuilding German industry as a "genuine peace economy" that was geared to "consumer needs." This principle should guide both production as well as distribution. It was with these aims in mind that the trade union representatives would contact the Economic Department of the North-Rhine provincial administration to learn what supporting materials existed and what preparations had been made that could be combined with "our plans." Böckler's conciliatory remarks should be borne in mind when a speech will be considered that he made a few weeks later.

By the end of the month, the Chambers of Industry and Commerce of the North-Rhine province had also come together to receive a report by Heinrich Kost relating to conversations that he had had with managers and trade unions in the mining industry.[26] While they focused on the big corporations, Pferdmenges, who also attended, reminded the meeting that labor arrangements must also include medium-sized and small firms. The meeting ended with a report by Niels von Bülow, the president of the Düsseldorf Chamber, on the preparations that were being made in Lehr's Oberpräsidium relating to formal works council legislation. The Iron Circle of WVESI met on the same January 31 at which secretary general Wilhelm Salewski summarized the discussion of the joint meeting on January 25.[27] His account was preceded by Reusch who mentioned that the mining directors had also formed a circle with the aim of contacting union leaders. He had recently seen Lehr who had promised his support, even if a detailed agenda still had to be worked out. Jarres was asked by his colleagues to write to Severing again in the hope that he would talk to the union leadership of the steel industry and might be helpful as a mediator. Dinkelbach also made a contribution in support of Reusch's approach, agreeing that the "main weight of our own efforts" vis-à-vis the trade unions should lie with Jarres.

On February 4, Reusch saw Jarres at his office with news that a committee of the Land Labor Office had discussed and ratified the text of the proposed works council law and had, without further consultation, forwarded it directly to the British authorities at Bad Oeynhausen.[28] When learning about this shortcut, both the Westphalian Labor Office and the mining industry objected. As they wrote to Lehr, the mining directors had themselves been planning to enter into direct negotiations with the unions. These maneuvers had in turn triggered similar moves by the steel industry. Reusch, as the chair of the Nordwest Group, now proposed to ask Lehr that negotiations between Jarres and Böckler be given the go ahead in parallel to those in the mining industry.

By the middle of February, some progress had been made along these lines. As was reported at another Iron Circle meeting on February 16, 1946, Reusch had been to see Lehr with the request that he help bring the two sides together.[29] Thanks to Severing's good offices, Jarres had meanwhile succeeded in making contact with Böckler, while Reusch reported that he had discussed with the Oberpräsident how a meeting could be arranged between the "leading enterprises." Anxious to be helpful, Lehr now invited the employers and the trade union leadership to come to his office on February 19.[30] According to Jarres's file note of the same day, the exchange was "clear and no holds barred (rückhaltlos), but harmonious." Lehr welcomed the meeting that, in his mind, held much promise for avoiding "chaotic conditions that would otherwise be inevitable." Jarres was the next speaker who declared that, following discussions among his colleagues in the iron, coal, and processing industries, there existed a desire to talk with recognized union leaders. Their aim was to create a basis of mutual trust, necessary in light of the current, inconsolable situation of the economy. There was also the hope that a worsening could be prevented and that there was a chance to achieve this. The meeting, he added, had not been called to forge an agreement but to remove the mistrust that existed on both sides. So many unacceptable proposals were being advanced at the works level by radical factions that the two sides must, at all cost, work out a high-level cooperative relationship in the near future. Together with legal experts, employers, and employee associations, the Land Labor Offices had written a draft for an employee representation with a set of practical rules. Even if there still existed divergent and negative opinions, it was nevertheless meritorious that a draft had now been tabled. The next step must now be to hear the basic ideas of the trade union side, so as to learn about the direction in which they were headed. Once this had been done, Jarres wanted to discuss with them how far and in what stages both sides might arrive at their common solution.

If the chair of the Klöckner supervisory board had stated his positions rather cautiously, Böckler was quite blunt. He began by pointing to a "strong mistrust" that the trade unions and all workers continued to harbor against the employers. Harkening back to the experience after the First World War, he reminded his audience of attempts at cooperation that had been made in the 1920s. The results had been "very disappointing" for the employees who had felt that they had been duped by the employers. Diplomatically skipping the Nazi period, Böckler then moved straight to his "unconditional demand" that employees and employers be put on an equal footing. There should be "complete equality" between the two sides of industry within the economy and how it was run. To be sure, his insistence on parity, he conceded, meant not only equal rights but also equal responsibility. He then juxtaposed his notion of "economic democracy" to the threat posed by the centralized Soviet system in the East. Yet, while employees were expected to change their attitudes and to abandon very radical measures, some strong guidance of the economy would be unavoidable. It could not be left to the individual anymore to decide what, how, and for whom an owner or manager was producing goods.

After this, the meeting spent some three hours debating Böckler's proposals. He was asked to explain how his program would work in practice and was also challenged to elaborate not merely on the implications of his proposals for big shareholding companies but also on his ideas relating to smaller businesses all the way down the line to single ownership. It became clear that Böckler had not given much thought to small firms and had only been thinking of publicly listed companies with management and supervisory boards. Professor Kuske, the director of the Economic Department at Lehr's Oberpräsidium, commented on the need for advanced economic training that many working-class candidates for board positions were largely lacking. After Karl Arnold, the leader of the Christian trade union movement, had spoken about the participation of union representatives on the boards of Chambers of Industry and Commerce, Lehr pointed out emphatically that the aim was also to have state authorities involved in directing the economy, but only to the extent that was absolutely necessary. Finally, he announced that another session of this group would take place at his office in the morning of March 11.

Not surprisingly perhaps, Böckler's demands had greatly alarmed Jarres with whom he had met for a personal exchange a few weeks earlier and from which he returned very satisfied, as they had agreed that all radical demands must be warded off. But now Böckler had been talking about parity and other measures that were bound to worry Jarres. On the day after the meeting of January 19, he therefore poured his heart out in a letter to Severing.[31] Although, as he wrote, the meeting with Böckler had started "harmoniously" and "an initial shadow of mistrust" had also been overcome, he then summarized Böckler's demands for parity in big corporations. Jarres had also been irritated that the union leader had no clear thoughts on how smaller, nonpublic shareholding companies would be treated. At the same time, he admitted that it would be no "misfortune" if the management boards of big corporations were complemented by an employee representative, provided this person had the necessary expertise and specialized knowledge combined with a strong personality so that he would not be dependent on the arbitrary and shifting moods of the workforce or the unions.

As Jarres reminded Severing, on an earlier occasion they had agreed that the candidate had to be independent of his sponsors and had to be of strong character, willing to go against the tide and to say "no." However, Jarres added, Böckler's "schematic demands" had gone too far and were unusable in practice. For all these reasons, he had a request, even after Severing had, however understandably, rejected Jarres's earlier plea to involve himself in the negotiations between employers and unions. Referring to himself as an "old man" who had not sought his present position, he appealed to Severing, as another elder statesman, to agree to use the weight of his prestige among the circles that were close to him in the general cause of a reordering of labor relations. In Jarres's view, the unions adhered to more than "theoretical wishful thinking," and their demand for parity representation was downright "dangerous." In short, Jarres hoped that Severing would exert a moderating influence on his "friends" in the labor movement so that the next meeting with Lehr in the chair could take place under more propitious circumstances.

After this, several weeks went by until Strohmenger, no doubt with Jarres's encouragement, invited Böckler to speak to the workers of Klöckner's Troisdorf Works.[32] The guest accepted but on the day of the meeting spoke for an exhausting

90 minutes. He started with a reference to the guilt of Weimar's industrialists who had supported Hitler financially, before postulating that the boards of the big corporations must have parity representation. He concluded that, although he had merely mapped out basic union principles, the labor movement had learned from the disappointments of the Weimar period. This time it would not be satisfied with a half loaf. Preparations were already being made to train suitable candidates so that the union's proposals would not flounder because worker representatives did not have the necessary expertise to participate in company governance. At the same time Böckler assured his audience that political neutrality would be strictly observed and urged them to adhere to the same high standards of behavior themselves. A "new world" could be built exclusively with "decent" people who would, as a matter of course, also show tolerance toward minorities. According to Strohmenger, there followed a discussion in a smaller circle at which the possibility of changes in property structures resulting from confiscations and other (Allied) interventions were also mentioned. Still, at the end of his remarks, Böckler reassured his audience that he would not take any action without prior contact with the Klöckner leadership.

The Challenge of Allied Law No. 22

I have spent some time to examine the difficulties that the two sides of industry, with Jarres and Böckler in the lead, faced in trying to explore and shape labor relations in the Ruhr region after the end of the Nazi dictatorship. The efforts relating to codetermination continued during the next few years. However, on April 10–11, 1946, the Allies gave West German industry and the unions a more tangible framework when the Control Council promulgated Law No. 22, by which works councils were officially established for the three Western zones of occupation. The problem was that the trade unions immediately voiced their dissent, especially in the steel industry.[33] At a meeting of works council representatives on April 24, they had, according to Strohmenger, "most vigorously" rejected the new law.[34] The German authorities were being urged by them to insist on a revision that conformed to current labor conditions. The old Weimar works council legislation, it was pointed out, had given more rights to the workers than what had now been produced by the Allies. As Strohmenger put it: "The progressive trade unionists do not want the right to negotiate, but demand a clear-cut right of codetermination" in all enterprises, with regard to "production, the distribution of goods," and the economy as a whole.

While Law No. 22 spurred the employers of North-Rhine Westphalia to form an association,[35] the trade unions held their second meeting of the zonal committee on May 30, 1946, at which it was revealed that the law had been a "huge surprise" to the unions.[36] Both its sparse text and its contents constituted, in their view, a "considerable retrograde step" that did not do justice to economic and political developments since the end of the war. The minutes of the meeting then offered a detailed, paragraph-by-paragraph critique, before reiterating at the end the law's retrograde character. However, they also conceded that the text left some room for further development.

It seems that it was these latter calculations that brought the two sides of industry together again in early June to discuss how Law No. 22 might be implemented and how far a consensus could still be reached between them.[37] The conference was introduced by Professor Hans-Carl Nipperdey, a well-known labor law authority at the University of Cologne. Subsequently, three approaches emerged from the discussions. The first possibility was that the Allies themselves would issue rules on how to operate the law. The second solution was for employers and the unions to conclude their own comprehensive agreements. Failing this, the third method was to forge agreements at company level. As further Allied instructions were deemed unlikely, the two sides of industry now explored the second and third options. Knowing that Jarres might be open to a company-level agreement, Böckler wrote to him personally.[38] He began, as he had done on earlier occasions, by reminding him of the German historical experience before 1945 and their past negotiations, before proposing that two worker representatives be added to the Klöckner Werke A.G. supervisory board. Jarres replied a week later, reiterating that a more "responsible participation" of the workforce would be "important and desirable." However, he then listed the difficulties that he saw in realizing this particular plan, as it would not be easy to arrive at a consensus among individual Klöckner Works. Moreover, the lack of clarity of the Control Council law had created uncertainties. Nor would it serve the cause (zweckmäßig) to arrive at an agreement that was merely confined to Klöckner. Jarres therefore proposed to take the idea not only to his supervisory board but also to his colleagues in the coal and steel industry with the view to achieving uniform guidelines for the entire region. He promised to get back to Böckler once he had learned more.

When making positive, but restrained, noises about the importance of Klöckner workers participating in the governance of the corporation in his letter to Böckler, Jarres will have had additional information about pressures within the enterprise demanding action on codetermination. Thus, on July 24 he received a letter from Harig, who, as will be remembered, had earlier spearheaded a faction of radicals at Hagen-Haspe. He now reported that the draft of a work-level agreement had been completed after many months of consultation with leading trade unionists.[39] Accordingly, Klöckner's works councilors had come to the view that the time had come to put their proposals forward. Following their talks with the management board, the document was meant to facilitate a "relatively frictionless cooperation." Jarres, the letter continued, would probably wish to know that both the trade unions and the British authorities favored a constructive treatment of the issue and the conclusion of a joint agreement. Having added some scary remarks about a threat to "labor peace" and the compulsion to act, Harig appealed to Jarres to show courage and make a decision that was in line with his "democratic attitude." It would not be difficult for him, Jarres, to persuade his colleagues to fall into line with the "wishes of the workforce."

Jarres responded a week later to point out that it was not the task of the supervisory board to enter into negotiations with the works councils with regard to the practical application of Law No. 22 and to conclude agreements.[40] Nor would the management board act without the consent of the supervisory board. However, Harig's draft would be put on the agenda of the next supervisory board meeting. Jarres also concurred with the view of the management board that the desire of the Klöckner works councils was perfectly justified. After all, the aim was to create a framework through which "labor peace" could be secured. Jarres added that such a framework would work best if it simultaneously provided basic guidelines for the larger region. This, he added, was what had emerged from the earlier negotiations under Lehr's chairmanship. What these had yielded was not to conclude local or individual works agreements that would endanger the desirable uniformity of a future higher level framework. Clearly unwilling to rebuff the works councils, Jarres wrote in conclusion that Klöckner would begin to examine the draft that the councils had submitted.

Two other letters demonstrate how unsettled and unpredictable the situation remained well into the autumn months until a solution was found in the winter. At that point the British authorities seized the initiative, even if they offered a solution that the trade unions liked and the employers hated. On the day of Jarres's letter to Harig, Josef Brisch, at this time a mayor of Cologne but evidently also taking an interest in employer politics, wrote to Strohmenger that he favored a progressive-spirited evolution of works constitutions and hoped that Strohmenger would reinforce his efforts in that direction.[41] At the same time, the employers, and Reusch in particular, had not spent their time sitting on their hands. On August 15, 1946, Reusch sent a letter to Jarres to which he attached a file note on the latest state of the negotiations between the employers and trade unions that had been going on above company level.[42] Reusch also reported that a committee had been constituted at the level of the Economic Advisory Council that the British had set up at their headquarters in Minden to consider a revision of the Shareholding Law. He added that, while Brisch and his colleague Peter Lückerath, the chair of the Düsseldorf trade union office, were, at least for the time being, holding on to the position that works council guidelines should be adopted at the higher level, the trade unions were "apparently" aiming to move the negotiations to the level of individual corporations. If this were the case, Reusch concluded, the employers would have to submit a draft of their own. Reusch thought that Jarres would be interested to know of this development in light of the plan to nominate workers' representatives to the Klöckner supervisory council. In putting this to his colleague, Reusch may have had news of employer-trade union talks a few days earlier at which the employers had announced that they were unable to support the notion of individual agreements and that the two representatives of the employers wanted to raise with Brisch the question of whether the talks should be continued.[43]

This was at variance, however, with what Heinrich Dinkelbach and Wolfgang Linz, both of them still on the management board of Vereinigte Stahlwerke, had been telling their VSt. colleagues on August 21.[44] Starting with the fact that, under the Weimar Works Council Law, a worker and a white-collar employee had been on the supervisory board of major corporations, this principle—the two men argued—should be revived in the current situation. They continued that it was desirable that the participation of the two works council representatives became law or was implemented through a more general agreement between the two sides of industry. As a comprehensive law could not be expected any time soon and a mutually agreed framework between employers and trade unions remained uncertain, the aim should be that at least some preliminary rules be established. However, Dinkelbach and Linz did not like the idea of special agreements inside the corporation and said that they would welcome a joint initiative instead. Indicating that they would not inform the works' representatives of their letter, they gave colleagues until September 1, 1946, to send a reply.

While it is not easy to make sense of these countervailing suggestions, the Iron Circle of WVESI learned at its meeting on August 29 that the high-level discussions between employers and trade unions had continued and the drafting of guidelines for the implementation of works agreements were being finalized.[45] It also emerged at this meeting that the Bielefeld Conference of the unions at the end of May had revealed that chances of a high-level agreement were slim. Reusch who chaired the session expressed his regrets at this development, adding that very difficult negotiations could now be expected at works level. Jarres concurred but remarked that the responsibility for this breakdown could not be laid at the door of the employers. In the end, the Iron Circle approved the document that the employers had drawn up, but then added that the whole issue had lost its significance because a British Controller had been appointed in the meantime to run the newly created North German Iron and Steel Control (NGISC) and supervise the steel industry.

Enter William Harris-Burland and Heinrich Dinkelbach, and Henle's Return from Eselheide

The appearance of William Harris-Burland did indeed create fresh uncertainties among both the employers and trade unions, Jarres included. This is why Strohmenger was asked to pay the controller an early visit, evidently in order to find out more about British attitudes toward Klöckner and the steel companies in general.[46] This conversation took place on September 11, 1946, as Strohmenger recorded in a file note and sent to the Klöckner management board two days later. As he put it, the British side had no objections to the signing of a works-level agreement, and so this document had subsequently been presented to the trade union leadership in Cologne which had accepted it.

As Strohmenger wanted to make certain that "peace and quiet" had finally been established and stop the reproach that the conclusion of this agreement had deliberately been delayed by the corporation, he advised that Klöckner give its approval without further ado, rather than wait for a more comprehensive general proposal from the employers at large. Should that latter document go beyond the Klöckner framework, it would be easy to adapt it accordingly. On the other hand, if the employers' proposal was no more than another attempt—as was to be expected, judging from the recent attitude of their associations—to undermine workers' efforts of gaining participatory rights, the Klöckner model had no chance of being adopted either.

If Jarres's aim of establishing some kind of participation for the Klöckner works councils had been thrown off balance with the arrival of Harris-Burland, another major change had occurred a few days before Strohmenger's note to the management board: Günter Henle had been released from Eselheide on September 9, 1946. It was again Reusch who, "visibly overjoyed," announced the good news at a meeting of the WVESI executive on September 19. Henle would be back in Duisburg in three or four weeks and thereafter would rejoin the sessions of WVESI.[47]

I have spent some time examining developments in the field of labor relations not only to record Jarres's trials and tribulations who, though in his seventies, had been working very hard to facilitate a fresh start with the works councils and the embryonic trade unions, but also to highlight the volatility of the situation in 1946. He was under pressure from the Klöckner workforce whose demands for equal representation in the governance of the conglomerate radicalized the initially more moderate claims of Böckler and his advisors in Düsseldorf and Cologne. In addition, there were the pressures that the three Western Allies exerted. First they introduced the rather vague Law No. 22 on works councils; then the British authorities took matters in their own hands by sending Harris-Burland, assisted by Dinkelbach, to negotiate an agreement with the unions that eventually gave the latter parity representation on the supervisory boards of the steel and mining companies. While Jarres was apparently prepared to adopt this British model, Reusch and several other managers vigorously opposed it, calculating that the eventual end of the Allied occupation would give them a chance to reopen the question of parity codetermination, now introduced by Harris-Burland. After all this, Jarres must have felt some relief that, with Henle's return to the management of Klöckner in early 1947, he would be able to give up his difficult role as loyal caretaker during Henle's internment. There was also the escalating Cold War and the creation of the Bi-Zone that gave, much to the annoyance of Harris-Burland, American politicians, and "steel people," a greater say in the restructuring of the Ruhr steel and coal industries.

Chapter 3 will therefore deal with how Henle, having taken charge of the Klöckner Werke A.G., dealt with the three other problems he faced upon arrival, that is, the decartelization, dismantling, and deconcentration policies of the Western Allies. All three issues raised further questions of a reordering of labor relations and codetermination on the basis of the parity that Böckler had been pushing for since the winter of 1945–6.

3

Decartelization, Dismantling, and Deconcentration

Against the background of Jarres's efforts to help forge a new relationship with workers and trade unions not only at Klöckner during Henle's internment, but also more generally between the Ruhr steel industry and labor after the end of the Nazi dictatorship, this chapter begins with an analysis of the role of the Western Allies in the reshaping of the West German industrial and financial system, before I return to the further evolution of labor relations at Klöckner and other steel corporations in the late 1940s. Among the three issues mentioned at the end of Chapter 2, decartelization provides the best way into this particular and complex field that is also interrelated with the codetermination issue and the beginnings of European integration. It also reveals the deep historical roots of Germany's economic relations with the United States, Britain, and France without which postwar developments in Europe cannot be understood. It finally clarifies why the Americans firmly insisted on the adoption of their preferred solution. After all, this was the country that had emerged from the war as the hegemonic power of the West and was now determined to have a decisive voice in postwar political and economic planning in Western Europe, also in light of the escalating Cold War with the Soviet Bloc. This meant that the British occupation authorities sooner or later had to fall into line.

German Cartels and the American
Vision of the Pax Americana

The threat of a reorganization of the Ruhr steel trusts and specifically Klöckner A.G. by the Western Allies first arose when the British Military Government issued Directive No. 5 on December 22, 1945. It decreed the withdrawal of ownership rights and separated the steel works from the corporation's mines, with the latter being put under the authority of the North German Coal Control (NGCC). The British next promulgated Directive No. 7 of August 20, 1946, that moved Klöckner's iron and steel works under the supervision of the North German Iron and Steel Control (NGISC).[1] This body, led by William Harris-Burland, an accountancy expert, in turn created the Treuhandverwaltung (TrHV), staffed by Germans, to help develop a reconstruction plan and deal with the implementation of Allied deconcentration policies. Heinrich Dinkelbach became the head of this agency, and his new role was received with suspicion among his colleagues. After all, in the spring of 1945, he had continued to serve on the board Vereinigte Stahlwerke (VSt.). Moreover, he had also attended the meetings of steel managers in the spring of 1946 that Jarres and Reusch had called to discuss labor relation with regional trade unions and works councils. However, in October 1946, Dinkelbach had changed sides and now resumed advocating for the plan that he had put to Henle in November 1945. Subsequently he had become even more firmly convinced that the steel industries had to be fundamentally reorganized. It may also be that, being a Catholic, he had been influenced by the ideas on labor relations reform that were being advanced by the Social Catholics under Karl Arnold and other Rhenish politicians as well as theologians.[2]

However, Harris-Burland was merely in charge of the deconcentration of the iron and steel industries. British mining policies took a different development. The dismantling and destruction of industrial installations that had begun straight-away in 1945 was, after the removal of the Soviet engineering teams from the Western zones of occupation, undertaken by other British agencies, but was vigorously opposed by the steel corporations as well as the population of the Ruhr region.[3] The French pursued a similar dismantling program in the southwest, targeting large manufacturing engineering and chemical corporations. There was a third program that the Western Allies and the Americans in particular began to tackle: decartelization. To begin with, they issued a total ban on the conclusion of horizontal agreements between independent firms that had been widespread in German industry before 1945. Henle became directly involved in debates on this issue, first between the Allies and German industry and, after the founding of the Federal Republic in 1949, between West German entrepreneurs and economics minister Ludwig Erhard, until an anti-cartel law was finally ratified by the Federal Parliament in 1957. The wrangling over cartels is of interest here not only for the shaping of the country's industrial system more generally, but also for Henle's views on the role of the Klöckner conglomerate in the national and international economy. This is why the cartel question is being analyzed first, before the related problem of deconcentration in the Ruhr will be examined.

The origins of the postwar debate on cartels date back to the late 19th century and a divergence that occurred at the time between the American and the German systems of capitalist market organization. During the economic depression of the mid-1870s, German companies, operating in the same branch of industry, had agreed to restrict competition among themselves.[4] They formed cartels to coordinate their production and also established syndicates that acted as sales organizations at prices agreed among the members of a particular cartel. The aim of these agreements among independent firms was protectionist and directed against both domestic rivals who were not cartel members as well as foreign competition. Theoretically, these arrangements should have come to an end once the depression was over and competition, the other fundamental axiom of capitalism, could be restored. However, by the 1890s, German entrepreneurs had come to like their cozy horizontal agreements so much that they continued to operate their cartels, while other branches began to copy them. Around 1910, almost 700 of these anticompetitive agreements had been signed. When cartels and syndicates were being challenged in the courts as protectionist, the Reich Court rendered an opinion in 1908 that, instead of banning cartels, declared them to be valid agreements under German law. This meant that if a cartel member wanted to leave the fold, it could be sued by the others for a breach of contract, while "undesirable" companies could under some pretense be kept out. In short, it was a rather peculiar type of capitalism that now unfolded in Germany.

This type must be juxtaposed to how the Americans organized the markets in the late 19th century when the country experienced an enormous expansion of its industries, especially those of the so-called Second Industrial Revolution, such as electrical engineering, chemicals, steel-making, and steel processing.[5] These companies now faced the same temptation as their German counterparts, that is, to try to coordinate their production and prices. There was also a growing trend to merge enterprises and to create huge corporations that aspired to, or even began to occupy, so dominant a position in the national economy that they became virtual monopolies. During the boom years of the 1880s and 1890s, some particularly successful businessmen did indeed build enterprises that began to hold a monopoly position. The aim was to destroy the competitors. By being able to dictate prices, they also affected the interests of ordinary consumers. These developments ultimately caused a rebellion, though not so much by smaller firms that were being wiped out by the giant "trusts" but by the American consumer and voter.[6] In the 1880s, these latter groups began to pressure politicians to pass legislation banning the formation of monopolies and cartels. Responding to these pressures, Congress passed, in 1890 and by a large majority, the Sherman Act that criminalized both the building of monopolies and the conclusion of protectionist cartels. It was reinforced by the 1914 Clayton Act that targeted, inter alia, price discrimination in the market place.

As a result of these pieces of legislation, American capitalism was not pushed, as might be expected, in the direction of a totally fragmented economy of small businesses but developed an oligopolistic market organization. This meant that, with cartels also banned, there now emerged several big corporations in a particular branch of industry that were competing against each other, while still leaving enough breathing space for small and medium-sized businesses. As this system took shape in the 20th century, it encouraged further economic growth as well as mergers, though always limited by Sherman. American consumers were also happy with this solution because competition, combined with the use of modern production technologies, stimulated firms to promote consumption by reducing their prices. The best example of this evolution is Henry Ford's Motor Company. He introduced rationalized car production and assembly lines. But instead of pocketing all the gains of rationalization himself, he passed some of them on to the buyers of his automobiles.[7] By the 1920s, his mass-produced cars had become affordable to ever larger numbers of consumers for whom they had still been too expensive before 1914. The existence of other carmakers, such as General Motors or Studebaker, secured competition within an oligopolistic market structure. Consequently, the United States experienced a mass motorization and mass production of other consumer durables, such as radios and household appliances that similarly reached ordinary consumers at affordable prices.

German capitalism had meanwhile taken a different path into the 20th century by expanding its pre-1914 system of anticompetitive cartels and syndicates to around 3,000 by 1930. Moritz Bonn, a well-known economist in Weimar Germany who had to flee the country after the Nazi assumption of power, pinpointed the difference very perceptively when in that same year he published a book entitled *Das Schicksal des deutschen Kapitalismus* (The Fate of German Capitalism) in which he wrote:[8]

> Ford's significance does not lie in [his] assembly-line [production] and a well-thought-out division of labor which the grown-up German children who visit America for the first time see as the *raison d'être* of American life. Rather it lies

in the sober fact which is propagated under the slogan of "social service" and hence somewhat removed from rational analysis. American entrepreneurs like Ford know that the masses will only tolerate an accumulation of great wealth in the hands of a few, if they [the "masses"] themselves derive a corresponding advantage from it. ... The authoritarian German capitalism, and heavy industry in particular, have never allowed others to participate in their earnings. ... As a result not only the ranks of those who wish to earn a share have been thinned out, but also the number of those has been reduced who in their hearts take a benevolent interest in the continuance [of capitalism]. Capitalism in America is certainly not superior ethically to Germany's. It is merely much cleverer economically.

These were perceptive observations that we shall have to remember when we come to the years after the end of the Nazi catastrophe and the reorganization of the West German economy.

When the Nazis came to power in 1933, they encouraged the formation of more cartels. It was simply more convenient for the Hitler dictatorship to deal with large associations than with innumerable independent companies, some big, but many of them quite small and yet vital for his rearmament program.[9] By the mid-1930s, most branches of the Nazi economy were cartelized. Recognizing by the late 1930s that Hitler was using this "coordinated capitalism" to prepare a major war and in 1939–40 even unleashed one, the United States was dragged into this conflict. It is often forgotten that, following the Japanese attack on Pearl in December 1941, it was Hitler who declared war on America.[10] Thenceforth, Washington waged this world war to destroy not only the Nazi regime but also the German industrial system that had furnished Hitler with the military hardware to wage it. It was no lesser person than US president Franklin D. Roosevelt who defined what was at stake when he remarked in 1944:[11]

> During the past half century the United States has developed a tradition in opposition to private monopolies. The Sherman and Clayton Acts have become as much part of American life as the Due Process Clause of the Constitution. By protecting the consumer against monopoly these statutes guarantee him the benefits of competition ... Unfortunately, a number of foreign countries, particularly in continental Europe, do not possess such a tradition against cartels. On the contrary, cartels have received encouragement from these governments. Especially, this is true with respect to Germany. Moreover, cartels were utilized by the Nazis as governmental instrumentalities to achieve political ends. ... Defeat of the Nazi armies will have to be followed by the eradication of these weapons of economic warfare. But more than the elimination of the political

activities of the German cartels will be required. Cartel practices which restrict the free flow of goods in foreign commerce will have to be curbed.

With the defeat of Germany, Japan, and Italy on the horizon, American strategic aims were therefore clear enough even before 1945: under Article 12 of the Allied Potsdam Agreement of August 1945 and also under Directive JCS 1067, issued by the US Joint Chiefs of Staff, cartels and monopolies were to be outlawed not only because they had contributed to the conduct of aggressive wars by the Axis powers; they were also considered dysfunctional to the competitive international economy that the United States, now the hegemonic power of the West, was determined to build after 1945. Apart from the proscription of cartels, virtual monopolies, such as the IG Farben Chemicals Trust or Vereinigte Stahlwerke (VSt.), had to be broken up into smaller units as well. Instead of a far-reaching fragmentation, they became organized as oligopolies to advance, as engines of strong postwar growth, international competition both at home and abroad. It is therefore important to stress that Roosevelt and his advisers did not have in mind a highly decentralized capitalism that was wedded to what came to be called "perfect competition." For the reconstruction of the West European economies, Washington wanted to promote large manufacturing units to achieve a rapid recovery that a welter of small companies was not thought to be able to provide. This is where the Sherman-style American system of market organization was to act as a role model for the West Germans.

However, when trying to implement these precepts as an occupying power in West Germany, the United States encountered strong opposition from many German managers who, after a short break, resumed their former positions at the head of still big conglomerates, especially in the Ruhr industrial region.[12] The other West European industries were also lukewarm about the American strategy. In the interwar period, they had also been busy forming cartels and were suspicious of Washington's postwar fervor to extirpate them. However, with the Germans having operated the most extensive system of cartels and syndicates, this tradition had become so deeply ingrained in Central Europe that many managers found it very difficult to imagine a competitive capitalism without cartels and syndicates, even one that was organized in terms of oligopolies.[13] Faced with this resistance, the United States began to use the superior power they had as an occupying power under international law. Accordingly, decision-makers in Washington who did not favor a prolonged punishment and ostracism of the West Germany, but wanted to reintegrate the Western zones of occupation into the emergent Western Alliance, began to persuade German managers to accept the ban on cartels and tried to "re-educate" them in American practices of market competition.[14] When they discovered that these managers ignored the ban, they intervened more forcefully, but found in the end that they could not finish their mission by 1949 when, faced with an escalating conflict with the Soviet Bloc, they founded the West German Federal Republic. The job of the reorganization of the market was now left to the Federal government and the newly elected Bundestag, although, having retained residual rights, the United States continued to take a watchful interest in the evolution of the West German debate and consecutive drafts of an anti-cartel law.

It was economics minister Erhard, a protagonist of the American anti-cartel model, who from 1949 onwards tried to stop attempts to revive the cartel tradition under the leadership of Fritz Berg, the president of the German Federation of Industries, prominently supported by the heavy industries of the Ruhr region.[15] It took Erhard almost a decade before his legislation that perpetuated the Allied ban on cartels became law on January 1, 1958, which, significantly, was named Law for Securing Competition (Wettbewerbssicherungsgesetz). It was a struggle that began with a number of false starts in the early 1950s so that Erhard's draft law had to be shelved until after the 1953 elections. The tug-of-war with the Bundesverband der Deutschen Industrie (BDI) then escalated in the mid-1950s. It was because of these delays that I decided to return to this issue later on in order to examine developments before and after 1953 and also to look at that point at the positions that Henle took.[16] Apart from codetermination and European integration, the ban on cartels was the third major controversy in which he helped modernize the West German industrial system and fit its structures into the Open Door international economy that Washington was determined to build. Suffice it to say at this point that in this respect Henle continued a tradition that his father-in-law had established before his death in 1940: his Klöckner Werke A.G. had never been firmly wedded to the traditional German cartel system. Instead Peter Klöckner decided to put together a diversified steel-making, steel-processing, steel-trading, coal-mining, and manufacturing-engineering conglomerate in which firms such as Klöckner-Humboldt-Deutz (KHD) were left to make their own strategic decisions with respect to investments, marketing, and so on.[17] Only Klöckner's coal and steel interests were part of a *vertical* integration, known in the Ruhr industrial region as Verbundwirtschaft that the US High Commission decided to break up with its anti-cartel policies.[18] Nor, unlike some of his colleagues, did Peter Klöckner join the mighty Vereinigte Stahlwerke that, like IG Farben Chemicals, had gained a virtual monopoly position that the Western Allies decided to deconcentrate after 1945.

Klöckner and the Politics of Deconcentration

This leads me back to the other two issues of the late 1940s that, apart from labor relations, profoundly affected Klöckner Werke A.G.: deconcentration and the dismantling of production facilities. The dismantling and the actual demolition of machinery was partly based on the stipulations of a plan that US treasury secretary Henry Morgenthau had submitted to Roosevelt and Churchill at the Quebec conference in September 1944.[19] It envisaged the reduction of Germany's future war-making potential by curbing its heavy industries. Although this plan was interpreted, first by Nazi propaganda minister Joseph Goebbels and after 1945 by some German managers and newspapers, as aiming at the re-agrarianization of Germany, recent research has shown that Morgenthau did not want to reduce Germany's economy and society that radically.[20] At the heart of this plan was the idea of preventing the country from being able to wage another war. Faced with the opposition of the War and State Departments, Morgenthau's vision never became official policy; but it gained some traction among the occupation authorities charged with initiating a policy of dismantling and industrial deconcentration.[21]

As a result, Klöckner Werke A.G. appeared on Allied lists of steel works that were earmarked for partial destruction or removal of machinery. Among them was the Stahlwerk in Osnabrück where one of the Siemens-Martin blast furnaces and assorted machinery were targeted,[22] while just a few miles to the south some 500 men were deployed to make repairs for the resumption of production at Klöckner's Georgsmarienhütte until its works were hived off from the main corporation by the British occupation authorities. As elsewhere in the Western zones of occupation, dismantling remained haphazard and unpredictable. Thus, machinery was taken from the KHD works at Oberursel near Frankfurt. By contrast, the "Humboldt Section at Cologne" was allowed to resume production of equipment to be used for the reconstruction of mines and bridges. It did not take long for the population of the Ruhr industrial region to mount protests against the destruction and removal of installations that could be easily repaired for the resumption of production in a still badly destroyed economy.

After a conciliatory speech that secretary of state James Byrnes gave at Stuttgart in September 1946, his proposals were enlarged when his successor

George C. Marshall made further promises in a major speech at Harvard University in June 1947. He announced the impending provision of considerable financial resources for the reconstruction of Europe, including the Western zones of occupation. Against the background of rising political and military tensions between the Western Allies and the Soviet Union, the contradictions of a policy of extracting reparations from West Germany and of deconcentrating its major corporations became more glaring.[23] This point was made not only through popular demonstrations and protest marches in the Ruhr region but also by German managers who welcomed delegations of American businessmen. They came to learn about economic rebuilding, but then learned about the contradictions of Western Allied policies.[24] These American businessmen and also a few journalists, such as Freda Utley who had published an influential book entitled *The High Cost of Vengeance*, advocated a halt to dismantling. There was also Joan Crane, who worked for US senator George W. Malone. After visiting Germany, she went home and persuaded Malone to lobby his colleagues in US Congress.[25] German managers also traveled to the United States to mobilize support for putting pressure on the British to abandon their dismantling program.

Among these visitors to the United States was Günter Henle. Later he "remembered precisely the numerous conversations" that he had had during his "first postwar trips to America."[26] He also spoke with various and "partly high-ranking gentlemen" in the State Department where he found "much understanding for the contradictory character of these things." Yet, these diplomats were not influential enough to bring about an immediate reversal. One of Henle's interlocutors even told him "not to take the dismantling so tragically," as he would be able to "replace the dismantled works" with new machinery and that "we would [then] dispose of the most modern installations of the world in a few years' time."[27] He was of course correct, but when witnessing on the ground the demolition of blast furnaces, rolling mills and other equipment, it was not easy for workers and managers to accept such consolations. This leads me to the third policy adopted by the Allies beyond decartelization and dismantling: deconcentration which occurred in two phases with regard to coal and steel. During the first phase the British called the shots as the occupying power in the Ruhr industrial region.

The next step is therefore to examine how far the British got with their policies in 1946–7. When they found it difficult to deal with heavy industry's resistance to deconcentration and moreover had to rely on American help to feed the populations of the region, as was their obligation under international law, they called on the Americans to come in with their greater economic capacity. In return for their assistance, Washington quite bluntly demanded a say in policy-making. This in turn led to the creation of the so-called Anglo-American Bi-Zone that provided food aid but also produced a more comprehensive program of industrial deconcentration.

Having encouraged Henle after the end of the war to repair his works and prepare them for the resumption of production, the new Labour government in London changed course in the autumn of 1945. As mentioned earlier, Henle was arrested and sent to Bad Nenndorf and Eselheide internment camps until September 1946. During this period, the British Military Government separated Henle's steel works from the mining companies of the Klöckner Werke A.G. The latter were put under a new authority, the NGCC. Eight months later, on August 20, 1946, Klöckner's iron and steel works were moved under the umbrella of the NGISC, with William Harris-Burland as the controller who in turn created the TrHV.

This latter agency was staffed by Germans under the directorship of Heinrich Dinkelbach, who had been a member of the management board of Vereinigte Stahlwerke before 1945 and had stayed on until the summer of 1945, assisting in the revival of the badly damaged steel giant. He had also attended the meetings of steel managers who Jarres and Reusch had assembled in the spring of 1946 to discuss labor relations with the regional trade unions and works councils. Dinkelbach had become convinced that, in light of their role under Nazism, the Ruhr steel industries had to be reorganized, even if his colleagues suspected him of being—as Harris-Burland put it—an Allied "collaborator."²⁸ As early as October 1945, he developed a "Dinkelbach Plan" for steel deconcentration that Henle, on receiving a draft, had flatly rejected as unacceptable.²⁹ When Harris-Burland opened his NGISC office in Düsseldorf in the summer of 1946 and clearly lacked a detailed knowledge of the complexities of the Ruhr industries, he hired Dinkelbach who brought along a few trusted German experts, mainly from his former employer, the Vereinigte Stahlwerke. They agreed to execute whatever the controller, liaising with the British ministry for Germany in London, told them to initiate.

Dinkelbach got busy, and in October 1946 his deconcentration plan was ready for presentation and early implementation. Four companies, including Klöckner Werke A.G., appeared on his list and, given the complexities of the steel industry and its Verbundwirtschaft links with mining, it contained endless details concerning the size of the newly created firms, their capitalization, relations with their former parent corporations, and with the coal industry. There is no need to describe the details of Dinkelbach's proposals here. Suffice it to say that it gave the directors of the steel companies that were earmarked for deconcentration plenty of points to criticize. As they saw it, the TrHV plan was not only too complicated and unmanageable but also destructive of an industry that was expected to assume a key position in the reconstruction of Western Europe at the dawn of the Cold War. Since it took some time for Henle and his colleagues to mobilize American support against Harris-Burland and Dinkelbach, they found themselves alone in the earlier-mentioned triangular relationship with labor and Harris-Burland, who, as London's man in Düsseldorf, had the authority to call the shots.

Perhaps in appreciation of this power-political constellation, the trade union's main committee for the British zone had adopted, at its meeting in Bielefeld on October 3–4, a resolution that reconfirmed the claims of the earlier conference in the spring, invoking once more the need to "democratize" the economy. Above all, it demanded that employee representatives be put on the supervisory boards of the steel companies on the basis of parity.[30] There should also be at least two representatives drawn from the respective works councils and chosen by the unions. Responding to earlier criticism, this time the proposals also included representation in limited liability companies and family-owned firms. Finally, the unions wanted a say in the nomination and dismissal of members of the management boards. All in all, it still was quite a tall order.

Ten days later, on October 15, Harris-Burland, anxious about the deep waters he was getting into, held a first meeting with a delegation of the unions to which he invited key people, that is, Böckler, Hansen, and Brisch. Dinkelbach had also come along.[31] The controller was the first to speak and read out a prepared statement in which he stressed that he was still studying the situation in the steel industry and that he was therefore not yet in the position to put a plan before them. Nor was it possible for him to predict what shape the iron and steel industry would take in the future. However, he had created a German TrHV under Dinkelbach to put forward proposals to be implemented as soon as possible. He insisted that there would be no change in property relations but that the interests of the workers would have to be considered, as he was beginning to pursue a program that his superiors in London had by now formulated. When it came to Böckler's turn, he spoke, as he had done on previous occasions, about the lessons that the German people had learned in two world wars concerning the role of big concentrations of capital in the economy that must not be allowed to recur. He expressed the hope that it would be possible to develop structures for both steel and coal that would be different from the past, even if it could not yet be said whether they would assume a more statist or a more communitarian shape. Above all, Böckler concluded, this time workers wanted to participate in corporate governance on the basis of equality, also considering that labor was now "the main factor still in existence in the economy."

Harris-Burland replied that he understood the union's "wishes" but that the actual work would be in the hands of his staff, including Dinkelbach and his team, and that they would observe a position of neutrality in the drafting of their plan. Böckler accepted this and referred to a letter that had been sent to Harris-Burland on October 12. Next came George Ernest Cusworth, the deputy controller, to explain the work that still had to be done. Several other trade unionists spoke to discuss such important questions as property rights and the rumored closure of several works with its implications for inevitable redundancies and the relocation of workers. Evidently worried by this, Böckler suggested that meetings be held on this and various other issues. Harris-Burland agreed that further exchanges were desirable before thanking the Böckler delegation for coming.

When Harris-Burland invited the trade union leadership to another meeting in Düsseldorf on Dezember 14, 1946, he introduced a staff member who had been specifically appointed to liaise with the unions.[32] Dinkelbach had meanwhile completed his plan that involved, as a first step, the removal of the following companies from their parent companies to become independent entities: Hoerder Verein in Dortmund Hoerde (Vereinigte Stahlwerke); the Bochum Works of the Eisenhüttenwerke (Otto Wolff); the Hüttenwerk at Oberhausen, belonging to Gutehoffnungshütte (GHH); and Klöckner's Haspe Iron and Steel Works. The TrHV director went on to explain those elements of his plan that were of direct interest to the assembled. He stressed that the idea was not to make repairs but to build a new framework. Above all, his plan was to highlight two aspects, namely that the owners were no longer in control of their properties and that "the workers will be inserted in honest and clear ways in the governance of the[ir] works." It seems that at this point Dinkelbach was still thinking of a nationalization of the Ruhr steel industries, most probably at the behest of the Labour government in London that was planning to take the British steel industry into public ownership at this time.

Harris-Burland and Parity Codetermination in the Ruhr Steel Industry

For reasons that will become clear in a moment, the TrHV's plan to nationalize steel was dropped. What remained was the idea of labor codetermination. While in 1945 the Social Democrats under the leadership of Kurt Schumacher also toyed with nationalizing coal and steel, Böckler had meanwhile changed his mind. For him the goal was to gain parity representation at the level of supervisory boards. As far as the management boards were concerned, Dinkelbach explained rather more vaguely that its members would have "the duty" to maintain a "good cooperative spirit" (gutes Einvernehmen) with the works councils. Böckler expressed his satisfaction at the appointment of Smith as the NGISC's liaison man and, following statements by his colleagues, reassured Harris-Burland that the unions would nominate only such works council representatives who had the necessary expertise for their new job and were of good character. It was also agreed that further details were to be discussed during the following week with two unionists, Erich Potthoff and Paul Strohmenger, who had been involved in the earlier discussions.[33]

The employers had meanwhile also heard that Dinkelbach's work had been completed and, knowing that they had taken a more conciliatory approach to codetermination, he thought it fair to inform Jarres and Henle first. They met on October 13, and the information they received was so disturbing to them that— with Henle still under a temporary British restraining order—Jarres wrote to Dinkelbach on the next day.[34] The details that they had been given confidentially, he wrote, filled him "with the deepest concern" (schwerster Sorge). He thought that the "fate that we are facing powerlessly in the German iron industry is taking its disastrous course." As he and his colleagues were not in a position to change anything, Jarres continued, he could only trust that Dinkelbach "had done everything and would do everything to save, under desperate circumstances, what could still be saved and be treated sparingly." Although he hoped that "economic rationality would be applied at least in broad terms," he approached impending decisions "with great concern" (grosser Sorge). He had but one request and suggestion that he asked Dinkelbach "kindly" to consider when it came to negotiating and making decisions, that is, that the Klöckner steel works as well as the other corporations continued to have ties with enterprises that were not directly part of iron and steel. He assumed that neither the Allies nor the German authorities had an interest in taking over such sideline works. With respect to the Haspe Works, he was thinking of its sulfuric acid factory and its Thomas slag grinder (Thomasschlackenmühle). While Jarres wrote that he would be happy to explain the details of such ventures, he also felt obliged to draw attention to the basic problems raised by the plans of the Allies, as he saw them. Having listened to these concerns, Dinkelbach, on December 18, gave an fuller oral presentation to the companies whose works had been earmarked for deconcentration.[35]

By early January 1947, other steel managers had also been alerted to Dinkelbach's plans, causing Hermann Reusch of GHH, to go straight to the top and to write to Oberpräsident Lehr on January 3, 1947.[36] He asserted that NGISC and TrHV were preparing the "socialization" of the steel industry. After Dinkelbach had taken "ever larger circles [and] especially the employee organizations" into his confidence, the GHH heavy weight Reusch felt obliged to inform Lehr of current developments. He began with a reference to Dinkelbach's very first proposal of October 1945 that had met with unanimous rejection by the steel corporations. Dinkelbach, Reusch continued, had now returned to these earlier proposals and was speaking of founding an array of new companies with a capital outlay of 100,000 Reichmarks. Apart from the fact that these entities were to have parity codetermination at supervisory board level, Reusch mentioned a "third pillar," to be provided by government representatives. He then listed other objectionable measures such as the idea of concluding leasing agreements between the former parent companies and the new firms, about which he was very uneasy. He also suspected Dinkelbach of being biased because he had recruited his team, with one exception, from among his former colleagues at the main office of Vereinigte Stahlwerke. However, with Dinkelbach having made an oral presentation of his plan on December 18, Reusch thought it better to wait until a written document was provided that could be more fully scrutinized than Dinkelbach's speech.

Subsequently, Reusch changed his mind and decided against waiting. Instead he invited Dinkelbach to talk to WVESI, which the latter declined on January 8.[37] Asking Reusch to understand his refusal, he explained that he had been told by John Hynd, the British minister for Germany in the Labour government, not to release the plan for public discussion. Clearly not happy with the delay, Dinkelbach conceded that it was becoming increasingly difficult to follow British directives. Worse, the official silence meant that tit-bits and speculations about the plan had already begun to circulate. All he could hope for was that Hynd's embargo would be lifted as soon as possible. Reusch's mistrust would have been even deeper, had he known that Dinkelbach was holding another, quite detailed meeting with Böckler, Potthoff, Strohmenger, and Skrentny on the very day when Dinkelbach declined to speak to WVESI.[38]

WVESI's members met on January 9 in the absence of TrHV documents or information that Reusch had been hoping to obtain from Dinkelbach on the previous day.[39] Instead Reusch reported to his colleagues in some detail on what he had learned of Dinkelbach's plans. While no resolution was passed, and judging also from notes that Paul Keller of Klöckner and Ludwig Gentz, a member of the association's executive, had been keeping,[40] the mood was decidedly rejectionist. Max Lobeck next reported on negotiations that had taken place with the unions in the middle of December at which the WVESI general secretary had referred to an earlier hope that a central agreement could be made with the employers. As before, what still remained to be settled was whether this agreement would apply to all industries or to the iron and metal industries only. According to the minutes of the meeting, members expressed "considerable dismay" (erhebliche Erregung) about the separate agreements that Klöckner, Mannesmann, and the safe manufacturer Bode-Panzer A.G. in Hannover had concluded, that granted a "certain codetermination" to their workers.[41] After this breach, there was a sense that some big corporations had left WVESI in the lurch. Chairman Karl Bungeroth ended the meeting by pointing out that pressure was indeed mounting day-by-day and that the trend was toward the conclusion of individual agreements that contained some form of codetermination,

How difficult it was to develop a common approach to this problem also emerges from a note that Hans-Helmut Kuhnke wrote to Henle on January 23, 1947, according to which the VSt. leaders had refused to sign a submission sent to Viktor Agartz, the director of the Zentralamt für Wirtschaft.[42] They were upset that they had not been given sufficient notice to consider a response by the full VSt. board to a letter that Klöckner and GHH had, on January 18, sent to the unions without the signatures of VSt. The inevitable result of this maneuver were tensions between Reusch and his VSt. colleagues that he said he was hoping to discuss with Jarres by telephone.[43] This being the age before the cell phone, he failed to reach the latter because he had gone to Bochum for a discussion with the directors of Klöckner's Viktor Mine. What also seems to have contributed to the general confusion was that on the previous day Dinkelbach had finally announced the reorganization of the first four companies that was to be undertaken within the "shortest time frame"[44] and in fact as early as the first half of February.

A meeting of the WVESI board that was hastily called for January 23 received a report from Reusch that, at Jarres's prompting, the directors of the four companies on the British deconcentration list had come together to exchange views and agree on a swift response of their own.[45] He added that talks had also taken place between William Asbury, the regional commissioner of the British Military Government for North-Rhine Westphalia, and the unions, and that Klöckner and GHH had sent the unions a proposal concerning their preparedness to introduce parity codetermination on their companies' supervisory boards and to fulfill the TrHV's deconcentration requirements. To put it more plainly, the aim was to offer the unions codetermination in return for their support against the steel corporations' opposition to deconcentration whose impact on Klöckner A.G. Jarres had outlined in his deeply concerned letter to Dinkelbach of December 14, 1946.[46] The earlier-mentioned letter by GHH, Klöckner, and Dortmund-Hoerde Iron Works to Agartz was then read out at the WVESI meeting. It contained a rejection of the TrHV's proposal while expressing a willingness to grant "full co-participation resp. codetermination rights" to workforces and unions. The ambiguity of these two terms cannot have been lost on the union leadership who could not but remember their earlier long and inconclusive discussions with the employers.

Evidently still hoping to get both employers and unions to accept his deconcentration plan, Dinkelbach now sent another invitation for a meeting with the unions to be held on January 29. It was attended by Böckler, Potthoff, and Strohmenger in the course of which Dinkelbach recalled the terms of his October 1945 proposal. He added that earlier on Jarres had "attached the greatest value" to achieving the participation of workers.[47] Dinkelbach continued that in a separate letter Jarres had recently requested a meeting between NGISC, the unions, and the steel companies affected by deconcentration. As far as Reusch's letter to Agartz was concerned that had been passed on to TrHV, Dinkelbach promised to write a matter-of-fact reply to the GHH chair with a copy for Böckler.[48] The latter now agreed to attend the tripartite meeting envisaged for February 6. The hiatus gave the employers a bit of time to prepare their arguments for this meeting. Moreover, Henle wrote a letter to Adenauer in which he gave the chairman of the Rhenish Christlich-Demokratische Union (CDU) the gist of Dinkelbach's plan that had meanwhile been made public. It committed both the British authorities and also the unions so firmly that Henle thought any counterproposals by the steel firms had no more than a very slim chance of being taken into consideration by NSISC.[49] Meanwhile, the employers' counterproposals relating to deconcentration and worker participation represented, as the unions had been explicitly told, a package that would lapse, if, as envisaged, Dinkelbach's reorganization was implemented by the middle of February. In short, the steel managers decided to fight very hard.

In light of these developments, the tripartite meeting of February 6 is crucial for an understanding of the subsequent development of both deconcentration policies and labor relations in the steel industry.[50] The exchange of views was opened by Harris-Burland who explained the design and the considerations behind the Dinkelbach plan. The aim, he said, was the "de-concentration of the big cartels[!] and corporations" and "to prepare the iron and steel industry" for a new organizational structure. The steps now to be taken with regard to the works at Oberhausen, Hoerde, Bochum, and Haspe were the first stage of a larger plan that, he added, had thankfully been developed by Dinkelbach. The latter, Harris-Burland continued, had also made the "excellent proposal" to facilitate union participation in the new companies and thus a "harmonious participation of all involved." The controller then gave the floor to the TrHV director who, he said, would also be ready to answer any questions. Dinkelbach remarked that he had little to add to his predecessor's explanations and ended his statement by repeating the dates when the four new companies would be established step by step from 8 February onwards.

After this, Reusch followed with remarks that minced no words as to his views on the proposed deconcentration program. In his eyes, many of the steel companies might, "under certain circumstances," still have a chance to survive as part of the industry, but "the rest would be an economic pile of rubble," a complete "wreckage." Without going into the details of his longer speech, only his concluding remarks will be mentioned here: he would welcome a postponement of Dinkelbach's plan until the steel industry's proposals could be worked out and submitted for consideration. Harris-Burland thanked Reusch for his intervention but could not refrain from adding that he had been in Düsseldorf for the past six months and that during this time no proposals had been received from the steel firms.

Being the main target of Reusch's attack, Dinkelbach began with an appeal to civility. He had been a "polite and friendly" person all his life and differences of opinion should be taken for granted and should be treated in a matter-of-fact manner. He then proceeded to refute Reusch's charge that he was planning the socialization of the steel industry. At no point, he insisted, had "Mr. Harris Burland" made a declaration to this effect. No less important and given the country's poverty, "nothing was to be destroyed that is good and useful." Deconcentration was to be guided by rational considerations in order to create "a healthier betterment." Even after Reusch's angry words, he asked all present to facilitate "harmonious cooperation."

The last corporate participant to join this rather disharmonious discussion was Karl Jarres who "sincerely" welcomed that this group had been asked to meet. After coming back to the issue of property rights, he conceded that no practical proposals had been put forward by the iron industry during the past six months but felt that NGISC and TrHV should take some responsibility for this. After all, it had been difficult to gauge what the Military Government was in fact hoping to achieve. Instead there had been confusion and lack of reliable information. Industry had been kept in the dark for too long, while all sorts of issues had been swirling around among the general public. Jarres went on to implore Harris-Burland to step back from his inflexible plan. Referring to the Potsdam Agreement, he accepted that, in light of the past, a reorganization of German industry had to be attempted, but the 1945 "Dinkelbach-Plan redivivus" was not the way forward. If the "power cake" of the German steel industry was to be carved up, it had to be done in a way that it "did not represent a danger to anyone anymore." However, this carving-up could not be done indiscriminately but only on a case-to-case basis and "jointly with those who are familiar with the complexities of a particular company" and with what had been "organically" tied together in the past. These firms, Jarres continued, were not corpses to be subjected to a post mortem but living entities now selected for "vivisection."

Clearly conscious of the Nazi period, Jarres, as an elder statesman, wanted to preserve "what is not expansionist" and might "constitute an economic threat with regard to monopoly or armaments." Based on these considerations, he wished to make proposals that do not merely originate with the employers but are advanced jointly with the workforces and the unions. Referring back to Reusch's remarks, he argued that industry should be allowed to discuss the cooperation between "capital" and "labor." If the employers had been rather late in taking these questions on board, it would admittedly have been better if they had sorted out these problems earlier on. Still, the delays were also due to the unsettled postwar situation. Referring to himself as "an old man," he concluded by appealing to Harris-Burland to postpone the Dinkelbach plan by two months during which "we" could "honestly and harmoniously" come to a practical agreement on deconcentration.

If Jarres's remarks were emotional and, as he confessed, coming from the "heart," Dinkelbach's subsequent contribution was no less so. To begin with, he felt obliged to state that Jarres had committed an injustice by stressing that he and his colleagues had only been informed of the plan on December 18. In effect, they had had at least two earlier conversations on the matter. But Dinkelbach also voiced his disagreement with Jarres on substance, stating in the end that his plan was merely an "intermediate solution" on a longer path of reaching a genuinely practical conclusion. Consequently, there would be plenty of scope for future negotiations and for arriving at a framework that took account not only of the interests of the steel companies but also of the unions, the workers, of West Germany, Europe, and, though he did not mention it explicitly, the Allies and the British government that, having won the war, had the power to insist on deconcentration.

Dinkelbach then outlined his strategy once more which led to a brief and rather testy exchange with Jarres. But in the end, the TrHV director emphasized that the whole reorganization would proceed according to "decent, reasonable, commercial principles" and that everything would be studied on the ground. Both the steel companies and the worker representatives would be given a chance to participate. Now that misunderstandings had been cleared up, all sides should move from the plan's conceptual stage to its practical realization. After all, he had pinned his good reputation to its eventual success, knowing that failure would mean the end of his career. What Reusch and his colleagues had misunderstood was to assume that the entire program was iron cast when it was much more a structure that could be modified.

It seems that Böckler, as the next speaker, saw this point when he began by stressing that for him it was not a matter of politeness or the lack of it, nor of feeling offended or not offended. He had no doubt about what needed to be done in light of "the horrific events of the recent [Nazi] past." Although there had been delays and admonitions by the unions had been ignored, the task of expanding the influence of the workers had not changed. The unions may initially have had their reservations about the Dinkelbach plan; but it was a plan that made a start also with regard to the "democratization of the economy" that was so essential to Böckler. Trying to calm Reusch and Jarres, he added that what he had heard from the controller and Dinkelbach was their willingness to examine fresh proposals. He then came back to a familiar theme by insisting that the unions be given "absolute equality with respect to all aspects of the economy." In other words, he was still expecting the employers to establish parity codetermination that the companies had been prepared to offer, if the unions sided with the steel companies in their quest for an acceptable solution to deconcentration. But given the endless discussions among the employers of whether to grant codetermination, the unions had given up. They were now looking to Harris-Burland simply to decree it. The controller who had to deliver steel deconcentration to his superiors in London was willing to issue this order in return for union support of the Dinkelbach plan. And this was the solution that Böckler was happy to accept in the knowledge that there was room for modifications not only with regard to the organization of the steel companies, but also in terms of the codetermination he so desired. In the end, Harris-Burland therefore struck a deal with Böckler, and the companies had no choice but to accept union parity. As far as the Dinkelbach plan was concerned, the steel companies were left with the chance to negotiate changes to what Harris-Burland began to implement from early February 1947 onwards.

In light of this outcome, it is not surprising that Reusch, whose GHH was directly affected by deconcentration, would continue to bear a grudge not merely against the British but also against the unions and remained opposed to the agreements that were eventually forged in 1951. Jarres and Henle by contrast showed a willingness to find a compromise. As has been mentioned, they had long been prepared to involve their works councils and unions in the governance of their enterprises. The latter who, after his release from internment and with his denazification procedures behind him, was slowly reinserting himself into the Klöckner conglomerate, had attended the first meeting of the supervisory board of the Haspe Works on February 12, 1947.[51] This was the new deconcentrated company whose workforce had long taken quite a radical stand on worker participation.

Accordingly, Henle came straight to the point when he stated that the management had been urged to cooperate within the enterprise. He admitted that there were reservations vis-à-vis the path that was being proposed. However, after a "conscientious assessment" the company was prepared to cooperate. After all, there was a larger consideration that had to be given first place, not merely in general, but also in the interest of the district and its thousands of workers. A further aim was the creation of a new social structure based on economic-democratic principles. Henle then referred to a statement of October 1945 in which he had put forward some ideas out of a sense of obligation toward family and the German people. He prefaced his further remarks by mentioning that one of his grandfathers had been of the "Israelite religion." As a result, he, the grandson, had been increasingly exposed to suspicion and persecution and had to give up his position at the German embassy in London. It had been his father-in-law who had taken him into the Klöckner Werke A.G. until he lost his position, this time on "Terboven's orders." However, since "the overthrow of the Nazi government" policies had been adopted for the "political purification" of the country as the way to gain the confidence of the occupation authorities. At the same time, he felt unable to ignore how he had been forced in the autumn 1945 to have his packed suitcase ready "by day and by night" prior to his arrest and internment. Henle then launched a vigorous critique of the absence of any security under the law and the rebuffing of legitimate complaints about a system of occupation that existed in contrast to attempts to establish a viable democracy. In short, he demanded more "truth and clarity" and the adherence to legal standards instead of arbitrariness. It seems that this rare reference to his family's predicament before 1945 was designed to convince his audience that his quest for a fresh start in labor relations was genuine, as his subsequent actions and decisions will confirm. It was a rare moment when Henle broke his silence about the past and gave an impression of the insights he had gained from his earlier life and work. It was also significant that he publicly expressed his thoughts to his workers rather than his colleagues.

Nor, given his own efforts of the previous year, was it surprising that Jarres was disappointed by the failure to forge an agreement with the unions until now. This emerges indirectly from a note that he wrote on the day of the dramatic meeting with Harris-Burland, Dinkelbach, and the unions.[52] After the formal exchange had ended, he expressed privately his regrets to Böckler that the unions had deserted the employers by not supporting the idea of postponing the implementation of the Dinkelbach plan. Böckler refuted this reproach and suggested further deliberations, since the unions were perfectly willing to examine practical proposals in cooperation with the steel companies. What had astonished him, though, was that, while Reusch and Jarres had made their views known, the other firms present had remained silent—a criticism that Jarres rejected. Complete unity, Jarres replied, had existed between them, and only the VSt. participants had found fault with Reusch's acerbic remark that their huge conglomerate was rightly listed for deconcentration. Once again, Ruhr steel politics continued to be full of tensions, many of which went back to a pre-1945 past that would not go away.

A circular that the union secretariat for the British zone sent out on February 18 shows how anxious the unions were to move ahead with codetermination.[53] It said that the Zonal Committee and Executive had passed a unanimous resolution that leadership practices that dated back to the Nazi period should be replaced by agreements that gave the works councils full codetermination rights in all company-related matters. Meanwhile, Reusch had some good news to report at a meeting of the WVESI Iron Circle on March 13, 1947:[54] Dinkelbach had indicated at the start of the meeting that NGISC and TrHV had decided that they wanted to evaluate the experiences with the four companies that had been selected for deconcentration. This meant that weeks and months would pass before they would proceed with the planned reorganization of other steel companies. Nor, Reusch finally remarked, could further decisions be expected before the end of the foreign ministers' conference that had begun in Moscow on March 10 and whose subsequent breakdown rang in the official beginning of the Cold War.[55] While many in the West had been expecting this break, Reusch did not say so explicitly. Still, it was not too difficult to see that the outbreak of the East-West conflict would reshuffle the cards in favor of West

German industry whose capacities would thenceforth be more urgently needed than before. After all, reorganizing and dismantling the heavy industries of the Ruhr region would thenceforth be even more illogical than these policies had been until now.

Pondering the outcome of the tripartite meeting on February 6, Jarres and Henle had also taken away from it a cue that proposals for modifications to the Dinkelbach plan would be welcome. Accordingly, they continued to meet with Harris-Burland and the TrHV director to discuss such matters as the lease agreement for the deconcentrated Haspe Works.[56] Jarres also contacted Böckler again to sound him out on this matter, adding that "we would furthermore welcome" an exchange of opinions on developments in the iron industry.[57] Would he please let him know, if, where, and when such a meeting could be arranged that would not have to be confined to the deconcentration issue. After further weeks in which Henle and his colleagues continued to discuss modifications to deconcentration, it was on August 29 that Gerhard Schroeder of the Klöckner Werke A.G. management board had some uplifting news for Henle, following a WVESI meeting on the previous day.[58] With reference to deconcentration, he had some "interesting and well-nigh revolutionary information": among the unions there was now a growing number of voices who were opposed to further deconcentration with respect to the separation of what they felt "belonged organically together." Moreover, "our[!] works councils" had independently come to the conclusion that deconcentration needed to be reassessed. A submission to this effect was being prepared for Böckler to consider. Finally, Schroeder had learned during discussions he had had with American visitors that they also felt that existing "organic ties" should be taken into consideration "very strongly." In short, it had become quite clear that the reorganization of the steel industry and West German industry in general was undergoing a gradual metamorphosis, as the integration of the three zones of occupation into the anti-Soviet alliance, spearheaded by the United States, unfolded.

However, there was one issue that did not change: the pressure of the work councils and trade unions to establish Harris-Burland's model of parity codetermination. Thus, the councils of the three remaining Klöckner A.G. works at Troisdorf, Düsseldorf, and Piesberg, supported by the main administration, forwarded to Jarres on January 15, 1948, a motion to introduce parity representation for the parent company's supervisory board.[59] Jarres responded on January 27 that he would support a codetermined participation of the workforce that gave them both a seat and a vote on the supervisory board, but no more.[60]

Deconcentration and Codetermination Phase 2

This is therefore the point at which we can move to the second phase in the evolution of the deconcentration and codetermination tug-of-war during 1948 and 1949 when the Americans appeared on the scene. As mentioned earlier, their participation in Ruhr industrial policy making must be seen against the growing difficulties of the British military authorities not only to get their restructuring proposals accepted but also to fulfill their obligations under international law of feeding the millions of Germans living in the Ruhr region. This is when the Americans began to use their agricultural surpluses and capacity to deliver grain and produce. They resorted to what has been called the "politics of food."[61] This meant that they demanded a say not just in the running of food aid programs, but also in economic policy making in the British zone more generally. Years later, Harris-Burland was still visibly angry during an interview when he talked about those "steel people" who turned up in Düsseldorf and began to throw their weight about, sidelining the British controller. In November 1948, the Anglo-American Law No. 75 was introduced that decreed the deconcentration not only of the Ruhr region's coal and steel industries but also of other branches of industry as well as the banking system. NGISC was turned into the UK/US Steel group and the TrHV was expanded and renamed, with Dinkelbach no longer in exclusive charge. Instead several trade unionists, two steel managers of the deconcentrated companies, and a number of civil servants were appointed. Henle was asked to represent the Altkonzerne but withdrew when he learned that ownership rights were still on the agenda and might be taken away.

Again the larger context of the American reconstruction strategy is important, with the underlying consideration in Washington being the determination to introduce the principles of American antimonopoly legislation in West Germany—the European country that, despite bombing raids and dismantling, still had the potentially most powerful industrial system.[62] This potential was to be mobilized for reconstruction in the hope that by promoting the American vision of how to organize and run a modern manufacturing economy would do the trick. The adoption of this vision in West Germany would then spill over into the neighboring economies. As Paul Hoffman, a former president of the Studebaker Corporation and now the administrator of the Marshall Plan, put it in May 1949:[63] decartelization filled him with "the greatest hopes" for the restoration of Western Europe's capacity to compete via Germany. The goal was to build in West Germany a type of "free competitive economy we have in the United States." Once this was done, West Germany would develop a "very effective economy" whose influence would spread beyond that country's borders, also making its neighbors more competitive.

It was typical of Hoffman's reconstruction strategy that he now began to organize so-called Productivity Councils.[64] They were established to promote trips by European industrialists and trade union leaders to visit American steel mills and car assembly lines in the expectation that they would take their insights back home and begin to introduce in their companies the practices that they had seen. As all these initiatives have to be viewed within the framework of the American strategy of creating an Open Door competitive world trading system under the hegemonic umbrella of American capitalism, it is not surprising that Washington's politicians pushed for the decartelization and deconcentration of German industry. As an occupying power, they had more leverage in West Germany that they did not have in London or Paris in the push for their industries to abandon their own protectionist traditions.

It is due to these calculations that "monopolistic" West German corporations, such as Vereinigte Stahlwerke and IG Farben, appeared in the crosshairs of the Office of Military Government US (OMGUS) and from 1949 in those of the US High Commission, established after the founding of the Federal Republic. However, before examining the evolution of the Allied deconcentration program after 1949, we have to go back to the development of labor relations after the founding of the Federal Republic.

4

The United States and the Completion of the Reshaping of West German Industry

If 1946 and 1947 were difficult years for the West German steel industry and also for Günter Henle at Klöckner, the following two years brought changes in international politics and also in the Western Allies' handling of the occupation that raised the hopes of the heavy industrial corporations for a better future. And if those early years were marked by patient and restrained discussion of the major problems of reconstruction, punctuated only occasionally by Reusch's angry interventions and Böckler's extensive expectorations with references to the dark years before 1945, the following years were, by contrast, more dramatic and involved top-level decisions that shaped the long-term future of the Federal Republic.

To begin with, there was another sign that the Cold War had started in earnest in Berlin's American, British, and French sectors with their over two million inhabitants when Stalin imposed a land blockade on the Western parts of the island city. Its people were now threatened with starvation, with Stalin clearly hoping that the West Berliners and the Western Allies would soon be forced to surrender. The three Western sectors had become a thorn in the dictator's flesh, as they threatened, with their open inter-sector borders, his control of the Soviet zone of occupation. East German citizens could freely travel to the Soviet sector of Berlin and then traverse on foot the borders into the American, British, or French sectors. They could also board a suburban train (S-Bahn) in the Soviet sector and alight at a station in the Western sectors to register as refugees. This big hole that the Western intelligence services were also happy to use for their activities had to be plugged, with East Berlin becoming part of the Soviet zone. The Berlin Blockade of 1948 was supposed to achieve this.

American Economic Leadership and the
Start of the Cold War, 1948–9

Faced with Stalin's blockade, General Lucius D. Clay, the US Military Governor, immediately recognized the danger of a major defeat, if the Soviet dictator succeeded. As he put it in a message to his superiors in Washington: "We have lost Czechoslovakia, Norway is threatened. We retreat from Berlin. When Berlin falls, West Germany will be next. If we mean to hold Europe against Communism, we must not budge … If we withdraw our position, Europe is threatened."[1] With road, canals, and railway links being disrupted, the Western Allies decided on April 2, 1948, to supply the city from the air.[2] Thenceforth British and American planes landed at Berlin-Tempelhof and Gatow airports every few minutes. On April 15, for example, they delivered close to 13,000 tons of supplies. It was only a year later that Four-Power negotiations finally ended the blockade. West Berliners remained forever grateful for this rescue operation. The estimated costs to the United States and Britain that had primarily been running the air lift were around $200 million.

The Berlin Blockade and other emergent flashpoints of East-West tension accelerated two major decisions that greatly benefitted West German industry. In June 1948, the Allies agreed on a formula designed to reform and stabilize the West German currency.[3] The Reichsmark was converted into the Deutschmark, and while this reform meant painful losses to German individual savings accounts, the reform put an initial 40 marks of the new currency in people's pockets to make their first purchases of food and other essentials. The black market on which, in addition to American aid programs, the population had increasingly been forced to rely for their survival in 1946/7 disappeared. Almost overnight the shops were filled with hitherto scarce goods, and there was plenty of optimism that West Germany would soon experience a period of prosperity. Although it took more time for the economy to stabilize and for the initial spike in unemployment to come down again, after years or even two decades of austerity, living standards began to rise again. The resultant optimism was embodied by Ludwig Erhard who, working at the Verwaltung für Wirtschaft, had supported the Allied currency reforms, first drafted by a number of American economists.

Those West Germans who, in addition to their savings, had assets in the shape of landed property or factories, even if war damaged, could look forward to an even brighter future, as American-financed economic reconstruction superseded Allied dismantling policies. These middle- and upper-class families could now mobilize their assets and rebuild production facilities with the help of external investments and loans from a banking system that was slowly resuming its traditional role. A report published in the American business magazine *Fortune* in October 1949 summed up quite neatly what was happening in the Rhineland at this time:[4] "The central workshop of Europe—the industrial complex of the Rhine and Ruhr basins—is now pulsing, if not at its prewar capacity, certainly with enough vigor to make the future of Germany a prime concern not only of Europe, but also of the US." The much stronger and bigger American trusts, the author continued, were considerably less troubled by this resurgence than French businessmen and politicians. They were beginning to realize that the Ruhr region in particular still constituted "the greatest concentration of economic power on the [European] continent."

While this quote is a telling confirmation of what has been said in the Chapter 3 about America's larger economic strategy, as articulated by Paul Hoffman and also by William Draper, Clay's economic adviser,[5] I'll be returning in greater detail in the Chapter 5 to the question of how the successes of German industry that were bound to worry West Germany's neighbors led to efforts by US high commissioner John J. McCloy to create a greater balance between the French and West German heavy industrial systems. There is also the role of the State Department in the integration of Western Europe and the shaping of what became the European Coal and Steel Community (ECSC) of 1951 to be considered.[6] For the moment, though, the Americans turned their attention to the political founding of the Federal Republic and the creation of a parliamentary-democratic constitution, the Basic Law. The first meetings of the politicians and lawyers involved in this initiative began, with Allied encouragement, in Herrenchiemsee south of Munich in the crucial year of 1948. Without going into the many articles of the final document, suffice it to say that it guaranteed in its first twenty articles such fundamental human rights as freedom of expression, of assembly, of religion, of movement, of choosing one's profession, and, with certain riders, of property.[7]

Article 21 is also significant in that it defined West Germany as "a democratic and social federal state" in which "all state authority emanates from the people" and "all Germans shall have the right to resist any person or persons seeking to abolish that constitutional order, should no other remedy be possible." If these 21 articles reflected the many bitter lessons learned from the Nazi past, the articles that followed enshrined in the so-called Basic Law many of the insights gained from the experience of the failed Weimar Constitution. By establishing a modern parliamentary democracy and economic system, some of the new principles will emerge later on from the debates on the shaping of labor relations. There are also the discussions relating to the Schuman Plan, at the end of which stood the creation of the ECSC of 1951. All this had a positive impact on the three major issues that had preoccupied the steel industry in previous years: dismantling, cartels, and deconcentration in which Henle also played an important part.

Of the three issues, the removal and destruction of industrial installations had by 1948 become increasingly irrational. After all, this was the time when the Americans, through the Marshall Plan and other aid programs, poured resources not only into Britain and France but also into the Western zones of occupation and from 1949 into the newly founded Federal Republic. These programs were supposed to boost production. The aim was not merely to create economic prosperity but also to counter the political and military threat that the Soviet Union and communist movements in Western Europe were said to pose to Western Europe. The idea was to stabilize the region by promoting the principles of democracy and improving living standards. Economic growth was to be stimulated, with the United States acting as a model of what a market economy was capable of achieving. No less important, American capitalism was being complemented by social policies that originated in Roosevelt's New Deal and continued after 1945. It is often forgotten that not only Western Europe but also the United States practiced welfare policies and the economic recipes of Keynesianism and public infrastructural investments. The American economy was being managed in a triangular relationship between government, the employers, and powerful trade unions. To be sure, there was some push back against this New Dealism by employers, but in the 1950s the political economy of the United States was quite different from that of the pre-1929 years, but also of the 1980s when it turned to Ronald Reagan's neoliberalism.

As to economic policy making in West Germany, it took Washington until 1949–50 to pressure the British Labour government to scrap its dismantling policies in the Ruhr region. Germany's companies were by that time on a path of expansion and—as American colleagues had told Henle in 1947—were free to acquire the latest technology for the modernization of their factories.[8] As has been mentioned, the German tradition of cartels was first undermined by a strict Allied ban on all anticompetitive arrangements between independent firms. This ban was subsequently adopted by the Federal Republic, although it took economics minister Erhard quite a few years to overcome big business resistance to it that Bundesverband der Deutschen Industrie (BDI) president Fritz Berg and the conservatives in the Ruhr steel and coal industries continued to put up.[9]

There were two other issues of the early postwar years that had not been definitively settled before the introduction of parliamentary government in 1949: codetermination, as demanded by the trade unions since 1946, and deconcentration of the big corporations. Both issues generated plenty of controversy, while the Americans continued to use their residual powers under the Occupation Statute to steer the semi-sovereign Bonn Republic under chancellor Konrad Adenauer in a direction that was in harmony with Washington's global quest of creating an Open Door international economy outside the Soviet Bloc.

The Debate on West German Labor Relations and Codetermination

Turning to labor relations, it will be remembered that not much progress had been made on codetermination, as demanded by Böckler in his meetings with Jarres, Reusch, and other steel managers throughout 1946.[10] The latter kept dragging their feet, while harboring hopes that the trade unions would support them in their attempt to stop industrial deconcentration in return for a limited worker participation in the governance of the steel companies. In the end, Böckler struck a better deal with Harris-Burland and Dinkelbach that sidelined the employers. With both men interested in making a start with four companies that had been earmarked for restructuring, they got the trade unions on board in return for the promise that they would put an equal number of workers' and union representatives on the supervisory boards. They also enlarged the management boards of those four companies by a worker director, assisted by another trusted employee, to look after social welfare. In short, it was in this way that a start was made with Böckler's much vaunted parity codetermination model of 1946–7. While Jarres very reluctantly accepted this model for Klöckner Werke A.G., Reusch at GHH continued to hope that it could be rescinded once the Allied occupation came to an end. Indeed, even after parity codetermination in the coal and steel industry had become Federal law in May 1951 (to be discussed in a moment), he continued his rebellion, convinced that union parity had been imposed by Harris-Burland and Dinkelbach. For the moment the question was, however, whether this 1947 model could be expanded to the rest of steel and coal and more generally to the big corporations in other branches of industry.

When, after the creation of the Bi-Zone, the Americans appeared in the Ruhr region, the newly formed (UK/US) Combined Steel Group was expected to see to it that Harris-Burland's work was completed. He continued to be assisted by a larger group of German experts reconstituted from Dinkelbach's TrHV on September 1, 1949, and renamed Treuhandvereinigung.[11] Although the founding of the Federal Republic complicated its work, the Allied High Commission that had replaced the Military Government agencies after the creation of the Federal Republic was determined to complete the deconcentration of German industry. On May 16, 1950, Allied Law No. 27 was promulgated to complete the breakup of corporations such as Vereinigte Stahlwerke i[n] L[iquidation], as it was now officially listed. While German resistance to deconcentration continued, John McCloy, the US high commissioner, encouraged the trade unions, the employers, and the Federal government to move ahead with their discussions on codetermination by suspending the agreements on labor relations that had meanwhile been made in two Federal states: Hesse and Baden-Württemberg.[12] The hope was that this suspension would clear a path for a comprehensive higher level settlement between the two sides of industry and the Adenauer government in Bonn. The trouble was that the chancellor was not keen to take a lead on the codetermination question.

Adenauer reasoned that since his Christian Democrat Union (CDU) had not won a majority in the federal elections of September 1949, he had to rely on a coalition with a number of smaller parties that gave him a very slim parliamentary majority. And yet, when he presented the program of his government before the new Bundestag on September 20, 1949, he felt that he had to include in it a reference to an issue that he knew was very controversial but required an early solution: parity codetermination as established by Harris-Burland in 1947 in parts of the steel industry. As the chancellor put it in his statement before the Bundestag, "Legal relations between employees and employers had to be newly organized in line with the times (zeitgemäß)."[13] He added that the "patronizing role of the state" had to be replaced by the "self-administration of the two social partners." A balanced compromise on labor relations between the two sides of industry was, Adenauer concluded, "the inevitable precondition for the revival" of West Germany, and this could be brought about only by a joint effort. The "social-political and societal recognition of the employees," he added, required "a reorganization of the property rights in basic industries." While the chancellor left the terms of the compromise pretty vague, it was clear that, in recognizing the instability of his government coalition, he had to shy away from seizing the initiative himself. Employers and unions had to find a peaceful compromise among themselves.

During a subsequent session of the Bundestag on November 4, 1949, the CDU deputy Josef Arndgen took up the chancellor's statements by suggesting quite unambiguously that the time had come to place the employee on an equal economic rights footing next to the entrepreneur as "his co-worker."[14] Quite in line with Adenauer's declaration, it was then for the Social Democrat deputy and member of the Deutscher Gewerkschaftsbund (DGB) executive Willy Richter to add that a new works council law was also needed that "anchored" clearly and firmly the right of codetermined equality in the "social, personal and economic spheres."[15]

Following Adenauer's recommendation, the question of modernization of labor relations was not taken up by the Bundestag. Instead Böckler, now chair of the DGB that had been founded in October 1949, was anxious to put the issue on the national agenda. Hans Bilstein, the president of the employers federation of the metal industries, subsequently mediated a meeting between Walter Raymond, the president of the employers federation, and Böckler on November 15, 1949.[16] It seemed to be a propitious moment to move forward. As Raymond and Bilstein noted afterwards, both sides had approached their conversation "from the start in complete openness" and had observed forms of conduct that were "mutually understanding and trusting"—a point made perhaps also in memory of the bitter confrontations between Reusch, Jarres, and Böckler during the debates with Harris-Burland and Dinkelbach in 1947.[17]

In particular, the employers wanted to know what the trade unions understood by "codetermination." Although Böckler had over the years repeatedly clarified his position on this question, Raymond and Bilstein mentioned the "marked disquiet" that had arisen among their colleagues as to its meaning. Not wishing to wreck the conversation, Böckler's reply was evasive, stating that the trade unions were in the middle of preparing a study on this subject that would be circumspect and comprehensive. He added his conviction that the supreme goal of their mutual efforts was to increase output. Codetermination should therefore never lead to industrial production being negatively impacted. After this, Raymond asked Böckler to put a hold on the DGB's publication on codetermination, as he was himself thinking of constituting a commission to discuss the issue. The trade union leader agreed and both sides exchanged assurances that they would continue to cooperate in full confidence. There would also be no press releases until their cooperation had yielded tangible results.

These negotiations finally began on January 9–10, 1950, in a quiet location at Hattenheim near Eltville on the Hessian side of the Rhine, not far from Wiesbaden and Mainz. They were chaired by Raymond and Böckler. While the notes of the meeting make interesting reading,[18] it is sufficient here to refer to a summary of those two days of discussions. Divided into seventeen paragraphs, the document stressed, to begin with, that the atmosphere had been "remarkably matter-of-fact and harmonious." However, it also became clear that, while there had been some agreement on the creation of a supra-regional "Federal Economic Council" and also on employee participation at the personal and social-welfare level, no consensus could be reached on what was called "economic" codetermination at company level. All Raymond and his colleagues were prepared to concede to the unions was to "recognize, in principle, rights of codetermination" at the supra-company level. The trade unions representatives took cognizance of the entrepreneurial position. They added that, in their view, the preconditions had been created for further negotiations, with the aim of ultimately arriving at a "good solution to the overall problem of equal rights for employees in the economy." In the meantime, the two sides of industry would work on proposals that would introduce codetermination rights on the personal and social level. Once these had been submitted, a further conference was to be arranged.

When the DGB held a postmortem on the Hattenheim talks on January 24–25, 1950, there were some critical comments as well as approval of the work that the DGB Economics Institute had done. At the same time there was no doubt that achieving codetermination as envisaged by Böckler was still a long way away.[19] The meeting then passed a motion that "the realization of codetermination both at supra-company and company level" was an "indivisible whole that does not allow for a partial regulation." All levels were to operate on the basis of parity "in order to implement the principle of absolute equality between capital and labor." It was also agreed to continue the Hattenheim talks.

It was probably inevitable that Böckler's reticence on November 15, 1949, notwithstanding, bits of information about the DGB's position on codetermination began to leak out. By March 3, 1950, these rumors were so ubiquitous that Raymond thought it necessary to write to Erich Bührig, a member of the DGB executive. He could no longer refrain, he wrote, from expressing his concern about the direction that the codetermination talks had been taking.[20] Apparently Adenauer's labor minister Anton Storch had also made contact with Böckler to discuss a draft of a codetermination law that the Federal government was preparing. The DGB thought this initiative to be helpful as long as the Hattenheim negotiations continued in the hope that an agreement between the two sides of industry could be struck. Perhaps seeing the larger issue, Storch now suggested that Böckler might wish to talk to the Allied high commissioners who were preparing Law No. 27 that was supposed to complete the deconcentration of the big corporations in all branches of industry. The labor minister may have hoped that the DGB might be able to influence the three high commissioners that this law would be less strictly applied. Böckler took up this suggestion, and a meeting was scheduled for March 29. While McCloy and his colleagues were no doubt interested in hearing Böckler's views on codetermination, it seems that Adenauer, on learning of it, felt that the Allies should be informed of the situation as he saw it, and so he wrote to McCloy on March 29.[21] He was probably relieved to hear that the meeting with Böckler had to be cancelled but also learned that the US high commissioner wanted to be helpful to the chancellor in finding a Federal solution by suspending the labor agreements that had been concluded at the Land level in Hesse and Baden-Württemberg.[22]

While this jockeying was going on, a second round of negotiations had been scheduled in Hattenheim for March 30–31. The notes of this meeting meticulously record the back and forth between the two sides in which a preliminary consensus was established for introducing codetermination at a supra-regional level, including the creation of a Federal Economic Council, an Agricultural Council, as well as Chambers of Industry and Commerce.[23] But the two sides could not overcome their differences on the most crucial point, that is, parity representation on the supervisory board of big corporations and the appointment of workers' representatives to the management board. The joint communiqué therefore merely recorded that the Hattenheim conference had ended without a result.[24] Informed by Raymond about this disappointing outcome, Adenauer was anxious to avoid moving the whole issue to the Bundestag and hence into the public realm.[25] On May 6, he admonished the two sides of industry not to give up and later invited them to a meeting in Bonn on May 24, 1950. Introduced by the chancellor himself, this time economics minister Ludwig Erhard and minister for labor Anton Storch had joined him.[26] Although the chancellor had to leave early, the meeting became a marathon lasting thirteen hours and ending at midnight.

By that late hour, there was at least a sense that a rapprochement had been achieved, and so the two sides agreed to meet again on June 2.[27] However, this meeting, too, merely resulted in an agreement to continue deliberations on June 9.[28] There were two more attempts to reach a consensus on June 23 in Bonn and on July 5–6, 1950, this time at Maria Laach, a remote retreat somewhat west of Koblenz, with Storch present on both occasions.[29] The notes of the second meeting merely recorded that it ended prematurely on July 6, when the DGB representatives declared that the talks were without purpose (zwecklos).[30]

Despite the many hours during which the two delegations had wrestled with different alternatives, it proved impossible to bridge the gap between what the DGB demanded and what Raymond—under pressure from industry's hardliners hovering in the background—was prepared to concede. The unions consistently demanded parity on the supervisory boards of shareholding companies with more than 1,000 employees. With regard to companies of between 500 and 1,000 employees, they were now satisfied with a representation of one-third of the seats. The most the employers were prepared to accept was a third for companies of all sizes. It was clear that other avenues had to be found to resolve this issue. This was also the conclusion of the DGB council when it met on July 15. On this occasion, the members resolved not to reject another invitation by the Federal government but to consider measures to fight for what were deemed well-founded claims for securing workers' rights in the big corporations.[31]

The Crisis of the Hattenheim Negotiations, 1950

Not surprisingly, the failure to reach an agreement at Hattenheim during the first and in all subsequent meetings inevitably created more uncertainty. Worse, as Hans Brümmer, a member of the metal workers' union executive, wrote to the DGB executive on August 2, 1950, the codetermination issue had meanwhile "landed" in the parliamentary sphere.[32] He was correct in the sense that both the CDU and the Sozialdemokratische Partei Deutsdchlands (SPD) had been preparing drafts of a codetermination law to be introduced in the Bundestag. To complicate matters further, the Federal government had been working on a draft of its own whose contents was kept secret.[33] On May 15, the DGB had published its draft of which they must have known that the employers would dislike it. The latter were, not surprisingly, also opposed to a CDU proposal envisaging a law that rejected the principle of parity altogether. If ratified, it would also have abolished the parity codetermination that the unions had won in 1947, thanks to Harris-Burland's fiat, in four steel companies, including Klöckner.[34]

With the DGB executive now thinking of countering this fundamental threat of the CDU proposal by coming out for a bare-knuckle fight in favor of parity codetermination, Böckler and also some of the more moderate steel managers scrambled to avoid a total train wreck that was bound to upset the social peace that had barely been established. At the DGB headquarters in Düsseldorf there was talk of the employers relapsing into traditional class struggle postures.[35] Worse, through an unnamed journalist, news reached the DGB that labor minister Storch had given a report to the Adenauer cabinet in Bonn about a power struggle inside the DGB between radicals and moderates that allegedly explained its contradictory policies.[36] Further hectic maneuvers ensued, and there was also the unsettling news that, with Böckler's approval, Hans vom Hoff had met with Raymond in Wiesbaden, allegedly to offer a compromise on codetermination. As no agreement had been reached even now, no further talks were expected. As to the Wiesbaden meeting, the source of this rumor was said to be close to the SPD and generally reliable. The rumors about splits inside the DGB may have fostered an impression that a power struggle was also going on inside the employers' camp. Raymond had tried hard to negotiate an agreement, but there were powerful hardliners among the employers who, while not wishing to go back to 1945 or favoring the retrograde CDU draft, certainly rejected Böckler's notion of parity for large shareholding companies. It seems that these hardliners had rallied around the recently founded BDI under the leadership of Fritz Berg who was supported by the irreconcilable Hermann Reusch. There also existed a faction of medium-sized enterprises whose leaders were vigorously opposed to the proposed expansion of parity codetermination to all branches of industry. What, in their eyes, Böckler allegedly had in mind was "totalitarian socialism," pure and simple.[37]

This view was very bluntly articulated by Otto Vogel, chairman of the management board of Schürer A.G., a medium-sized food-processing company in Augsburg, Bavaria, and vice president of the BDI. Speaking at a rally of the Employers' Federation (BdA) on November 8, 1950, he thundered that the DGB headquarters in Düsseldorf would become the power center of the entire economy.[38] To him this amounted to "a monstrous totalitarian claim to power the likes of which we have not seen since Adolf Hitler and [Nazi Labor Front leader] Robert Ley." This earlier history, he asserted, merely represented "the preliminary stage of a much greater unfolding of power." With Vogel having thrown the gauntlet by resorting to totally untenable comparisons with Nazism, Böckler promptly mentioned the speech with considerable indignation at a meeting of the DGB executive on November 21.[39] He then tried to boost morale among his colleagues by stating that this time they would not budge. Reporting to his colleagues on the worsening situation, vom Hoff mentioned that the Allied high commission had been in touch with German government agencies about the transfer of Allied rights. He added that the DGB welcomed such sovereignty transfers, though only if these negotiations made certain that the companies covered by Allied Law No. 27 also included parity representation on their supervisory boards and a corresponding composition at the management board level.[40] Vom Hoff then revealed the DGB's larger calculation: if it were possible to find a "satisfactory regulation," achieving the aims of the trade unions for the rest of the economy would "no longer be quite so difficult." It seems that he was too optimistic about getting help from the high commission, as may be gauged from the work that the Treuhand had meanwhile been doing with respect to the deconcentration of the remaining steel corporations, with VSt. most prominently on its list. At a meeting on November 24, 1950, Dinkelbach, supported by his colleague and banker Gotthard von Falkenhausen, had remarked, in the presence of Böckler and vom Hoff, that the Allies would not include, in their impending executive order, "a legal basis for codetermination in the sense of parity." Rather they were taking the view that this was a matter for the Germans to settle among themselves.[41]

This news was not the only disappointment for vom Hoff and his colleagues. They will also have been aware that on July 27 the CDU's proposal to abolish codetermination altogether had been given its first reading in the Bundestag, and that, together with the SPD's draft, it would now be winding its way through various parliamentary committees toward an eventual final vote.[42] Nor was it good news for the DGB that Erhard, a key minister, who, unlike Adenauer, had never been particularly sensitive to trade union concerns, had taken the view that codetermination was a matter for the Bundestag to decide.[43] Böckler felt that, in light of these developments, the DGB had to take a firm public stand. With the leaders of the Metal Workers' Union at his side, he announced that their claim for parity codetermination would be submitted to a vote to the members on whether to call a strike against the attempt to scrap codetermination. The Miners' Union was similarly mobilized and promised to hold a strike vote as well. On November 23, Böckler informed Adenauer of this plan.[44]

Adenauer, having failed for months to get the two sides of industry to come to an agreement on codetermination among themselves and now faced with a massive threat to strike, had no choice but to intervene in the escalating crisis. A strike was bound to damage the still fledgling domestic economy. No less important, his negotiations with West Germany's European neighbors on the Schuman Plan, to be discussed in a moment, were reaching a critical stage.[45] Disruptions, as threatened by the trade unions, would inevitably raise suspicions among West Germany's neighbors about the stability of the Adenauer coalition and the prospects of completing the negotiations for an ECSC that had been going on since May 1950. On November 27, the chancellor told Böckler in his reply that the path the DGB was taking threatened to unleash nothing less than a constitutional conflict.[46] A strike, he added, could only have as its aim to hit economic growth and to push a decision eventually to be made by freely elected deputies in the Bundestag in the direction of a support for the "wishes" of the DGB. Böckler took until December 11 to respond, but his position was as unyielding as ever.[47] He flatly refuted Adenauer's argument that the right to strike was limited to questions of wages and work conditions. Referring to Article 9 of the Basic Law, he insisted that the proposed strike over a question that touched the fundamental rights of workers was perfectly legitimate.

The chancellor now realized that, instead of writing protest letters to Böckler, he had to take more direct and constructive action. With his economics minister not being the right man to be sent to Böckler and relations between Storch and the unions also having soured after the failure of the Hattenheim talks, Adenauer sent Robert Lehr, now his Minister of the Interior and a man who was well familiar with the complexities of codetermination from his contacts with Henle in 1945–6. Appreciating how critical things had become, Lehr even took the trouble of visiting Böckler at his home on November 26, a Sunday,[48] taking Karl Arnold, one of the leaders of the Social Catholic movement and now minister president of North-Rhine Westphalia, with him. According to the protocol of the meeting that the DGB executive held in the morning of the following day, Lehr spoke of a "wish" to invite the trade union leadership to a meeting with prominent entrepreneurs for an exchange of views on codetermination.[49]

As Böckler was himself still hoping for a peaceful outcome without a strike, he agreed. Lehr also promised to recruit a small group of influential steel industrialists; Arnold volunteered to send out the invitations which, given Arnold's position in the trade union movement, Böckler will have taken as another positive signal.[50] However, he did not leave Lehr and Arnold with the slightest doubt about the trade union's response in case an understanding with industry and the government failed yet again. As before, the aim was threefold: to secure a parity agreement for supervisory boards and the position of the worker director on the management board of the big steel companies along the lines of the Harris-Burland solution; to make certain that the companies (still to be recast by McCloy under the terms of Allied Law No. 27, including the mining industry) would also become codetermined. Thirdly—although this was not mentioned in public—codetermination for all branches beyond the Ruhr heavy industries. The meeting then agreed that—apart from Böckler, vom Hoff, Walter Freitag, Erich Bührig, and Hans Brümmer—August Schmidt, the chairman of the miners' union, would join the delegation.

At this critical juncture there arose two further complications: Adenauer was told by one of his ministerial counselors that Lehr's meeting could only be launched with the approval of the Bundestag committees that were charged with the proposed legislation on codetermination.[51] Otherwise the conversations that Lehr had in mind would complicate relations between the government and the members of the Bundestag who were very conscious of their constitutional role in this matter. After all, any agreement would ultimately have to be cast into a bill to be discussed and ratified by Parliament. Moreover, if the trade unions were confirmed in their view that codetermination, while a matter to be negotiated between the two sides of industry, could also be achieved through strike action, the unions' hand would be greatly strengthened. However undesirable all this was to Adenauer, time was running short so that Lehr tapped several steel entrepreneurs, among them Hans-Günther Sohl of VSt. (in Liquidation) and Günter Henle, of whom Lehr knew from his long-standing earlier contacts that he was certainly not a hardliner like Otto Vogel.

A first meeting was scheduled for November 30. On the day before, Sohl wrote to Lehr that, having talked to Henle, he had to ask the minister for a postponement of the meeting.[52] His justification was that, after the meeting with Böckler, Lehr had mentioned that the DGB leader did not really wish to hold the proposed vote by the metal union members to approve a strike. Even if Böckler wanted to hold back, Sohl and Henle had come to the conclusion that the union as a whole was willing to strike. After all, their vote on this matter was supposed to take place on November 29 and 30. This date had left Sohl and Henle to wonder if this really was a good moment to start Lehr's bilateral talks. But appreciating what was at stake, Sohl ended his note by stressing again that he and his colleagues were prepared to come to a mutual agreement with the trade unions on the composition of the supervisory councils of the new core companies that still had to be created under Law No. 75. At the same time, he could not restrain himself completely and added that the "stubborn" demand for parity on supervisory boards and the institution of a worker director on the management board would have to be dropped. Realizing that to express this view before the proposed meeting would put a serious damper on a barely restored dialog, Sohl suggested that, in order to avoid a setback to Lehr's initiative, the trade unions should not be informed about these hardly novel positions but should merely be told that the request of a postponement was due to difficulties of finding a date that everybody could make. Judging from Henle's busy schedule, this was probably not just a diplomatic excuse.[53]

However, before Henle's role is examined with reference to the negotiations that followed in the middle of January, the larger context in which these discussions took place must be considered. After all, Sohl and Henle were not the only ones trying to resume contact with Böckler and to put their views to Adenauer. In fact, one of the central points to bear in mind for the crucial weeks of December 1950 and January 1951 is the lack of consensus among the employers and their organizations. Unlike the trade unions whose aims were straight-forward and simple, the employers' associations were lobbying hard to make their divergent views known. Furthermore, there were the ministers in the Adenauer government who raised their voice until, it seems, the chancellor invoked the constitutional rule that he alone determined the guide lines of government policy. Finally, there were attempts to draw the Allied high commission into the fray. Although the US high commissioner took a special interest in the codetermination debate and was told by one of his advisers that the model that the British had introduced in 1947 had allegedly been "very successful," McCloy decided to remain strictly neutral on this issue.[54] In his view, this was something for the Germans to settle among themselves. The only interest he had was that the aims of the Law No. 27 on the deconcentration of the remaining steel and coal corporations and their cartel-like ties, known as Verbundwirtschaft, be cut or at least curtailed.[55]

Given the scramble on the side of the employers, it is not surprising that Fritz Berg, the president of the recently founded BDI, as well as Raymond, decided to write to Adenauer.[56] They accepted, they said, Lehr's strategy of bringing just a few representatives of the coal and steel industries together for talks with Böckler. Berg was no doubt correct when he added that the situation was very serious, indeed. Raymond, having received a copy of Berg's letter, also warned of dire consequences, if the chancellor caved in. Alfred Petersen, the president of the German Chambers of Industry and Commerce (DIHT), asked if the association should follow the lead of Berg and Raymond and issue a statement of its own or try to find common ground with the other industrial interest groups.[57] When one of the participants proposed to counter the strike with a lockout by the employers, as had been the practice in the Weimar Republic, Petersen thought it inappropriate to take a position on the strike. Apart from the industrial associations, there were also individual corporate managers who thought that they could help forge a consensus with the DGB.

Prominently among them was Hermann Winkhaus, the deputy chair of the Mannesmann management board. He had responded to feelers that he reported the miners' union had put out to him. A meeting with them was promptly scheduled for December 20, but had to be postponed.[58] With the Christmas holidays coming up, the trade unions had, according to Winkhaus, suggested a meeting early in the New Year, which in fact took place on January 8.[59] While Böckler welcomed talks in a larger circle from both sides that was accordingly scheduled for January 11, Winkhaus continued to maneuver on his own until he began to realize that his "circle of friends" had been outpaced by Sohl and Henle.[60] As he wrote to Böckler on January 9 and to his Mannesmann colleague Wilhelm Zangen a week later, Adenauer had meanwhile indicated that he wanted to take the reins himself and work with corporate leaders who were not only directly involved in both deconcentration and codetermination issues but were also close to the chancellor.[61] Feeling that he did not quite belong to this circle, Winkhaus decided to drop out. None too happy with this outcome, he wrote that what had made his retreat easier for him were bitter memories he had of the past: having been interned by the Allies for two years in 1945, he had sworn to himself not to meddle in this kind of politics. Of course, should he be asked to participate in the impending negotiations, he would be very willing to serve. In other words, it was not just the experience of being sidelined by his colleagues; what rankled Winkhaus no less deeply was his treatment by the Allies in the early postwar years. This was an aspect of the psychology of postwar industrial politics that deserves further investigation by other scholars.

Chancellor Adenauer Takes Charge of Settling the Codetermination Conflict

By early January 1951, it was thus clear that it was Adenauer's turn. When, after his exchange with Böckler on the legality of a mass strike and after both the miners and steelworkers had overwhelmingly approved strike action, the chancellor realized that he could not leave codetermination to others and that he had to find a group of leaders in the Ruhr industry who would help him negotiate a compromise with the DGB. Not surprisingly, his choice fell on Henle who, considering the positions on labor relations that he had taken up in earlier years, was willing to contribute to a solution. Perhaps even more significantly, he had begun to ponder the possible terms of a grand bargain. It is not that Henle was prepared to accept Böckler's demands hook, line, and sinker; but as Hans-Helmut Kuhnke, director of Klöckner & Co., wrote to Gerhard Schroeder, a director of Klöckner Werke A.G., as well as to Karl Jarres, a member of that company's supervisory board and Henle's mentor after 1945, on December 7, 1950, he wanted to meet them again to go over the problems with them.[62] He had also formulated an offer to be put to the trade unions: the supervisory board would have a 6:5 split, that is, six shareholder representatives sitting next to five of the worker representatives. He also wanted to accept a worker director, though not as a full member of the management board, as demanded by the unions.

After the unions had announced on January 4, 1951, that the strike would start in the evening of January 31, there was not much time to bring the two sides together under Adenauer's chairmanship. When the DGB Federal Committee met on January 12, Arnold was invited to join as a "tested friend."[63] Adenauer had been in touch with Böckler, and on January 17 the chancellor invited the industrialists for a preliminary discussion at which it was agreed to invite five delegates from the two sides.[64] They were Henle, Wenzel (for VSt.), Kost, and Hueck for mining and finally Robert Pferdmenges, Adenauer's close friend and a member of the Klöckner supervisory board.[65] Receiving the DGB delegation for its briefing on the following day, the chancellor referred in his introductory remarks to the earlier disputes between the two sides of industry over codetermination but stressed that he had always felt that a special arrangement had to be made because of the crucial position that coal and steel traditionally occupied in the German economy as a whole.[66] At the same time labor relations in the Ruhr region had been tense in the past and, as he admitted, had not changed. As the threat of a strike was still hanging over the country, it was clear that Adenauer wished to avoid one at all cost. Accordingly, he decided to remind the delegation not merely of the domestic repercussions of a strike but also of the critical stage that his negotiations had reached to promote European reconciliation and integration and to create the ECSC. Although Böckler will have taken Adenauer's statement as a hopeful sign, he nevertheless used the meeting to justify once more why parity codetermination was indispensable to the DGB.

Displaying his earlier optimism, the chancellor replied that he had not come to this meeting "to defend the entrepreneurs" but hoped to steer the matter toward a solution that was in the interest of the West German people as a whole. He then became encouragingly frank, stating:[67] "I am in favor of parity for the supervisory boards together with the insertion (Einschaltung) of the government." Even more strikingly, he declared that he stood by the Ahlen Program of February 1947 in which the CDU had denounced concentrations of economic power and had favored a participation of the workforce in company governance. In his conclusion, he even went so far as to suggest an agreement between the two sides of industry under which the supervisory boards of the steel companies would have four shareholder representatives and four nominated by the employees. Finally, three seats were to be reserved for the public sector. The chancellor then added that he expected a parallel solution to be adopted for the mining industry. Although no concrete decisions were made, the meeting agreed that Adenauer's office would put out a brief statement that a meeting had taken place and that both sides were "hopeful" of a positive outcome on codetermination. After this, the DGB lost no time to nominate the members of its team: Böckler, vom Hoff, Freitag, Deist, and Heinrich Imig, the deputy chair of the miners' union.

The two delegations of five members each came together in the chancellery on January 19, at 10 a.m.[68] Adenauer attended only in the beginning, but in line with his remarks at the meeting on the previous day he made a telling gesture that Sohl reported in his memoirs: [69]he asked Böckler to sit next to him, with Pferdmenges and his colleagues seated across the table. Interestingly enough, the DGB chief, apparently remembering his conversations with the VSt. manager in 1945, asked Adenauer that Sohl be included. However, the agreement had been for no more than five representatives per delegation, and with Wenzel being the more senior colleague, Sohl had to stand back to accommodate Henle as the second steel representative as well as two mining managers, Kost and Hueck. It certainly was all very carefully balanced. When Adenauer left the meeting, he must have been hoping that he had prepared the ground well both in terms of representation and of an agenda for a settlement—the goal that had become a major challenge to his political skills, moral authority, and capacity to reach compromises not only with respect to labor relations but also to the parallel task of integrating the Federal Republic into Western Europe and more specifically into the ECSC.

After Adenauer's departure Böckler suggested that Pferdmenges take the chair, and the delegates spent the day to exchange their respective negotiating positions. As on previous occasions, Böckler reviewed the history of codetermination as far back as the interwar period and again demanded parity representation in company governance. When it came to the composition of the supervisory boards, the employers suggested four representatives from each side, plus one to be sent by the Federal government and two more who were not owners but nonetheless well familiar with the company in question and close to the entrepreneurial side. By contrast, the trade unions proposed five representatives from each side, with an eleventh member jointly chosen by the two sides. Other delegates offered variations to these two models. For example, Pferdmenges preferred two neutral chairs, of whom one could be a government representative. It was apparently later on that the employers specified the qualifications that the eleventh person was expected to have. He—and this was still very much a male-dominated world of big business—was to have no ties to either side. He was to be of impeccable character and to have a good knowledge of the national economy or of economics. The subsequent discussion also yielded a positive result with regard to the worker director on the management board. The employers accepted such a person, even in cases of firms where the board as a whole had just three members. As neither side expected an agreement after the first day, and it had by then become 7 p.m., another meeting was arranged for January 22 that had to be postponed till the 25th.

The postponement was due to a lack of agreement between the two sides on January 19 whose specifics are difficult to extract from the record of the meeting but can be gauged from a file note of a meeting that Henle and his four colleagues held in Bonn with their DGB counterparts on January 22 with reference to points that had been left open.[70] According to this document, Kost and Hueck saw no problem with a codetermination agreement that covered all mining companies. However, as far as steel was concerned, both Wenzel and Henle insisted that the document should apply only to companies that fell under deconcentration Law No. 27. No other corporations were to be included, and this was also to hold for subsidiaries of companies that were not involved in iron and steel production. Henle and Wenzel merely conceded that processing plants that were subdivisions rather than separate entities under Law No. 27 core corporations would be included. Apparently the DGB representatives agreed to these differentiations in principle but did not give their explicit consent.

It seems that Henle was especially keen to lock in this particular solution, as it affected his Klöckner Werke A.G. and its links with Klöckner-Humboldt-Deutz, the manufacturer of heavy vehicles and other engineering equipment. To Freitag, on the other hand, this matter was no more than a side question that could be settled later on. Deist merely made a vague comment on the issue. If this demonstrated once again that the delegations had very different interests, leaving Henle dissatisfied, there was at least general agreement between the two sides that, on the basis of a 5:5 division on the supervisory board, the professional qualifications of the eleventh member would have to be those that Deist had proposed, that is, it would have to be someone who was trusted by all sides, possessed experience and expertise in the coal and steel industries, and was also known for his "ability to have a conciliatory influence in difficult situations." Henle's file note ended with the statement that the position of the worker director was discussed exclusively with respect to the mining industry.

So, the worker director was yet another issue that had to be settled with respect to the steel companies.

The dating and origins of a memo for an "agreement on the codetermination question" appear in a note at the bottom, stating that it was "dictated by … Henle, Pferdmenges, Kost, Wenzel and Hueck" on the day of their meeting with the DGB.[71] As that meeting had ended at 7 p.m., it is possible that the employers decided to record their positions on the number of seats on supervisory boards, the electoral terms for the eleventh persons, and, thirdly, the worker-director question immediately thereafter. On the other hand, if this internal agreement was produced before the meeting with the DGB, its details were not revealed to the union representatives. All we have therefore is a "dictated" statement that the five men agreed among themselves on a 5:5 split of seats for the supervisory council, plus a proposal for the distribution of the five employee representatives (two workers, one white-collar employee, and two nominated by the trade unions) and further details relating to the appointment a worker director. Yet, the position of this worker director was not to be equal to that of the other members of the management board; instead he would be responsible for welfare issues as defined by the "guidelines" adopted by the management board as a whole. Moreover, he would also be expected to keep the personnel files of blue-collar workers as well as white-collar employees who were covered by a separate agreement that their union had made with the employers' association, the BdA.

While this meant some progress, the specifications did not amount to equality and were therefore bound to lead to questions from Böckler and his colleagues at the next joint meeting that Adenauer hoped would finally end in a joint agreement so that the strike could be called off. However, the chancellor was again besieged by inquiries and warnings from various employer associations that had been excluded from the meeting on February 19. Thus, the advisory council of the association of the North-Rhine Westphalian metal industries held a meeting on January 20, 1951, at which Hans Bilstein, its chair, stated that, in light of the negotiations in Bonn, he no longer reckoned with a strike.[72] The idea of a lockout that some circles had been mooting was therefore also fast becoming a nonstarter.

However, in the subsequent "lively" debate, chaired by Bilstein, mention was made of motions that had been introduced by the chemical unions demanding codetermination for their industries. The meeting promptly deplored such demands, but also the lack of a united front among the employers, as neither the BDI nor the Bundesvereinigung deutscher Arbeitgeberverbände (BdA) were legitimated to speak for the coal and steel companies. In other words,

Bilstein's association did not want to be bound by decisions that were being made elsewhere. It was also awkward for Adenauer that Raymond felt obliged to send a telegram in which he expressed the fear that the terms of the coal and steel agreements with the DGB would have repercussion for other branches of industry.[73] Finally, the North-Rhine Westphalian Landtag caucus of the Free Democratic Party (FDP) informed the chancellor that if the DGB's notions of codetermination were adopted without the "participation of legislative bodies," this would be tantamount to a breach of the constitution and that the chancellor, in the FDP's view, would be abandoning the foundations of democracy.[74] Nor would a settlement without an involvement of the legislature find a majority among the political parties. In other words, any agreement on codetermination had to be put through the Bundestag or risk the end of the government coalition.

Rattled by these criticisms and the threat to his position as chancellor, Adenauer, having received a copy of what the steel industrialists had put together on January 22, knew that more hurdles lay ahead, once the two delegations had at last found a consensus on codetermination. He therefore asked Henle and Pferdmenges to determine up to what limit they were willing to make concessions.[75] Putting pressure on them, but himself also under pressure, Adenauer reminded them of the "pledge" (Zusage) they had supposedly given to the trade unions in early 1947.[76] Henle replied that the latter had rejected this offer at the time and that it had therefore lapsed.[77] If, he added, "we had really made mistakes," then "we do not wish to repeat" them "in 1951." With their differences of opinion persisting, the two left Adenauer "visibly dissatisfied." Having told Böckler that he favored parity and desperate to forge an agreement, the chancellor called a special meeting of his cabinet for January 24, hoping to obtain the backing of his ministers.[78] Franz Blücher, as minister for the Marshall Plan, voiced qualms about how an expansion of codetermination would affect the credit worthiness of West German companies. With Jakob Kaiser, the minister for All-German Questions, joining him, it was Erhard who came to the rescue. He dropped his earlier concerns by stating that matters had advanced so far that a divergence from the path taken hitherto was no longer possible.

Armed with this somewhat dodgy ministerial backing, the chancellor opened what was the second and final meeting between the two groups, presumably wondering how it would end. The minutes of this meeting trace the back and forth between the two sides and need not be recorded here. After more than five hours of debate, the participants agreed on a press announcement stating that, with the chancellor in the chair, they had come to an agreement on codetermination in coal and steel. Furthermore, the Federal cabinet had met immediately thereafter to resolve that a draft law would now be transmitted to both the Bundestag and Bundesrat.[79] The particulars of what ultimately and after further debate in the Bundestag would be put on the statute book were hammered out by a Redaktionsausschuss made up of Kost, Henle, Schroeder, vom Hoff, Deist, Lorenz Höcker, the legal counsel of the Deutsche Kohlenbergbau-Leitung (DKBL), and Hans Korsch, the legal counsel of the DGB.[80] Again, we can omit a detailed account of the committee's "guidelines relating to codetermination in the coal and iron-making industry," except to reiterate that the proposal was for an eleven-member supervisory board and for a worker director as a full member of the management board who was expected to work, like the other members, in "closest consensus" with the board as a whole.[81]

Parity Codetermination and Its Ratification by the Bundestag

With these "guidelines" in place, it is interesting how the two sides assessed the results of their negotiations. Henle's position emerged from a letter that he wrote to Pferdmenges on January 31 in which he took the view that, with regard to codetermination, "parliament and government" had been "run over by a power factor within the state (eine Macht im Staate)."[82] Adenauer's "great personal success" in settling the issue could not, he added, distract from this fact. Meanwhile, the DGB had come to a more optimistic conclusion when its Federal Committee met.[83] As vom Hoff reported on this occasion, parity had been accepted and the role of the trade unions had been recognized. The problem of the worker director had also been settled within a "satisfactory framework." The strike could therefore be called off. Significantly, vom Hoff considered this success to be a start "on the path [toward establishing] codetermination in the economy as a whole." Later on, Freitag highlighted the great contribution that Böckler had made to this success ever since 1945 and thanked him profusely. In his reply, the DGB leader stressed that they all had opened the door for the pursuit of a continuing struggle to expand the new system of parity codetermination to all industries. If he had wished for anything, it would have been greater solidarity, something that he hoped would come to exist in the future. He then spoke about the importance of finding representatives for the supervisory boards and for the position of the worker director. They would not only have to be well prepared for their job but also feel a strong sense of responsibility and be "decent" (anständige) men. In conclusion, Böckler could not resist making a remark about those managers who had succeeded over many decades in keeping "alien elements" away from their companies. Perhaps thinking of Reusch and other hardliners rather than Henle or Sohl and imagining their long faces, he wondered what their attitudes might be now that codetermination had been agreed.

The months of February to the middle of May were taken up with laborious negotiations in the Bundestag.[84] With Henle being a CDU deputy, he inevitably witnessed how the draft legislation wound its way very slowly through an array of committees during its first and second readings. It was only on February 14 that he made a longer speech that started with a reference to his involvement in the January negotiations by stating that it would obviously not be appropriate for him as a participant to defend or criticize the results of negotiations led by Adenauer.[85] Instead he thought it more important first to turn to the past, before looking into the future. As to the past, he reminded his colleagues of the conversations that Lehr had initiated in 1946. He admitted that they may not have yielded results but they had not been useless. After all, they had made it possible for "leading men from both sides" personally to get to know each other and to exchange their thoughts on "important economic and social problems." These, Henle continued, formed the background to the deconcentration policies that Harris-Burland and Dinkelbach had imposed. It was in opposition to their policies that Klöckner, the Otto Wolff Corporation, and GHH had formulated their own counterproposals. This had been the context in which they had first proposed "co-participation rights" for employees. Henle specifically mentioned Jarres's letter of January 18, 1947, to Böckler that had contained suggestions for a recasting of the supervisory boards.[86] If an agreement had come about at the time, Henle felt the Ruhr steel and coal companies would have been spared the *via dolorosa* of deconcentration. In fact, he felt it could have been avoided altogether.

Notwithstanding the subsequent failure of these early contacts, Henle continued, the steel companies had maintained their interest in a "co-participation and codetermination" of their employees. This is why they had never given up on the idea of continuing negotiations that had now borne fruit in the agreement of January 25, 1951. Given the serious consequences that a failure would have had this time, it had been better to come to an understanding, whereas a cancellation of the talks by one side or the other would simply have been irresponsible. As one of the participants in the codetermination talks, Henle was willing to accept criticism, as those earlier times when this was forbidden were, "thank God," over. Indeed, he added, he shared the critical comments of some of the peculiar circumstances in which the discussions had taken place. The concessions that the corporations were prepared to make went right up to the limit of what was still acceptable to them. He and his colleagues had acted in the hope that an agreement could be achieved and that a strike would be unnecessary, also in light of the "serious times that we are living through." And yet there was a moment in the middle of March 1951 that demonstrated that Adenauer did not observe a strict neutrality and that Sohl, the outsider, had kept in close touch with the Klöckner leadership in an effort to tip the scales, if only slightly, in favor of the employers: on March 10 Pferdmenges had called Sohl with the news that he had met Adenauer "in a small circle" for a discussion of codetermination at which the issue of the eleventh man had once more come up.[87] After this, the banker and friend of the chancellor thought that "the matter would be settled in our sense."

The codetermination drafts passed the various parliamentary hurdles at considerable speed. The third reading began in May, and the law was passed on the 21st.[88] It left a possible expansion of the law to other branches open, although the employers had repeatedly insisted that this window had been explicitly closed. It took until 1976 for another highly complex law to pass the Bundestag that expanded codetermination beyond coal and steel and shifted the balance of power between employers and unions slightly but preserved the ultimate influence of the former. Moreover, the actual implementation of the 1951 law still required further negotiations relating in particular to the mining industry to be analyzed in Chapter 5, also with regard to Henle's position on the future of Verbundwirtschaft between coal and steel.[89] With the basic framework of codetermination in place, another understanding between the two sides of industry was waiting to be negotiated and to be cast into a law. This time the issue was the rights and duties of the works councils that had played such an important role in the postwar reconstruction of the economy. Eventually their role would be recognized in a Works Constitution Law (Betriebsverfassungsgesetz [BVG]), ratified in 1952. While the codetermination drama unfolded at the end of January 1951, there were finally the problems of Law No. 27 covering deconcentration. These were in turn related to the negotiations on the ECSC that Adenauer had used to push the West German coal and steel corporations into an agreement on codetermination. Chapter 5 will therefore have to deal with this complicated question in which Henle once more played an important role.

5

The Origins and Creation of the European Coal and Steel Community

If Chapter 4 examined the conflicted history of the codetermination debate in 1950–1 and its resolution by the Mitbestimmungsgesetz of May 1951 that introduced parity representation for the trade unions in the coal and steel industries as well as the position of a worker director on management boards, this chapter revolves around two related issues that also required settlement at the same time: Law No. 27 that was supposed to complete the Allied deconcentration process of the big corporations. Secondly, the solution that was found cannot be separated from the origins of the Schuman Plan, announced in May 1950 and finally agreed by the governments of six West European states a year later, thenceforth known as European Coal and Steel Community (ECSC). Again Günter Henle played an important role in its shaping and ratification process.

Previous chapters have examined the first phase of Allied policies of breaking up a number of major corporations as stipulated in the Potsdam Agreement of August 1945. After months and years of rather haphazard decision making by individual zonal military authorities, the next phase eventually became enshrined in Allied Law No. 75 of November 10, 1948, that replaced the British Law No. 56 of February 1947.[1] Up to that point, Britain had forged ahead with the deconcentration of four steel corporations under the direction of William Harris-Burland, the head of North German Iron and Steel Control (NGISC). He was assisted by the Treuhandverwaltung under Heinrich Dinkelbach.[2] With the formation of the British-American Bi-Zone, NGISC was replaced by the UK/US Steel Control through which the Americans began to oppose some of the more far-reaching plans of the Labour government in London that envisaged the expropriation and nationalization of Ruhr mining and steel-making. The Office of Military Government US (OMGUS) under General Clay, with William Draper as his economic adviser and Paul Hoffman as the administrator of Marshall

Plan funds for the reconstruction of Western Europe, the Americans began to call the shots in the Allied deconcentration effort. Washington, faced with the beginning of the Cold War against the Soviet Bloc, wanted to use the potentially still very powerful Ruhr industries as the main engine to revive the other West European economies. However, while rejecting British-style nationalization, OMGUS, like Harris-Burland, was convinced that Ruhr steel and mining had to be reorganized. It was not just a matter of banning the formation of cartels, syndicates, and monopolies that Clay had decreed; apart from the four companies that the British had earmarked, a number of other conglomerates, such as VSt. and IG Farben, were deemed too big and therefore had to be broken up. The Allied Law No. 75 was supposed to achieve this objective.

British-American Conflicts Relating to Dismantling and Deconcentration

It was probably inevitable that tensions would arise between the British and American deconcentrators, the more so since the British military authorities in the Ruhr continued to dismantle production facilities that both OMGUS and also West German corporate managers as well as their workers considered to be counterproductive in light of the rapidly changing international situation and the perceived Soviet threat. Robert Lehr raised this question at a meeting with Lt. General Sir Brian Robertson, the British Military Governor, on October 18, 1947, on which we have a detailed account by Günter Henle. This time he acted as a member of the Economic Council that had been constituted as a voice of the officially licensed political parties in the three Western zones of occupation.[3] The occasion was the recent publication of the list of enterprises that the British had decided to dismantle, and Sir Brian told the meeting in no uncertain terms that he was in no mood to discuss this list. The dismantling would go ahead regardless of German objections. To reinforce his point, he invoked his American colleague General Clay who had allegedly stated that, if these policies encountered German resistance, it would be more difficult to convince the American public that they should continue to provide material and financial aid to the West Germans. At the same time, Sir Brian promised that he would do his best to provide foodstuffs and other necessities and that Clay would join this effort. Turning to his audience, he then stressed that law and order could be reestablished only through a joint effort. If, as he had been reading, German participation was deemed a "collaboration," he would have to say that comparisons with pre-1945 events were quite inappropriate. If the Germans thought that dismantling was undertaken because Britain was afraid of German competition, they should look at the list. To be sure, Sir Brian concluded, Anglo-German competition would be unavoidable in some branches, but the situation should be examined unsentimentally. It was his plan to work with Germans in a spirit of fairness.

Robert Lehr next responded to these remarks, highlighting how he had worked "loyally" with the occupation authorities after the end of the war. He warned that the list had unsettled the German population and that people would only accept German leaders like him, if he could demonstrate that he had done his best in his negotiations with the more powerful occupation authorities. He continued by pointing to flaws in the British calculations of actual German steel capacities, proposing that the figures should be corrected. When it was Henle's turn, he also insisted on the need for reliable statistics, before drawing attention to the fact that the list was tilted toward machine engineering and its base, that is, steel-making. The development of the economy as a whole, he continued, depended "decisively" on the extent to which these sectors were being dismantled. In the end, Henle, too, pleaded that the steel industry be given more time to respond to Sir Brian's list. At this point the British general, anxious to avoid long arguments, agreed that he would give the Germans two weeks to respond and that in the meantime his experts would meet with the German side to come up with accurate capacity calculations.

While Clay and the Americans are likely to have heard about this meeting, it is doubtful that they were happy about Sir Brian's hard line on the dismantling issue. American businessmen visiting the Rhineland and various commissions sent by Washington certainly assessed the situation differently. They found that dismantling was irrational. To them it was clear that the practice had to stop as soon as possible. Washington wanted Western Europe united economically and ideally also politically, also in light of the escalating East-West conflict. It was only after the founding of the Federal Republic, endowed with limited sovereignty rights and after the election of Konrad Adenauer as chancellor, that his influential voice was added to this opposition. On November 22, 1949, he finally succeeded in halting the British removal and destruction of industrial installations.

However, this did not mean that the deconcentration of VSt., IG Farben, and other corporations had been abandoned. After all, the decision-makers in the United States pursued the construction of an Open Door international economy without protectionist cartels and monopolies. They favored an oligopolistic market structure in which large companies would compete against each other, as was the tradition in the United States.[4] This vision clashed not only with British dismantling policies but also with London's alternative Imperial vision of the postwar world economy. Labour as well as Britain's Conservatives wanted to secure the country's future not as part of Western Europe but by fostering their long-standing ties with the Empire and Commonwealth. The trouble was that this had become a dodgy project after 1945 not only because it was anathema to the United States as the hegemonic power of the West, but also because decolonization had definitely set in and was bound to continue. Britain, by contrast, continued to live under the illusion that the Empire and Commonwealth was a viable alternative to the Pax Americana. This miscalculation became crystal clear during the Suez crisis of 1956 when US president Dwight D. Eisenhower stopped the reassertion of colonial ambitions in London by telling prime minister Anthony Eden to leave Egypt without delay or, instead of sending the US navy, he would sink the pound sterling.[5] Eden got out of Suez very quickly.

However, back in 1949–50 the weakness of Britain's international position had not yet dawned on the Labour government in London, the Conservatives under Winston Churchill, and the British political and economic elites more generally. Worse, Washington and London did not see eye to eye, and not just because Attlee's socialism did not mesh too well with American New Deal capitalism. To make the coordination of Allied policies in West Germany even more difficult, the French appeared more prominently on the scene in 1948. They had more or less successfully begun to sort out their own domestic problems and, no less important, in 1946 had launched an industrial modernization program directed by Jean Monnet. Especially the steel industries of northern France were to be strengthened. At the same time Paris, remembering the Nazi occupation, watched American policies of reconstructing and recasting the Ruhr region with apprehension. In order to raise the French voice in the Allied inter-zonal administration, they pushed for the Bi-Zone to be expanded to a Tri-Zone.

After this had been achieved, the French government promptly demanded a say in the reorganization of West Germany's heavy industries. Apart from discussions of more long-term alternatives, such as the internationalization of the Ruhr region, there was the immediate issue of deconcentration of coal and steel that would result in a weakening of the economic power of the Ruhr region. To accommodate the French, Law No. 75 was changed to Law No. 27 that focused on completing the liquidation of six major steel corporations. The Bi-Zonal UK/ US Steel Group became the Tri-Zonal Combined Steel Group, while the TrHV was enlarged, with Dinkelbach still in the chair, but this time surrounded by some ten additional Treuhänder.[6] Originally Günter Henle had been asked to join but refused. He felt unable to give up the management of the complex Klöckner empire, as required under the new trustee rules. Professor Alfons Wagner who had at first also been included in the group, resigned in January 1951 when he could not agree with the Steel Group's plan to cut the traditional Verbundwirtschaft link between coal and steel, an issue to be discussed later in this chapter.[7]

McCloy's Indirect Support for Codetermination

However, before I analyze the solutions that were found under American leadership in line with the prescriptions of the tripartite Allied Law No. 27, there is an interesting sideline to be considered, relating to the codetermination settlement. It is revealing of the dominant vision of West German industrial reconstruction inside the Allied high commission that had replaced Allied Military Government after the founding of the Federal Republic in 1949. To establish this republic was another major decision made in Washington when in 1948 the US government encouraged the West Germans to draft a Basic Law, that is, a constitutional document. Once it had been ratified, elections for the Bundestag followed in the autumn of 1949. After the new parliament had been constituted, a majority of deputies elected the Federal government with Konrad Adenauer as chancellor.[8] Apart from organizing a working parliamentary democracy, labor relations were the other major issue in which General Clay had become involved in 1948–9.[9] In order to facilitate an agreement between "capital and labor" at an inter-zonal level, he had suspended the clauses of the Works Council laws with which two federal states, Baden-Württemberg and Hesse, had introduced separate codetermination systems in these two Länder. Clay's successor, US high commissioner John McCloy, had upheld this suspension. With Böckler's claims for parity still on the table, it is not surprising that the DGB chairman tried to get McCloy to side with the unions in their struggle with the employers to lock in the DGB model of parity representation in the supervisory boards of the big steel and coal corporations as well as the position of a worker director at management board level.

In the hope of strengthening its position, the DGB had meanwhile also mobilized the American Federation of Labor (AFL) and its influential president Walter Reuther.[10] He and his colleagues in the Congress of Industrial

Organization (CIO), while dead opposed to any socialization experiments, had built participatory arrangements into the collective bargaining agreement that they had concluded in various branches of industry back in the United States. It was only that they had not cast these agreements into formal laws, as in West Germany.[11] Responding to their German colleagues, Reuther's AFL had come out in favor of the DGB's version of parity codetermination, although it was unhappy about "Clay's policy of suspension" in Hesse and Baden-Württemberg. However, with the Federal Republic established and the Hattenheim negotiations, mentioned in Chapter 4, underway in early 1950, the US high commissioner agreed with Reuther on a moratorium that gave Adenauer breathing space in his quest to forge a comprehensive codetermination law for the Federal Republic as a whole. The problem was that the Americans had set a very short deadline of April 1, 1950, for the passage of this law. Should the chancellor fail to meet it, McCloy had promised Reuther to end the suspension of the two Länder laws. On April 4, Böckler informed McCloy of a letter he had written to Adenauer that the Hattenheim negotiations had reached a dead end. Four days later, McCloy promptly reinstated the codetermination laws in Hesse and Baden-Württemberg. According to Henry Rutz, the AFL's European representative, this decision marked a "great success for the German trade unions."[12] It certainly created two regional precedents and spurred Adenauer to make an even more strenuous effort to get the two sides of industry to reach a comprehensive agreement on codetermination.

However, the appearance of the AFL also gave the West German employers time to alert their American friends. Like their West German colleagues opposed to any kind of parity, the American business community and its lobbies, with the National Association of Manufacturers (NAM) in the lead, began to voice its criticisms. In the meantime, the codetermination crisis inside the Federal Republic had grown more serious. As will be remembered, there was Otto Vogel's very polemical speech before the BdA in Munich on November 28, 1950, followed by an overwhelming vote by the metal workers and miners in favor of calling a strike.[13] NAM reacted to this threat by raising the scary prospect that American investments would be drying up, if West German industry became codetermined. After earlier rumblings, this opposition finally became so strong that on January 31, 1951, NAM president Karl Bunting officially wrote to Heinrich Krekeler, the West German consul general in New York, to express his concern about codetermination that, as we have seen, had by then at last been agreed on between Böckler and the steel and mining companies and had been moved over to the Bundestag to be cast into a properly ratified law.[14] Of course,

Bunting assured Krekeler that he did not wish to interfere in a decision that was to be put to a democratic vote by elected West German deputies. Yet, he felt obliged to let Krekeler know that American investors had been following labor relations in West Germany with "growing disquiet." The consul general no doubt reported Bunting's visit to Adenauer without delay.

With both AFL and NAM appearing on the scene, it is not surprising that McCloy felt a need to get more information on the threatened strike of the metal workers and miners. To find out, he sent Harvey Brown, the director of his labor office, to meet with trade unionists. Subsequently, he also had a long conversation with Walter Freitag, Hans Brümmer, and Max Bock at the very end of 1950.[15] They told him about "the deplorable conditions" in the steel industry in 1945 and the position of the then British Military Governor that one of the answers to this situation would be a wider cooperative arrangement between management and union representatives. The delegation added that "during annual meetings of a number of decartelized steel plants mention had been made of the surprisingly beneficial results [gained] from this new type of managerial organization (codetermination)" on which both management and union representatives had even been "congratulated." Harkening back to German history before 1945, Freitag then confirmed the trade unions' determination to push their claims. With the experience of the Imperial and Hitler periods behind them, the DGB was now very firm that this time the unions would "do everything" within their "power to keep the German people from being sold down the river for a third time." Brown came away with the conclusion that "never before was it so necessary that we do everything possible to prevent German organized labor from losing faith in the American element of the Occupation Powers." This is also why Brown felt that, if the labor movement was not given support, "we would not have that much-needed influence, necessary in making the German labor movement a greater force for democracy." He might have added that the trade unions could also be useful mediators in McCloy's quest to complete deconcentration.

Brown's report made McCloy wish to hear the DGB story himself, and so, on December 14, 1950, he asked Freitag, Matthias Föcher, the deputy chair of the DGB, August Schmidt and Franz Grosse of IG Bergbau, and Heinrich Deist as a member of Treuhand group for dinner at his private residence in Bad Godesberg, followed by a discussion that took place in a friendly and personal atmosphere.[16] This was surely an extraordinary gesture of good will by McCloy in which Brown and two other High Commission for Germany (HICOG) experts participated.[17] The meeting spent some time talking about codetermination, with Schmidt insisting that his mining union was no less keen to see codetermination accepted than IG Metall. Raising the question of the role of the Stahltreuhänder, the high commissioner rejected the idea that they could be members of the supervisory boards of corporations that were being created under Allied deconcentration plans. The third item on the agenda was, significantly enough, concerned with "decartelization and de-concentration" in the context of "the Schuman Plan." McCloy reiterated "very cautiously" that he would uphold his neutral position with regard to codetermination. Only if this proved impossible, would he make a decision that did not violate "the interests of the employees." According to his file note, Deist felt that McCloy understood the claims of the trade unions and was prepared to meet them more than halfway.

Jean Monnet and the Origins of the Schuman Plan

Deist's evaluation of the meeting was too optimistic. With the AFL pushing on one side and NAM on the other, McCloy increasingly found himself between a rock and a hard place and decided to tackle deconcentration without enlisting the DGB. However, there was yet another reason why deconcentration had to be resolved. To understand the pressures that McCloy was under in 1949–50, it is important to look at the French picture and, in this context, also to consider the career and role of Jean Monnet. As a French businessman, he had been opposed to the Nazi occupation of France and had fled to Britain in 1940 to join the French government in exile led by General Charles de Gaulle. With the British holding out even after the desperate evacuation from the beaches of Dunkirk to get the defeated expeditionary force home across the Channel, Prime Minister Winston Churchill appealed to US president Franklin Roosevelt to supply the last bastion against the Nazi conquest of Western and Northern Europe with weapons and food. When this was granted, first on a cash-and-carry basis and later under the Lend-Lease program, Jean Monnet was invited by Churchill to go to Washington as a member of the "British Purchasing Commission" to continue "those services in connection with supplies from North America which have been so valuable to us during the time when you were chairman of the Anglo-French Coordinating Committee."[18]

Living in the US capital, Monnet had many opportunities to learn not only about the huge industrial and financial capacities of the United States, but also about American plans for the future, especially once the country had entered the war and it had become clear that the defeat of Hitler and his allies was only a matter of time. While in Washington, Monnet held his ears close to the ground and learned about Washington's blueprints for the establishment of a new international order and the creation of an Open Door multilateral world economy after the defeat of the Axis powers. As he put it during a hearing of the Economic Affairs Committee of the Conseil de la République in December 1949:[19]

> We are in a world undergoing a total transformation. You can no longer think of the future in the context of the past. We Europeans are still haunted by past notions of security and stability. Today the principal idea is that of [socio-economic] expansion. That is what is happening in the United States. They are always ready to evolve and search out progress.

Returning to France after the end of the war with these impressions, Monnet realized that the French economy was poorly prepared for the competitive capitalism that American planners had in mind when they pondered the integration of German industry into Western Europe as part of a comprehensive Pax Americana. With the punitive period of the Allied occupation of Germany gradually being replaced by reconstruction, Monnet, having observed Washington's economic policies and knowing about the relative weakness of the French economy in comparison to that of its German neighbor, persuaded the French government to launch the "Commissariat du Plan, de Modernisation et d'Equipement" in 1946.[20] The title of this organization gives its mission away. With Monnet at the head, it was to encourage and push French industry to increase its productivity and to overcome its protectionist and anticompetitive traditions by preparing itself for the American-dominated Open Door. The northern French steel industry deserved particularly favorable consideration. The efforts of Monnet's commissariat certainly encouraged change at the level of installing more modern equipment. Apparently, in the context of these efforts, several steel works in northern France formed the "Union sidérurgique du Nord de la France (Usinor)" in 1947. This association was supposed to facilitate the purchase of both warm and cold rolling mills from the United States. On March 3, 1949, the Brussels newspaper *Le Soir* published an article on the construction of modern French broad-band rolling mill.[21]

While French heavy industry underwent a more or less successful modernization process, partly financed by American aid, it was no secret that by 1948 the big corporations of the Ruhr region had once again become serious competitors, as John Davenport had reported in the American business magazine *Fortune* in October 1949.[22] Still traumatized by the memories of two world wars and witnessing the rebirth of the Ruhr industries, it was perfectly understandable that France was looking for ways to contain the rising economic power of its Eastern neighbor. It was also of concern to Paris that Britain, while still dismantling industrial installations, was increasingly focused on reviving its Imperial and Commonwealth interests rather than helping advance West European unification and reorganizing West German industry. And as far as the United States were concerned, it was clear enough that, unlike the French, they did not feel particularly threatened economically and demographically by the size of the German companies in comparison to giant corporations such as US Steel, General Electric, General Motors, or Du Pont Chemicals.

In light of developments across the Rhine, Paris now began to pursue two strategies. The first one was to try to tie German heavy industry firmly into an institutional framework and thus to forestall a repetition of German attempts at domination like in the first half of the 20th century. This goal came to be enshrined in the Ruhr Statute of April 28, 1949, that established an International Ruhr Authority (IRA) and, apart from the United States, Britain, and France, also included Belgium, Luxembourg, and The Netherlands.[23] The newly founded Federal Republic acceded in September 1949. West Germany was thus kept in a minority position. Paris also secured the continuation of coal deliveries from the Ruhr region as reparations for the losses suffered during the Nazi occupation. If the original intention had been to deal with the "problem of the Ruhr" through the IRA, it was soon replaced by a plan that French foreign minister Robert Schuman, on the advice of Monnet, announced on May 9, 1950.[24] It proposed the close integration of the French and German coal and steel industries, subsequently enlarged by the steel and coal industries of the Benelux countries and Italy, though without Britain. As has been mentioned, London decided to rely on cooperation and trade among the members of its Empire and Commonwealth instead. And yet the Schuman Plan was not merely born from a fear of West German industrial power. Rather it was created to block another development that Monnet had observed with alarm in 1949. With the French zone of occupation in southwest Germany located right next to Alsace Lorraine, French and Germans had begun to revive their cultural relations of the 1920s. While these new contacts had some effect of bringing the two sides together after the horrendous years of the German occupation of France, they were soon complemented by efforts of economic reconstruction that were arguably an even more powerful driving force than cultural cooperation.

With the Cold War now starkly looming in the background, it was not surprising that the two sides of industry should remember not merely the intellectual and academic ties that had existed during the Weimar years when Gustav Stresemann and Aristide Briand concluded the Locarno Pact in 1925, but also the unique complementarities in raw materials and industrial production. There was Lorraine with its iron ore deposits, on the one hand, and coal mining in the Ruhr, on the other. During the mid-1920s it therefore made sense to the managers and owners of coal and steel companies to cooperate and to do so in ways that were familiar to them: cartels and syndicates. While this tradition of market organization was highly developed in Germany, French heavy industry had also resorted to cartelization.[25]

So, if cartels existed as an integral part of the national economy, why not establish international cartels, as had happened in 1926 with the conclusion of the International Raw Steel Cartel (IRC)?[26] However, from the start this particular cartel was a precarious experiment and did not last for more than a few years before it collapsed. When the Great Depression hit the steel industries hard, another attempt at cooperation was made in the shape of the International Steel Export Cartel of 1933. As the American steel industry had also lost confidence in the principle of competition in those years of crisis and had resorted to high protective tariffs, steel managers across the Atlantic actually joined ISEC attempt at private regulation of production and prices. The ubiquitous rise of nationalism in the 1930s killed ISEC, and it was only in the late 1930s that the United States returned to oligopolistic competition at home. This return now became the strategy underlying the postwar Open Door international economy that secretary of state Cordell Hull, an avowed internationalist, had been furthering.

As we have seen above, the cartel tradition was still alive after 1945, and not just in West Germany but also in French heavy industry. French industrialists, worried by both American and German economic power, were by the late 1940s busy building cartels again, while their West German colleagues were rebelling against the Allied ban against their own cartel practices. In these circumstances, the two sides began to talk to each other again. Was Franco-German cooperation through a transnational European cartel perhaps a path to growth that would also weaken the competitive pressure of the big American corporations? It is with such calculations in mind that by 1949 prominent French and Rhenish industrialists were reaching across the Rhine outside the governmental sphere. Their confidential conversations were facilitated by Georges Villiers, the president of the French peak industrial association, the Conseil National du Patronat Français (CNPF) and other French and German industrialists, including Henle.[27] Among his and his colleagues' interlocutors were such influential men as Walter Schwede of the VSt. management board, now in liquidation, of whose covert conciliatory attitudes toward French industry during the Nazi occupation the French business community had favorable memories.

On the West German side, WVESI had started its own research into the idea of closer cooperation and the creation of a common market for steel. Of course, they were thinking of an arrangement between private corporations in which government would have no direct role. Meanwhile the French foreign ministry, worried about a possible return to the interwar IRC, had been toying with the creation of a "pool"[28] in which the two sides would cooperate as equal partners, supported but also supervised by expert civil servants. So, by the winter of 1949–50 all sorts of concepts were swirling around Paris and Bonn and soon began to reach the press. On January 21, 1950, the Düsseldorf *Industriekurier*, a newspaper with many connections to Rhenish heavy industry, after starting with the usual appeal to European unification, made the following comment: [29]

> In particular this constructive idea [of unification] is most likely to be achieved via an interlude of national cartels within an international framework. And, in view of the strongly cartelized French industry, this is possibly even the only avenue. However, this requires corresponding organizations in Germany for [the preparation of] an economic understanding, for example, with France about production and market differentials.

Less than a week later, Ernst Friedlaender wrote in the West German weekly *Die Zeit*—in those days still a more conservative voice—that "in the view of influential European experts international cartels in particular had a great deal to contribute to promoting the integration of Europe which the American Marshall Plan administrator [Hoffman] has so expressly demanded."[30] By the spring of 1950, *Industriekurier* reported on negotiations between French and German industry representatives that included Belgian and Luxembourgian steel interests to explore the possibility of a "European steel cartel."[31] Accordingly, the Bonn correspondent of the newspaper met with a Frenchman who had an "excellent insight into the conditions of the French iron industry." Their conversations "touched upon the most important questions of the present time, i.e., the problem of re-establishing a European steel cartel, the question of checks on German steel [production] and the French attitude toward the [still restricted] German steel quota." Participants at these meetings, the correspondent added, were representatives of an "anti-Monnet" faction.[32]

This telling report evidently pointed to tensions and conflicts that had meanwhile arisen between Monnet and French heavy industry. As he had insisted many times, he did not intend to revive ancient industrial traditions but wanted to modernize the economy, with the United States serving as a model in broad outline and not to be slavishly copied. He had listened to Paul Hoffman who, while not wishing to get directly involved in European negotiations, had been nudging Continental European politicians when he declared on October 31, 1949, that they should "create single large market within which quantitative restrictions on the movement of goods, money barriers to the flow of payments and eventually all tariffs are permanently swept away."[33] Monnet had equally strong views on how Western Europe should be reshaped in terms of its economic organization. Here he was totally opposed to the formation of cartels and agreed with economics minister André Philip that such "congrégations économique" must be a thing of the past.[34] In this sense, the American historian Hans Schmitt was certainly correct when, in analyzing the origins of the ECSC, he wrote that worries about a revival of ancient European traditions "acted as a powerful stimulus on the planners of a European union under new auspices and institutions." On May 3, 1950, Monnet provided a very clear statement of his calculations when he declared that the plan he had drafted in previous weeks would solve "the question of the domination of German industry, whose existence would inspire fear throughout Europe, would remain a source of constant disquiet, would ultimately prevent the unification of Europe, and plunge Germany once more into the abyss." By contrast, his plan would create "conditions of joint expansion in a competitive relationship" for both French and West German industry, while avoiding "any form of domination."[35]

The Schuman Plan Negotiations, the First Phase

French foreign minister Robert Schuman who hailed from Lorraine and was therefore well familiar with the history that Monnet was alluding to, was thus easily persuaded to announce on May 9, 1950, a plan that came to bear his rather than Monnet's name. Its publication led to hectic diplomatic activity. Though first conceived as a Franco-German initiative, the Schuman Plan quickly became a West European enterprise. This meant that, after Adenauer had agreed to participate, the Benelux countries and Italy began to assemble delegations for the impending negotiations in Paris. Only Britain signaled that its international priorities lay elsewhere, and London was therefore also not among the eventual signatories of the ECSC treaty. While Monnet was hardly unhappy about Britain dropping out, it is interesting to compare how he and his West German interlocutors put their negotiating teams together. On his side, Monnet relied primarily on trusted collaborators, such as Pierre Uri of the Commissariat du Plan as well as Hervé Alphand and Etienne Hirsch, while keeping the CNPF and other industrial associations at arm's length. Thus, Jacques Ferry of the Chambre Syndicale de la Sidérurgie Française, though "near the negotiations," gained influence with Monnet only "because of his expertise and intelligence" and also his strong pro-European beliefs.[36] Adenauer took a different approach and initially even went so far as to consider appointing Ludwig Kastl as head of the West German delegation. A former member of the Reichsverband der Deutschen Industrie during the Weimar period, he was rather more an unreconstructed representative of the German cartel tradition. As late as 1963, he contributed an article on his "Cartel Experiences and Insights" to a volume that he edited under the title of *Kartelle in der Wirklichkeit* (Cartels in Reality). In it he argued the cartels had withstood the test of time well.[37]

Not surprisingly, the French expressed their unhappiness with Adenauer's choice, and Monnet went to see the chancellor on May 23, 1950, to urge him "not to send technical experts, if possible, but [to select] as delegates personalities who thought in European terms and who had a wide economic horizon" to prevent the Schuman Plan from being "filibustered (zerredet) by problems of a technical kind."[38] Responding to this request, Adenauer picked Walter Hallstein, a professor at Frankfurt University where he taught the Law of International Economic Relations. There was also a consensus among the Bonn ministries involved in the Schuman Plan negotiations that the government delegation should, "in view of the importance of the task," lead the negotiations "during the first phase" and should not resort to simply distributing "general tasks to the industrial circles."[39] When at a later stage more detailed questions arose, the participation of experts from industry was to be facilitated "in such a way that the government delegations issued clearly formulated special tasks in mixed Franco-German committees of experts."

In light of what happened over the summer of 1950, it is probably fair to say that Adenauer tried to heed Monnet's advice on the composition of the West German team of experts. Günter Henle who agreed to chair the steel advisory group, certainly met Monnet's criteria. He was not only known to have sought cooperation with the DGB in the late 1940s when the trade unions were trying to reorganize labor relations,[40] but Adenauer also trusted him from the days when Henle agreed to serve on the Economic Council and was elected to the Bundestag on a CDU ticket in 1949. Henle certainly favored European integration. However, as the key person in the Klöckner conglomerate whose deconcentration had not yet been completed, Henle had a direct interest in the course of the Schuman Plan negotiations. Hallstein was also surrounded by other experts such as Max C. Müller, who had worked in the secretariat of the International Steel Cartel in the 1920s, and Clemens Middelviefhaus, another cartel specialist. A heavy weight with whom the leader of the West German delegation to Paris had to wrestle was Fritz-Aurel Goergen.[41] During the war he had proven an energetic activist in Albert Speer's armaments production machinery who after 1945 began to rebuild the Phoenix steel works in Duisburg.

Finally, there was the WVESI with its deep knowledge of the history of the European steel industry, going back to the 1920s and even as far as the pre-1914 period. It had a secretariat that was well equipped to write detailed memoranda on the Schuman Plan, of which it produced several. The first one published before Schuman's announcement was dated April 11, 1950. It accepted rather flexibly that the "liberalization of the world economy" would be better "in the long run" than "the mutual isolation of the national economies."[42] It then highlighted the view that "we shall be better able to survive free competition in a liberalized" international economy "once we have completed our investment program." Nor should "the principle of equality" be "killed off from the start in the process of the liberalizing measures that are to be taken." Moreover, not only Britain and France, but also Belgium and Luxembourg, "had cartel-type agreements that are increasing the competitive strengths of the[ir] iron and steel industries vis-à-vis our own." This is where the Americans should bring to bear their influence or "we shall be confronted from the start with a serious factor of inferiority which requires correction and consideration within the framework of existing liberalization plans."[43] Another WVESI memorandum of June 5, 1950, again started with pessimistic prognoses of an alleged German inferiority. Reminding the reader of the greater dynamism of the German steel industry in the past in comparison to that of France, it focused on the powerful position that the president of the Schuman Plan's proposed supervisory High Authority would occupy. As this person could "hardly" be expected "to be a German," he might use his powers to fix production levels in order to restrict capacities "at our expense in favor of the French." Given these anxieties, WVESI finally suggested a return to international cartels: "If the American aversion to cartels could be overcome at an early stage," their formation would only be temporary, as they "would become irrelevant through the practice of a coal and steel union."

The persistent pursuit of a cartel solution is also reflected in a third memorandum that WVESI produced on July 4, 1950. Again it referred to the powers of the High Authority, but wanted governments to sign no more than a general international agreement as soon as possible that contained the undertaking to pool the coal and steel industries and create a High Authority that had the right to intervene in the management of a private economy.[44] However, the actual work would be done by a "directorium of industrialists of all participant countries." To back all this up, the Walzstahl section of WVESI composed a forty-three-page analysis, enriched with statistics and addressed to the economics ministry in Bonn.[45] It was written on the basis of notes kept by the secretary general of the former IRC and in the hope that "these materials will perhaps be of interest in the context of the Schuman Plan."

What must have been encouraging to these steel experts and their colleagues in the Ruhr mining industry was that their counterparts at CNPF and in French heavy industry had been conducting parallel research along similar lines. Although the magazine of these industries was entitled *L'Usine Nouvelle*, the ideas that it promoted were not particularly novel and certainly at variance with what Monnet and Hoffman had in mind. No less alarming to Monnet, the magazine's issue of May 18, 1950, reported extensively on the cartel system of the interwar period.[46] The advice they had for Monnet's drafting committee in Paris was similar to that of WVESI, that is, to develop just a broad framework and to leave the implementation of the Schuman Plan to the experts in private industry. It was also notable that, if the lobbies initially had to rely on what was reported in the press about the negotiations in Paris, on July 13 *L'Usine Nouvelle* revealed that things had clearly improved: French industry experts now were in daily contact with Monnet.[47] As to the German side, the growing influence of private interest groups surfaced during a meeting at Erhard's economics ministry on July 7, 1950, on whose agenda was an item relating to "requests of enlarging the committees of experts."[48] Although some participants had misgivings about this proposal, it became known that Adenauer had meanwhile taken the view that his government should not be "petty" when it came to the composition of these specialized committees.

Monnet Asks the Americans to Help Complete the ECSC

It is not difficult to see why Monnet was bound to be very unhappy about these challenges to his original script, with outside pressures having become stronger and stronger. As he had explained at a meeting of the Schuman Plan's "inner delegations" on June 24, 1950, the lobbyists were to consult their governments and also inform their respective groups. These would then respond and put forward their own positions.[49] This is why it was all the more important "not to lose sight of the overall interest" of integrating Western Europe's coal and steel industries. In light of the complexity of the subject matter, there was also the danger that the negotiations would drag on. It seems that Monnet at first hoped to overcome this danger by having intensive round-the-clock meetings. Hallstein told his colleagues in Bonn that negotiations proceeded "with such intensity at the moment that it was impossible to have a break."[50] Consequently, it was difficult to predict when the German delegation would be available to travel to Bonn and see the Adenauer government for an in-person report. It is difficult to know how much progress was being made during these marathon sessions, except that by the summer the delegates were so exhausted that it was time to press the pause button. Monnet did not take a rest, though. Facing the continued pressure from the cartel-minded lobbies, he used this respite to take two steps: he asked the Americans for help with his negotiations and decided to sideline the industrial pressure groups quite unceremoniously.

The archives still await detailed evaluation as to how this exclusion was engineered. We merely have two statements from men who had access to relevant information, even if their accounts are retrospective. To begin with, there are reports by Pierre van der Rest who had been part of the Belgian delegation. As he revealed in January 1952, it was after the summer of 1950 that "the experts of industry" were no longer able to participate "directly … in the negotiations."[51] All they could do was to keep in touch "with the official delegations from the background." There is also Hans Dichgans's book *Montanunion* in which he wrote that "the experts … wanted to solve these problems, despite all misgivings, through agreements among producers, through cartels." They were also opposed to the creation of a High Authority, through which Monnet wanted to put a check on cartels in which private corporations rather than a supranational institution were in charge.[52]

Given the power of the lobbies, Monnet had come to realize that he could not succeed without the direct support of the Americans who he knew were bent on destroying the European cartel tradition for good. To draw them into the Schuman Plan negotiations required some diplomacy after Washington had been surprised by the original announcement in May 1950, even if McCloy, speaking in London before the Pilgrim Society in early April, had again urged the West Europeans to integrate.[53] It was also awkward that Schuman's initial proposal looked to US secretary of state Dean Acheson as if another protectionist bloc was to be created. His first reaction was therefore quite reserved, and John Foster Dulles, who had been temporarily appointed as acting secretary of state, merely reinforced this stance with the words:[54] "It is too early for us to give the proposal our approval because of the possible cartel aspect and known previous French efforts to secure detailed control over investment policies and management of the Ruhr coal and steel industry." Averell Harriman, then the US special representative in Europe, also counseled that the "cartel angle needs careful watching."[55] However, Monnet was able to reassure the US state department that a common market for West European coal and steel would include guarantees of open access for nonmembers, including American industry. As the French newspaper *Le Monde* reported on November 11, 1950, the task was now "to inscribe anti-cartel articles in the treaty project."[56]

After their return from the break, the delegations again worked hard to produce a draft treaty. They were able to do this without the earlier interference by industrial interest groups, while remaining very conscious of Washington's cartel suspicions. On December 7, 1950, the French delegation submitted the text of two articles that had appeared in an earlier draft but had now been renumbered as Articles 60 and 61.[57] The submission was prefaced by a paragraph that summarized what was at stake in the quest of getting the whole project across the finishing-line:

> It is the essential economic purpose of the Schuman Plan to satisfy the demand of the community by establishing a market which provides enterprises with a constant incentive to increase their production capacities and the quality of their products. The means to this end is [the] promotion of competition. Insofar as the special characteristics of these industries and changes in economic conditions require intervention, this can be initiated only by a public authority. The establishment of private monopolies as well as the formation of cartels would lead to a petrification of existing conditions and would result in the dominance of private interests in the place of the pursuit of common aims. The High Authority can only put a stop to this, if it has sufficient powers and exercises these with constant vigilance.

Accordingly, the new Article 60 was directed against "price-fixing, production controls, restrictions on technological progress or a division of markets through agreements between producers." Together with Article 61, the aim was "to do away with forms of organization which lead to the suppression of competition and to private interests being provided with political influence." Reflecting long-standing American positions on competition, these articles explain why the *Kölnische Rundschau* reported on December 22, 1950, that "the Americans had recently expressed their great interest in the satisfactory conclusion of the [Schuman Plan] negotiations." Indeed, Hallstein had stated as early as the end of October that "Herr Monnet's ideas are probably influenced by the American desire that all cartel-like institutions be rejected—a desire that gains special weight due to the fact that it is supported by the funds which the US are to provide at a later stage."[58] The draft had now met American concerns for openness so that Western Europe would be a productive part of the new economic order that Washington was determined to build.

The other major problem that still had to be settled before the ECSC treaty could come into effect was the power of the West German corporations and their planned deconcentration under Law No. 27. West German industry, pointing to the Soviet threat, the founding of North Atlantic Treaty Organization (NATO), and Washington's request for a West German military contribution to the defense of the West, had become even more insistent that breaking up the big corporations was as irrational as the dismantling of industrial installations had been in previous years.

Looking at the Cold War, the instabilities within the international system resulting from decolonization, and the need to integrate Western Europe, if not politically, at least economically, West Germany's big corporations, recognizing how indispensable they had become to the United States and its economic reconstruction effort, decided to apply the leverage they thought they had gained against Monnet's urgent attempt to get the Schuman Plan accepted by its six-members—in itself a big job. The Adenauer government was a particularly weak link in the European governmental chain, as the failure of the Schuman Plan would be a major setback for the chancellor's policy of tying the Federal Republic firmly to the Western community of nations. However, Adenauer was not without leverage himself. As we have seen, the winter of 1950–1 was also crucial for an agreement on parity codetermination with the trade unions and thus for a restructuring of labor relations.[59] And so he used the Schuman Plan to put pressure on heavy industry to accept the codetermination compromise, arguing that if the negotiations with the DGB failed, it would seriously undermine his European diplomatic design.

Early signs of a crisis on this latter front appeared in September 1950 when Hermann Reusch suddenly withdrew from the circle of West German Schuman Plan experts. He left in anger in light of Monnet's sidelining strategy and also the continued pressures from the US high commission in connection with the deconcentration Law No. 27.[60] Worse, on October 1, 1950, after the resignation of Gustav Heinemann over another issue, Robert Lehr, who was Adenauer's favorite candidate to become his successor as Federal minister of the interior, made a speech before the Bavarian foreign trade association in which he railed at

Monnet's plan to set up a High Authority, bluntly calling it *dirigiste*.[61] Moreover, Lehr made positive references of the 1926 IRC and complained about the burdens that Monnet's treaty would impose on the Ruhr coal industry, if it was to be obliged to pay for the proposed closure of inefficient Belgian mines. The speech created a considerable stir and was widely reported in the press, as his words were taken to represent the views of the Adenauer government. Hallstein hurriedly told journalists that "Herr Dr. Lehr's statement is of a private character."[62] To reinforce this message, Günter Henle was wheeled out as chairman of the West German group of steel experts, who had spoken at the same conference and had made "a perfectly positive statement on the Schuman Plan," allegedly without having had contact with Lehr beforehand.[63] To provide concrete proof that Lehr had not spoken in an official capacity, the secretary general of WVESI personally took "Dr. Henle's speech to Paris" to show it to Hallstein and the president of the French steel association in an attempt to mollify "the latter's vivid misgivings about the [suspected] German attitude."

Against the background of these upsets, Henle now argued all the more forcefully that, given the international power constellation, his colleagues in the Ruhr region had no choice but to accept both parity codetermination and the proposed ECSC treaty. What lent force to his argument was that he once again openly referred to the catastrophic course of German history between 1933 and 1945. The insights gained from the Nazi period simply required that attempts to dominate Europe from the center must never be made again and that a different kind of political and economic order had to be created both at home and in relation to West Germany's neighbors. As we have seen, this is how Henle helped Adenauer to forge a codetermination compromise between the DGB and the coal and steel companies in January 1951.[64] And when, at that same moment, the Schuman Plan negotiations similarly reached a point at which the project was either threatened with collapse or achieving a breakthrough, it was again Henle who raised his voice. As he put it later—mindful of American attitudes—the ECSC was designed to introduce to coal and steel the "first European anti-trust law." In other words, he indirectly took the Sherman and Clayton Acts as a model, adopted by the United States before 1914, as a framework for securing a competitive, if oligopolistic, market economy without cartels and monopolies. Like Henle, Hallstein was similarly hoping for a "positive turn" and warned specifically against attempts by the mining industry to keep its sales organizations.[65] Cartels and syndicates, even if placed "under the strictest supervision of the state," were as suspect to Monnet and the Americans as ever. "A clear-cut 'German No,'" Hallstein added, would be tantamount to a most unfortunate "*Katastrophenpolitik*."

If such dire warnings that Bonn received indicated that there were limits to the influence and power of the Ruhr region's heavy industries' ability to shape West German domestic and foreign policy, they became very clearly visible during the winter months of 1950–1. The big corporations had also overestimated the leverage they possessed against deconcentration and the implementation of Allied Law No. 27, after the Combined Steel Group announced on November 30, 1950, that some twenty-nine companies were to be created. Put differently, the Ruhr coal and steel badly misjudged the strength of the alliance that Monnet had forged with the Americans. This bond related not just to Washington's eventual approval of the Schuman Plan, after Monnet had inserted anti-cartel clauses into the draft treaty, falling in line with the American vision of an Open Door Western world economy. It was also the result of a recognition by McCloy and his experts that France and also the Benelux countries had to be helped to mitigate their fear, ancient and now again very acute, of German industrial power. Unwilling to curb West German economic might by policies of deconcentration that contained the Germans as draconically as envisioned in the Morgenthau Plan, Washington was nevertheless prepared to use its residual powers as an occupier after the founding of the Federal Republic to deconcentrate the big German corporations to a level that roughly put them on a level playing field with French industry. The calculation was that this would reassure Paris, Brussels, Luxembourg, and Den Haag that the dangerous imbalances of the past had been rectified.

Concluding the Deconcentration of West German Industry

This leads me to the final part of this chapter and to American deconcentration policy relating not merely to coal and steel but also to other branches of industry, such as chemicals, electrical engineering, and finance. It also takes me back to the US high commission that was primarily charged with this task. However, this rather complex story becomes more intelligible if a start is made with an assessment that Sidney Willner, the head of the decartelization branch at the US high commission, offered at the time.[66] His words were reported in an article in *Deutsche Zeitung* at the end of January 1951. Willner claimed that he had looked "very carefully" at the problem of concentration in the French industry as compared to West Germany's, as discussed at the end of the previous section. Although he had found various "integrations," in "none of the cases in France did the participations go so far as to be able to exert a control that restricted competition." Instead his analysis had led him to the conclusion that "the concentration of French heavy industry" was about "equivalent to that of Germany after deconcentration" had been achieved across the Rhine. Implying that it was not a perfect balance, Willner conceded that German industry might still suffer a number of disadvantages. But to him this was not a "particularly important" problem, "because all cartels" in the ECSC countries would "automatically become 'illegal' after the ratification of the Schuman Plan." What Willner did not mention was that once the ECSC treaty was ratified, Allied restrictions on West German production would also lapse. So, if French heavy industry was really ahead of the Ruhr region, the West Germans would still be able to catch up within the newly competitive framework once it had been adopted by all members, banning cartels and supervised by a High Authority. In the end, all sides underwrote a grand ECSC compromise that, against the backdrop of a much larger international crisis and the subsequent Korean War, was in many ways also a fudge to settle the matter once and for all.

If Willner had revealed the principles that the US high commission used as a lever vis-à-vis West German industry, I can now examine how Allied Law No. 27 was in fact applied to different branches, not just coal and steel. I start with chemicals before moving on to the reorganization of coal and steel, including the treatment of Henle's Klöckner conglomerate. As far as IG Farben was concerned, this chemicals giant had occupied a dominant position in its branch during the "Third Reich." After 1945, this triggered, first of all, the prosecution of several board members at Nuremberg that Joseph Borkin examined in 1978 in his bestseller *The Crime and Punishment of IG Farben*. It was the first book to analyze this issue.[67] It was followed in 1988 by a much more balanced study by the American historian Raymond G. Stokes who recounted how IG Farben was broken up into four companies: Bayer at Leverkusen next to Cologne on the other side of the Rhine and Farbwerke Hoechst just west of Frankfurt. Further south at Mannheim-Ludwigshafen were the factories of Badische Anilin- und Sodafabriken (BASF). The smallest firm was the Casella & Co. Farbwerke, originally a limited company that had joined the other three in 1916 as part of an Interessengemeinschaft (IG) before the founding of the large IG Farben conglomerate in 1925. No less notable is the title of Stokes's book: *Divide and Prosper*. While there was German resistance to IG Farben's breakup, Allied deconcentration laws turned out to be a blessing for this branch. While Casella proved to be too weak to survive in the new competitive world that the United States were building, Bayer, Hoechst, and BASF thrived and began to compete as oligopolies on the world market, challenging such big players as Du Pont and

Imperial Chemical Industries (ICI). Over time all of them grew into enterprises that were in fact bigger than IG Farben had been in the interwar period.[68]

The electrical engineering industry was treated rather lightly by the Western powers. Siemens, now in Erlangen, and Bosch in Stuttgart did not have the size of IG Farben and underwent a relatively insignificant deconcentration.[69] The three big banks (Deutsche, Dresdner, Commerz) were split up into twenty-five smaller institutions before they began to reconcentrate.[70] Next to IG Farben, the Vereinigte Stahlwerke, the other virtual monopoly, was also prominently earmarked for deconcentration and broken up into two dozen companies. The German owners and managers complained at the time that they were too small and fragmented to be viable. But again, by exploiting the boom of the 1950s and especially the need for steel during the Korean War, they rapidly expanded their steel-making and steel-processing capacities and began to merge.[71] Thus the August-Thyssen-Hütte (ATH) started off as a torso, but within a few years had added blast furnaces and rolling mills. By the 1960s, it had grown into the largest steel corporation in Western Europe, competing on the world market next to the United States and Japan.

No less important, this time ATH was built as a diversified American-style steel trust that had shed most of its traditional ties to the Ruhr mining industry. Because this Verbundwirtschaft looked like a cartel to the US high commission, McCloy insisted on largely separating coal and steel and also on the dissolution of the syndicated Deutscher Kohlenverkauf (DKV) sales organization.However, Heinrich Kost, the head of the DKBL, resisted Allied policies vigorously, which in turn delayed the completion of America's deconcentration plans. Still, at the end of this process, Verbundwirtschaft had largely folded. The ATH and other steel companies began to buy a good deal of their coal on the world market where it was often cheaper. The Ruhr mining industry initially continued within the framework of twelve smaller companies that operated successfully enough under the umbrella of Gemeinschaftsorganisation Ruhrkohle (GEORG). But by the late 1950s, demand for Ruhr coal declined, resulting in a crisis that was exacerbated by the rise of oil as a source of energy for industrial as well as domestic consumers. Coal saw a brief recovery in the early 1960s after which it experienced another steep decline that the Federal government tried to cushion with the help of subsidies and retraining programs for jobless miners.[72] With the rise of the automobile and other consumer durables, demand for the making and processing of specialized steel remained strong until these industries were also hit be problems of worldwide overproduction in the 1970s and 1980s.

If this was the large picture, Henle's Klöckner Werke A.G. also got caught up in the deconcentration policy, first of the British occupation authorities and then of the UK/US Steel Group. On June 18, 1947, Georgsmarienhütte, south of Osnabrück, became an independent shareholding company whose traditional ties with Klöckner had been severed.[73] The same happened to the Stahlwerk A.G. just up the road in the city of Osnabrück, where a meeting of shareholders approved its new status, with its specialty of casting locomotive wheels and other railroad steel products. While the demand for such products was more volatile, Georgsmarienhütte benefited from the steel boom that encouraged a cautious expansion when two Siemens-Martin blast furnaces were added. Meanwhile the Quarry Works at Piesberg were not hived off, while the Haspe Works near Hagen were among the first four companies to be severed and reorganized by Harris-Burland and Dinkelbach as an independent shareholding company.[74] The treatment of Klöckner-Humboldt-Deutz (KHD), a subsidiary of the Klöckner Werke A.G. that held virtually all the shares in this company, was also painful for Henle. Its deconcentration was complicated by the fact that KHD had two major shareholders, Klöckner & Co and the Dutch NV Handelmatschaappij Montan in Den Haag.[75] The Allies demanded that these ties should now be cut, with one firm merely owning the shares in the coal and steel firms and the other being the exclusive shareholder of KHD, the machine engineering complex.

Henle reacted to these deconcentration policies in two ways: he was one of very few industrialists in the Ruhr region who repeatedly openly admitted that Allied policies were an adverse reaction to Nazi period and that, given what had happened before 1945, these policies were understandable and justified. As he put it in his memoirs:[76] "It must be said as a matter of justice that dismantling and de-concentrations were self-inflicted consequences of what the Hitler-madness has done to the entire world." Could one expect after this, he continued, that the victors "would so soon after the end of the war be exclusively or predominantly guided by political reason and economic insight?" At the same time, he felt that the Allies had cast their deconcentration net too wide. In his view, the Vereinigte Stahlwerke giant had to be broken up, even if the Allies could have done it more efficiently and less bureaucratically. But Henle wondered whether the reorganization that was forced upon Klöckner was really necessary and complained that it took him endless journeys to Allied offices and to ministries in Bonn to negotiate a "reasonable solution" for his diversified corporation. To his dismay, different works were put together in a unitary corporation (Einheitsgesellschaft) that left the individual units at Osnabrück, Georgsmarienhütte, Piesberg, Haspe, and the Viktor/Ikern mine in Castorp-Rauxel, as well as a number of other smaller ventures without their former cohesion. Worse, the name Klöckner was changed to Nordwestdeutscher Bergwerks und Hüttenverein. Only the works at Troisdorf and Düsseldorf stayed with the headquarter in Duisburg.[77] On May 30, 1953, Klöckner's deconcentration had finally been completed.[78] Henle's complaints about the treatment he received were probably justified and therefore soon reversed. When on November 1, 1953, the Nordwestdeutsche Bergwerks und Hüttenverein and its subsidiaries were finally released from Allied control, a shareholder meeting quickly resolved to give the Einheitsgesellschaft its former and time-honored name of Klöckner Werke A.G.

More than once did Henle view the reorganization of West German industry, and of heavy industry in particular, against the backdrop of the Nazi period without ever publicly mentioning the discrimination he had suffered, because of his Jewish family background. Instead he became a major advocate of a policy of reconciliation and cooperation between West Germany and its Western neighbors and the French in particular. A good digest of his thinking can be found in a memorandum that he wrote on September 18, 1948, at the very beginning of which he defined the need for cooperation among the West Europeans as an imperative.[79] He then considered the importance of the Marshall Plan that in his view was suffused in a spirit of "international economic understanding and supplementation." Of course, this understanding also had a political dimension to it. Once again he reminded readers how "National Socialism in Germany had proven more powerful" and had resulted "in domination of the one by the other, until this attempt tipped over into catastrophe." As to the postwar period, Henle stressed that the Western powers had been rather slow in recognizing that Germany was divided into four zones and was an industrial nation that had lost its agricultural regions in the East. As a result, the Western zones had become "a second England," but lacked the resources that would enable it to contribute to the reconstruction of Europe. For Henle, West Germany had no choice but to boost its industries and to support itself through "export-profits." Consequently, West Germans should be allowed to compete on the world market, but should also seek cooperation to avoid an "unbound competitive struggle" that was problematical to him also on political grounds.

At the same time, Henle's memorandum showed much understanding for French hesitations to loosen "the shackles of the German economy." He understood France's "security needs," but, he wrote, the West Europeans, instead of being involved in a traditional power struggle, now found themselves as part of a defensive response against the Soviet Union. For him the question was as to whether West Germany would become a more permanent "protective bulwark" against this external threat. In his view, it was vital for Western Europe to cooperate with the full participation of West Germany and its industries. Although he did not say so, it was not difficult to see that his Klöckner conglomerate, by promoting European cooperation, would benefit from this larger vision. As Werner Bührer has argued, Henle was prepared to engage in novel forms of economic cooperation. Like Sohl, he envisioned "Europe" not as a value as such, but as the "political legal framework … for a larger and unified economic space."[80] His support of the Schuman Plan was grounded in these considerations. To be sure, he was not just favoring the construction of a new Western Europe as such, but also saw that a rebuilt Klöckner A.G. could be expected to thrive in a united Europe.[81]

However, there is one final point to be made about Henle's role and thoughts during the dramatic years between 1945 and 1951. He was clearly very conscious of the burdens of the Nazi period and the lessons to be learned from it. Yet the debates with his colleagues and with the Allies were never just about safeguarding economic interests but also about the need of make mental changes. At a critical point in January 1951, Walter Hallstein reminded his colleagues that they needed to have regard for "the American mentality" when it came to deconcentration and decartelization and that the conservative Bergassessoren of the Ruhr region simply had to adapt to.[82] Socialized into the peculiar pre-1945 German system of market organization, they had great difficulties adapting to the postwar world, which the American side had to take into account. Edward Mason, the Harvard economist, articulated this very clearly in 1946 when he wrote that in the absence of permanent occupation new principles cannot simply be imposed but would have to be implemented by the occupied themselves.[83] It seems that McCloy and most of his staff accepted this notion and the significance of psychological factors that were at play on both sides. Working at the US high commission, Robert Bowie in particular would drive a hard bargain when it came to the *Umbau* of the Ruhr industries.[84] But the HICOG experts also appreciated the need to affect an economic reorientation in parallel to the political one that they were also pursuing.[85]

Henle did not have his colleagues' difficulties of adapting to a new world in which the United States was the hegemonic power. The positions he came to represent were partly related to his sociocultural background and his experiences under the Hitler dictatorship. Nor was he a typical Ruhr steel industrialist. Based on firm ethical and also religious values related to his upbringing, his diplomatic career and also his years as a deputy in the Bundestag had taught him the art and value of compromise. To him life did not merely consist in making and selling steel products. As he put it in the subtitle of his memoirs, he was also a "friend of music" and, as an accomplished amateur pianist, established an internationally esteemed music publishing firm. If his Jewishness had made him an outsider under the Nazis, he remained one also among his conservative colleagues such as Hermann Reusch, and the fact that the latter had studied philosophy, rather than mining, may have reinforced his conservatism. This means that a closer look at the biographies of these men often makes it difficult to generalize and to assess who they were and what values they embodied at a time that had seen great upheaval.

The recognition that Henle had gained in the postwar years and his successful reconcentration and diversification of the sprawling enterprise during a period of economic expansion and prosperity enabled him to live a life that was certainly more secure and less racked by vagaries than the years after his removal by the Nazis from his post in the German foreign office and in 1941–2 from his family's steel corporation. This means that the years up to his death in 1979 were considerably more stable, though by no means less busy. The next and final Chapter 6 will therefore focus on those later years and especially on the 1950s and 1960s when he was directly involved in the management of the Klöckner conglomerate, its reconcentration, and its impressive success in the domestic and international markets, although he never allowed himself to be totally absorbed by his steel business, as his work for his music publishing house demonstrates.

6

Some Concluding Topics for Future Research

Günter Henle was no doubt right when he titled a chapter in his memoirs covering the decade following the struggles over the reorganization of the West German steel industry and of labor relations "The Good Fifties."[1] The late 1940s and early 1950s had certainly been full of drama for him, for the Klöckner corporation, and West German industry more generally and there had been many "unpleasant worries."[2] The deconcentration measures that the Allies decreed contained "quite a few bitter pills,"[3] but the years from 1953 onwards were years of reconstruction, reconcentration, and expansion that kept Henle busy. One of the bitter pills he had to swallow was that, while he had remained a partner in Klöckner & Co., the steel trading firm that the Nazis had allowed him to keep in 1942, he was banned for five years from assuming a seat on the supervisory board of Klöckner A.G., the public steel-making part of the conglomerate that Peter Klöckner had built up before the Second World War. It was also aggravating that this corporation had not only been deconcentrated but also been forced to change its name. It was only in 1953 that this conglomerate was able to issue a joint annual report and allowed to revive its more time-honored brand name. At their annual meeting in 1954 the shareholders were very happy to restore the "Klöckner" name. What had been happening to him and his family during the two decades or so before also explains, I hope convincingly, why I decided to give this book its seemingly contradictory title. His life and work had indeed been that of the "Insider-Outider of Germany's Heavy Industry" in the first half of the 20th century.

The following chapter (Conclusion) does not conclude with Henle's subsequent life and work up to his death in 1979. Nor is it is a comprehensive analysis of the history of the Klöckner trust. His manifold activities as an entrepreneur, politicians, and patron of high culture will have to be analyzed in other studies that also evaluate the company archives, deposited at the Federal Archives in Koblenz as well sources held by the Klöckner Family Foundation in Düsseldorf and by Klöckner-Humboldt-Deutz (KHD) and other parts of the

Klöckner empire. This concluding chapter will merely highlight a few aspects of Henle's work that will have to be researched more deeply by other scholars.

Reintegrating Steel-Making, Machine Manufacturing, and International Trade

The reintegration of the KHD manufacturing arm posed some difficulties. Before 1945, KHD had been a virtually fully owned subsidiary of Klöckner Werke A.G. The complication arose because Klöckner & Co. had been a major shareholder in Klöckner Werke A.G. together with the Dutch NV Handelsmatschaappij Montan, which was founded in the 1920s by Peter Klöckner and held a one-third share in Klöckner Werke A.G.[4] Den Haag-based company had been sequestered in 1945 by the Dutch government that insisted that the two firms must be separated. In lengthy negotiations with the Hague Günter Henle managed to get the Dutch share released against a one-time payment. There was also the obligation that the ownership had to remain with a Dutch family foundation. Subsequently, the Dutch holding company became a major shareholder of Klöckner Werke A.G., whereas Klöckner & Co remained the major shareholder in KHD. With the European economy booming in the 1950s, the holding companies in Den Haag and Duisburg thrived, but after the withdrawal of earlier Allied occupation power restrictions, they began to cooperate more closely. Meanwhile Klöckner & Co. remained a limited company privately owned by the Peter Klöckner family foundation (established in 1937) and by Günter Henle, who was also its chief executive. Given Henle's role at the center of all three companies, he and his colleagues felt no immediate need to initiate a merger, but continued their amicable cooperation, while strengthening their positions in their respective fields of specialization.

Although the Allies had dealt a blow to the continuation of Verbundwirtschaft, Klöckner succeeded in holding on to some of its mining interests. These supplied the steel-making and processing units at Osnabrück, Georgsmarienhütte, and Haspe but were also connected to the mines at Castorp-Rauxel with one new development: Henle built a coal-fired power station at Rauxel that delivered electricity to parts of the Ruhr region. Once the coal crisis hit in 1958, the Klöckner mines at Rauxel, but also those at Viktor-Ickern and Königsborn, underwent a modernization program that enabled them to weather the slump of the late 1950s that was followed by another boom in the early 1960s.[5] As the grid of roads and highways (autobahns) was also expanded in the wake of the Bonn government's decision to reinforce West Germany's infrastructure, the Piesdorf quarries similarly became profitable, with cement and plastics factories added somewhat later. Finally, Klöckner's mines continued to supply coal to its steel works and rolling mills in Westphalia and in the Rhineland. Eventually, Klöckner A.G. would also have works in Kehl near Strasbourg in the southwest and at Göppingen, east of Stuttgart in Württemberg, a center of the metal bashing and machine-tool industry.

The drawback of the Westphalian works was that they had no direct access to major rivers or canals; to overcome this disadvantage, Henle began to plan a steel mill near the Hanseatic city of Bremen on the Weser river and close to the North Sea.[6] After plans for alternative locations on the Rhine at Wesel near the Dutch border had been dropped, both the management and supervisory boards approved the Bremen project in the autumn of 1954. By 1957, Klöckner operated three Siemens-Martin Works whose steel was processed by a warm broadband rolling mill complemented by a cold broadband rolling mill and with the next phase of expansion taking place from the early 1960s. In short, supported also by the city of Bremen and its own plans to expand its port facilities, the Klöckner works came to rely on what Henle had learned during his visits to American steel corporations. The Bremen works grew into a heavy industrial complex that could take iron ore deliveries from Sweden, but increasingly also from Brazil and other parts of the world. For Henle it was but a small step from this point to the ordering of Klöckner-owned freighters. The first one had a 30,000 brutto registered ton capacity. Over the next three years, the Weserport facility was equipped with highly automated unloading equipment for freighters of up to 70,000 brutto registered tons.[7] Within eighteen months the port, following an expansion of the automated rail loading facilities, achieved a turnover of 3.6 million tons of iron ore, two-thirds of which were distributed to the various Klöckner Works.

However, the conglomerate, while involved in steel-making and steel processing, also built up its manufacturing operations at KHD.[8] Counting on the expansion of civilian travel and commercial trucks, the works in Cologne decided to develop air-cooled powertrains of up to 340 hp. Diesel locomotives required considerably larger water-cooled four-stroke engines of 1,500 hp, while freighters needed engines of 4,000 hp. KHD had traditionally also been manufacturing heavy road and off-road vehicles, such as trailers, agricultural tractors, buses, fire engines, and caterpillars, all of which grew into a lucrative business. Between 1948 and 1956–7, KHD's turnover increased fivefold, while earnings from exports benefited from the Open Door international economy that the United States continued to promote. Peter Klöckner had begun to move into southern Germany during the interwar period, and in 1936 he finally acquired the Magirus truck and bus factories in Ulm.

All the while both the Klöckner A.G. steel enterprises and KHD were integrated with the third pillar of the conglomerate, the family's trading arm of Klöckner & Co. After Allied dismantling and deconcentration had stopped and the ECSC had been ratified, Henle, with the family having been freed from Allied legal constraints of ownership, devoted himself to the management and supervisory duties of Klöckner Werke A.G. and its subsidiaries as well as to his partnerships in Klöckner & Co. The international market offered competitive opportunities, although the High Authority in Luxembourg would scrutinize and, if justified, block attempts at excessive reconcentration through mergers and acquisitions. With Monnet as president, the ECSC High Authority also monitored attempts at re-cartelization and banned them, except in temporary emergencies that were allowed under the 1951 treaty.

Practicing Codetermination

In this new climate of expansion and competition, Henle encouraged the rationalization of production in his works and factories but did so in close contact with the trade unions. In those works that were being governed by parity codetermination, Klöckner A.G. began to implement the May 1951 law that Henle had helped craft and get on the statute book. The supervisory boards were put together and worker directors appointed to the management boards of the companies listed on the stock market. In fact, in line with earlier agreements made with Harris-Burland and Dinkelbach, the deconcentrated Stahlwerk Osnabrück A.G. had concluded a Works Agreement on February 9, 1950 through which half the members of the supervisory board represented the unions together with nominees by the local government.[9] The management board was made up of three directors: a commercial, a technical, and a (union) worker director. There was also a works council, now required under the 1952 Works Constitution Act, that had to be consulted about company matters.[10]

The reforms meant that the Klöckner A.G. and its subsidiaries, such as KHD, were dependent on the majority consensus of the supervisory board. At the same time, the management board with its worker director was involved in the corporation's strategic decision making. The works council had to be consulted, although it did not have direct decision-making powers. It took some time for this novel institutional framework to be consolidated, but as the system of labor relations had by 1951–2 become the law of the land, Henle tried hard to make it work and to establish cooperative labor relations, especially also with the chairs of the works councils, elected by the workforce.[11] In his memoirs he writes very positively about Böckler and also Ludwig Rosenberg, though less so about Freitag.[12] As a member of the Bundestag until 1953, he also established many close working relationships within the CDU/CSU (Christlich-Soziale Union) parliamentary caucus and with leading Social Democrats, such as Fritz Erler and Carlo Schmid.[13]

Apart from working with the DGB and the metal workers union, Henle tried to strengthen collegial contacts, some of which went back to the wartime period. The crucial support he received from Karl Jarres and Robert Lehr has already been discussed. The months of internment at Bad Nenndorf and Eselheide had created fresh solidarities with other steel managers held there. Among them, Hans-Günter Sohl was particularly close to him, and their relationship was strengthened by their collaboration during the codetermination and ECSC debates as well as their accomplished playing of the piano.[14] However, while Sohl and other colleagues supported Alfried Krupp and also Friedrich Flick and Hermann Röchling after they had been sentenced during the Nuremberg Trials as war criminals and sent to prison,[15] Henle seems to have kept his distance from his colleagues' efforts to obtain the early release of these Allied prisoners. It would be interesting to investigate how far this was related to Henle's wartime experiences not only with regard to Hitler's anti-Semitic policies toward "mixed marriages" like his own but also with men who, like Flick and Röchling, had been committed to the Nazi regime and its brutal occupation policies.[16] Only his attitude toward Alfried Krupp and Berthold Beitz was different. As mentioned in the introduction and reflected in this book's title, it is yet another intriguing story in the annals of the Ruhr industry that Henle's son Peter married Beitz's daughter Susanne. It is certainly remarkable that these two insider-outsider families should tie the knot.

Henle's election first to the Wirtschaftsrat in 1948 and then to the Bundestag in 1949 kept him busier than he had bargained for. His frequent drives back and forth between Bonn and Duisburg left him so overworked that he decided not to stand again during the 1953 Federal elections. The retreat from politics allowed him to focus not merely on Klöckner's development but also on promoting a modernization of West Germany's business culture. Apart from his attempts to improve labor relations, he also promoted modern management practices to take root in industry more generally. By the mid-1950s, a debate on these questions was in full swing among corporate leaders. The issue was as to how far American practices of corporate governance should be introduced to West Germany. A number of prominent leaders advocated that a younger generation of managers should not merely study Volkswirtschaft and Betriebswirtschaft at German universities but also attend the Harvard Business School for training, as the Harvard University professor Carl Joachim Friedrich had recommended to his brother Otto.[17] There is the example of Ludwig Vaubel who joined the management board of Vereinigte Glanzstoff-Fabriken A.G. in Wuppertal in 1953, a subsidiary of the Dutch Algemene Kunstzijde Unie N.V. (AKU). To gain a firsthand impression of how younger Americans were taught management methods, he had attended Harvard's advanced management course in 1950–1 and now recommended this training to his colleagues.[18] He also formed the Wuppertal Circle whose members discussed problems of how to organize and run a modern industrial enterprise.

This was also the time when American ideas and notions of team work were taken up in the columns of *Der Arbeitgeber*, the organ of the Bundesvereinigung deutscher Arbeitergeberverbände (BdA) and other publications.[19] While teaching in university economics departments continued along rather traditional and often quite theoretical lines, other companies booked their younger generation of managers into seminars at the Harzburg Academy.[20] It was run by Reinhard Höhn, a former SS-Gruppenführer, whose curriculum, while, of course, no longer espousing Nazi ideas, followed the "staff-line" principles of the Prussian army.[21] Especially former Wehrmacht officers thought Harzburg offered a better training than West German universities, and it was not just the conservatives in the Ruhr coal and steel industries who still adhered to more autocratic concepts of industrial leadership and who would send their promising employees to Höhn's establishment in the foothills of the Harz Mountains south of Braunschweig. For example, Rolf Hermichen, a member of the management board of Karstadt, the department store chain in Essen who was in charge of personnel and had been a Luftwaffe fighter pilot, thought that courses at the Harzburg Academy offered the best education for his managers.[22]

Given his own career and efforts at reintegrating West Germany into the world economy, it is not surprising that Henle would turn to other circles, such as the Unternehmer-Gespräche that took place in the spa town of Baden-Baden, south of Karlsruhe. Founded by Wolf-Dietrich von Witzleben, the chairman of the management board of Siemens & Halske, now headquartered in Erlangen, northeast of Munich,[23] this was one of several forums where the elite of German industrialists would meet for informal exchanges of ideas on topical subjects and the big issues of international politics and the global economy. While foreigners were occasionally asked to give lectures, this was a more exclusive German affair. However, we have already seen that Henle was everything but an advocate of autarky. His enterprises required him to look beyond West Germany's borders, and he had always been a supporter of political and economic internationalism ever since his years as a diplomat in the Weimar Republic.[24]

However, before delving more deeply into how Henle expanded Klöckner A.G., KHD, and Klöckner & Co. into a conglomerate that competed on the international stage and led him to undertake extensive travels not only to North America but also to Latin America, Asia, and Africa, his many contacts and his influence inside West German industry must be examined.

It is not surprising that he used his memoirs to discuss the network of banks upon which he relied to obtain the financial support that he needed for the postwar expansion of the corporation. In the first instance, he mentioned the role of Deutsche Bank (DB) that had been the "Hausbank" way back in the years when Peter Klöckner had built up his diversified industrial empire. "P.K.," as he was known to his family, served as a member of the bank's supervisory board until his death in October 1940. Henle no doubt wished to continue the tradition after he had met Hermann Josef Abs in the late 1930s who had become the bank's key person on the management board together with Karl Kimmich, the other DB board member whose advice Henle sought at a critical time in the early 1940s. He met Abs again in the internment camp at Bad Nenndorf. The Western Allies split DB up into three entities that Abs managed to reverse in the 1950s. DB redivivus established its new headquarters in Frankfurt, and Henle's cooperation with Abs resumed after their release from internment when Abs joined the KHD supervisory board. When, upon his retirement, Abs became a member of the DB supervisory board, Karl Klasen, his successor, worked closely with Henle and became the vice chair of the KDH supervisory board next to Henle as its chair.

Another board member was Hans L. Merkle, the man who restored the international position of the Robert Bosch electrical engineering firm in Stuttgart. However, as Henle pointed out, the availability of formal board positions was limited by the Betriebsverfassungsgesetz (BVG) that decreed that one-third of the twenty-one supervisory board members of big corporations like Klöckner were reserved for employee and trade union representatives as part of the codetermination compromises that had been forged in 1951 and 1952. There was space though at Klöckner for Ernst von Siemens, once the chair of the management board of the electrical engineering firm of Siemens & Halske before its merger with Siemens & Schuckert, on whose supervisory board he later served as the chair and with whom Henle enjoyed a "close personal connection."

Conversely, Henle accepted invitations to join the supervisory boards of a number of other big corporations, among them some of the major insurance companies. The largest among them was Allianz that operated not only in the domestic market but also internationally. Given the growth of Klöckner & Co. as the conglomerate's international trading arm, it was no doubt useful to be connected to the commercial insurance world. Based in Munich and also linked with the Bavarian Rückversicherungs-Gesellschaft seems also to have had a nostalgic significance, as it gave him the opportunity to return to his own Bavarian family roots. Henle's seat on the supervisory board of the British-owned Albingia Versicherungs-A.G. in Hamburg gave him a foot in the door to the important London insurance market.

Apart from the earlier-mentioned connections with the Dutch AKU and Henle's cooperation with Ernst Hellmut Vits, now its German chair of the management board of Vereinigte Glanzstoff-Fabriken, his other involvement in a major foreign-owned corporation was with the Swedish ball bearing trust, based at Göteborg and its SKF subsidiary at Schweinfurt in Bavaria. This connection went back to Peter Klöckner whom the Swedes asked to chair the Schweinfurt supervisory board. After his father-in-law's death, Henle continued the tradition in 1942, but, given the vital importance of ball bearings for the production of Nazi Germany's military machine, was ousted by the Nazis and later witnessed the almost total destruction of the SKF factories by the US air force. However, it did not take the parent company long after 1945 to rebuild and resume production of ball bearings in Schweinfurt, with Henle once more on its supervisory board.

Organizing the reconstruction of the steel-making and steel-processing works of Klöckner A.G. after its deconcentration by the Allies, Henle—as we have seen—established close relations with his colleagues in the Ruhr steel and coal industries. But as competitors they could not and would not have the kind of formal connections as Henle had with DB, Siemens, or Allianz. After 1951 there was also Monnet's High Authority watching all of them under the competition and cartel clauses of the ECSC treaty. However, the managers of major steel and coal companies met not only socially, including at hunting parties and dinners, but perfectly legitimately also held informal gatherings, discussion "circles," and interest-group associations to discuss mutual problems. As long as the occupation authorities laid down rules and regulations, they also devised strategies for responding to the structural and organizational changes that the Allies were insisting upon. It has also been mentioned how their situation as a group defeated by the Second World War created solidarities that were partly rooted in the long common history of the Ruhr industry, but also in the experience of working under the Hitler dictatorship. Yet, relations were not invariably harmonious. The introduction of codetermination, inevitably perhaps, generated tensions even before the dramatic debates of 1950 and 1951 related to the reordering of labor relations and the demand by workforces and trade unions for greater participation in the running of the new enterprises. Similar disagreements arose over the shaping of the ECSC, with Henle, the insider-outsider, playing a key role in both of these developments.

However, it would be wrong to underestimate how deeply ingrained was the sense of tradition and of belonging to a "community of fate" that was forged by Germany's pre-1933 history, by the devastating Nazi experience and the pressures exerted by the Allies to abandon at least some of the Ruhr industry's time-honored practices and attitudes. Henle's memoirs reflected this in the sense that he began his recollections with references not just to Peter Klöckner but also to some of the other major figures in the Ruhr region during the years up to 1945. He recalled that he met VSt.'s Albert Vögler, Ernst Poensgen, and Hermann Wenzel, though not Walter Rohland. He had warm words for Poensgen, who, together with Jarres, had helped negotiate the deal with Koerner and Terboven in 1942, calling him a "grand seigneur of distinguished stature" with "the physiognomy of a philosopher." Wenzel, like Poensgen, also retired early during the war, worn out by the pressures for total war and hardline Nazi organizers of industry, such as Paul Pleiger. While Poensgen used his international contacts and reputation from the 1920s to plead with the Allies for a mild treatment of the Ruhr industries, Wenzel took a more active role between 1945 and 1947 in attempts to stop a punitive treatment by the Allies. How far these men and Vögler who, as chair of the supervisory board of the VSt. and ally of armaments minister Albert Speer, may during the war have held a protective hand over the "non-Aryan" Henle requires further research.

There follow in Henle's memoirs the names of a few members of his own generation. He was particularly close to Hans-Günther Sohl. He also praises Otto Wolff von Amerongen, who inherited the convoluted business conglomerate of his father Otto Wolff after the war. There was also Wilhelm Zangen, the long-serving chief executive of the Mannesmann Corporation. While it is puzzling that Henle did not talk about his Jewish family background and the anxieties he must have felt during the war when the regime started its deportations to the death camps and husbands of "mixed" marriages were rounded up, as the

Rosenstrasse incident demonstrated in 1943, he did refer to two men with whose fate he was well familiar. Thus, he recalls the member of the Krupp Directorate in charge of raw material provision, Arthur Klotzbach, who resigned in 1937 in the face of mounting anti-Semitism and died disillusioned soon thereafter.

The other colleague whose background is also not mentioned by Henle is Richard Merton. Here the link was through the latter's membership on the supervisory board of Vereinigte Glanzstoff until his death in 1960. Merton had escaped from Nazi persecution to Britain. But instead of referring to Merton's well-known Jewish family history, Henle merely reports that Merton returned to Germany soon after the end of the war to chair the supervisory board of the Frankfurt Metallgesellschaft, a conglomerate even more diverse than Klöckner, specializing in engineering, chemicals, mining, and commercial trading worldwide. As Henle put it, Merton arrived in Frankfurt soon after the war, "unburdened by a look into the rear-view mirror." He added that he was of "great service" during the reconstruction of the West German economy "thanks to his circumspection and extensive foreign connections," especially with Britain. Other relationships were more informal. Thus, there seems to have been a mutual affinity with Kurt Lotz, the manager of the German subsidiary of the Swiss Brown Boveri & Cie conglomerate. And finally, there are Henle's remarks about Friedrich Flick, whom the Allies tried at Nuremberg on account of his close collaboration with the Nazi regime and the profits that he reaped from it. Although, unlike some of Henle's colleagues, he was not among Flick's supporters when he served a term in prison, he nevertheless wrote of Flick with some admiration when it came to the ways in which he rebuilt his empire after being forced by the Allies to sell off his coal and steel interests by shrewdly shifting into manufacturing. Thus, Flick acquired a major share in Daimler and other booming companies of the Second Industrial Revolution. By the 1970s, he had become one of the wealthiest and most powerful industrialists whose past and current methods few dared to criticize.

Henle's Transnational Networks

The end of the British occupation of the Rhineland and the founding of the Federal Republic facilitated friendlier relations between London and Bonn as the seat of the Adenauer government and its quest to become fully integrated into the Western community of nations. It is in this context that British and West German politicians, academics, and intellectuals decided to establish informal conversations at Königswinter, just across the Rhine from Bonn and Bad Godesberg.[25] Henle, displaying his excellent English, began to attend these meetings and to give lectures on European integration. He also traveled to the Second Westminster Conference in 1954, held to explore the possibilities of closer ties between the British Commonwealth and the embryonic West European economic community.[26] However, it seems that he felt no strong commitment to these attempts to increase a mutual Anglo-German understanding. His reservations may in part have been related to his memories of the British occupation, the harsh treatment he received at Bad Nenndorf, and London's policy of breaking up the Klöckner conglomerate. As he wrote in his memoirs, though, he felt no "anger" (Groll) at his internment.[27] At the same time, his family background and fate under the Nazis may have contributed to his early release from Eselheide. His wife will later have told him how agonizing it had been for her having been unable for weeks and months to find out where the British had taken him. Nor did Henle receive any special dispensations when it came to the British reorganization of Klöckner A.G. and Klöckner & Co. Finally, there was his active support for the creation of the ECSC from which Britain had distanced itself from the start. London's strategy to revitalize traditional links with the Empire and Commonwealth was anathema to Henle's vision of Western Europe's future.

In the face of his difficulties with the British, he began to look toward France as a more congenial partner for industrial cooperation, dating back to the 1920s. In those earlier years, this cooperation had taken place through the formation of the International Steel Cartel and later the International Steel Export Cartel. But times had changed after 1945, and just as Henle favored the installation of a competitive economy at home, he worked for a European Community that was open to multilateral trade. Hence his prominent role during the negotiations in Paris and Bonn to forge a compromise between the six governments and the industrial groups that lobbied hard against Monnet's High Authority. Once the ECSC was in place, Henle recognized that Franco-German relations needed constant nurturing. More than once tensions arose, as during a meeting at the end of March 1954 hosted by Pierre Ricard, the president of the French association of steel industrialists. On this occasion, Adenauer, who also worried about French opposition to the anti-Soviet European Defense Community, again relied on Henle when he asked him to lead the West German delegation.[28] The latter happily continued his diplomatic efforts. In December of that year he returned to Paris to participate in a conversation on Franco-German economic relations. It had been organized by the Centre d'Etudes de Politique Etrangère, and this time a larger number of politicians, academics, and journalist from both sides had been invited. Henle came home feeling that relations had clearly seen further improvement.

The tensions were to some extent similar to the teething troubles that Monnet encountered during his first years at the High Authority. Given that the ECSC was a very novel experiment in transnational institutional cooperation, it was perhaps inevitable that problems and misunderstandings would occur. Although Henle was critical of some of Monnet's supervisory decisions,[29] he certainly wanted Western Europe to take the next steps toward closer integration and therefore also welcomed the drafting of the Rome Treaty that enlarged the ECSC to the more comprehensive European Economic Community (EEC) at the end of 1957.[30] When Britain's Imperial and Commonwealth bloc policies and also their European Free Trade Zone (EFTA) ran into trouble, the Conservatives under Harold MacMillan prepared an application for British membership in the EEC. This time it was the French president Charles de Gaulle who lay across the tracks of an EEC enlargement. Dismayed, Henle wrote to Adenauer, advising him that he could and should play the role of mediator, even if Paris demanded a high price for its approval of a British entry.

There were two ways in which Henle continued to encourage the integration of West Germany and its industries into the Western community of nations: with the rise of the Federal Republic on the international stage, he attended official receptions and dinners in Bonn in honor of prominent politicians from all over the world.[31] More importantly, with the Royal Institute of International Affairs at London's Chatham House before his eyes, Henle became convinced that the Federal Republic needed a similar institution, that is, an institute that conducted research into a wide range of contemporary problems and also invited prominent speakers from abroad to meet German experts and politicians. Accordingly, Henle became involved in the founding of the Deutsche Gesellschaft für Auswärtige Politik (DGAP).[32] Soon influential politicians came to Bonn to talk about their policies and perceptions of the world, among them Julius Nyerere, then chief minister of Tanganyika; U Thant, the secretary general of the United Nations; and Abdel Khalek Hassouna, the secretary general of the Arab League.

With air travel becoming easier in terms of visa requirements and more comfortable, Henle, often accompanied by his wife Anne-Liese, began to travel outside Europe. His earliest trips took him to North America where he first used his contacts to nudge Washington to remove the restrictions on his industrial conglomerate. But once these problems had been settled, he was regularly traveling abroad, wearing two hats: one related to the Klöckner A.G. as a steel-making and steel-processing enterprise; the other as the head of Klöckner & Co., the international trading company. Thus, in the autumn of 1955, he undertook an extensive journey to Latin America, partly to secure iron ore deliveries, especially from Brazil.[33] But he also went down memory lane to Argentina where he had been a senior counselor (Legationsrat) at the German embassy during the 1920s. Frequently combining tourism with business and having traversed the Andes into Chile, he also visited Peru, where Klöckner had just built a joint venture with local businessmen to produce steel pipes. His trip also took him to Panama and Cuba and back to Europe via New York for more business conversations. In North America, Henle also connected with the Canadian Alcan Corporation, a major producer of aluminum. In 1966, Alcan and Klöckner founded the Klöckner-Alcan-Aluminium GmbH & Co. in Düsseldorf through which he expanded his interests beyond steel-making and processing.

In the spring of 1957, Henle undertook a longer trip to Asia with his wife and daughter, soon after celebrating the fiftieth anniversary of Klöckner & Co.[34] The turnover of his trading house with its 5,000 employees had meanwhile risen to an impressive 1.9 billion marks, and it was time for him to visit the Far East. He stopped over in India where he saw Nehru again, before moving on to Hong Kong and Tokyo. He returned via the Philippines where KHD had just finished building a cement factory. Colombo was his last stop. In the autumn of 1961, Henle and his wife traveled to West Africa to visit Senegal, Sierra Leone, and Liberia, where he inspected one of Klöckner's iron ore export firms.[35] The couple then traversed the continent via Ruanda-Burundi to see Kenya and ultimately also Addis Abeba. Judging from the notes that he kept, it was a memorable journey. In February 1966, Henle went on a separate trip to South Africa, again combining business and pleasure.[36] Given his family background, mention should finally be made of his trip to Israel, even if it took him until November 1965 to arrange it. He and his wife saw the widow of Chaim Weizmann as well as a number of academics and industrialists.[37] The couple also attended a concert in Tel Aviv, during which they were surprised to hear many German words spoken around them, also at a subsequent reception in honor of the artists. As Henle put it in his memoirs:[38] "We encountered interesting interlocutors whom one does not meet on a daily basis." But they also felt "very distinctly how much culture and intellect the Nazi regime had maliciously expelled and destroyed."

Henle and the Debate on West Germany's Ban of Cartels

While the ways in which Henle dealt with these burdens of the past will be examined again later in this chapter, this is the point to return to the evolution of the debate on cartels. This issue has been discussed in Chapter 3 with regard to Allied attitudes in the 1940s.[39] But from 1948 onward, Washington had left it first to the Verwaltung für Wirtschaft (VfW) and, after the founding of the Federal Republic, to the government and the Bundestag in Bonn to put a ban on cartels and syndicates, that is, horizontal agreements between independent firms over prices, production levels, marketing, and other anticompetitive practices.[40] They knew that Ludwig Erhard at VfW and from the autumn of 1949 as head of the economics ministry was not only an Atlanticist keen to establish close relations with the United States but also agreed that the German cartel tradition had to be stopped. From his earlier work, he was also aware of the resentments that many entrepreneurs, large and small, felt against the Allied pressure to abandon the cartel tradition. As the Bipartite Control Office (BICO), but also reformist employers, such as Otto A. Friedrich and Dietrich von Menges, discovered in meetings, the tradition had become so much part of the mental world of many managers and owners that they resisted the ban and even tried to circumvent it. Time and again BICO had to intervene to break up a cartel that some branches had covertly reconstituted.[41]

Soon after taking charge of his ministry, Erhard therefore asked a number of his civil servants to write a draft under the chairmanship of Paul Josten. Evidently inspired by what came to be known as "ordoliberalism" and promoted by Professor Walter Eucken and his colleagues at the University of Freiburg the Josten Circle that had intensified its work in the spring of 1949 not only recommended a total ban on cartels and syndicates but also wanted to secure what was called "perfect competition."[42] Accordingly, Josten proposed to prevent the resurgence not only of monopolies but also of all larger concentrations of economic power. An office was supposed to keep monitoring proposed mergers and acquisitions and if they reached a threshold that threatened perfect competition, they would be broken up by a court order.

It is not surprising that this proposal met with the vigorous opposition of all larger corporations that—as has been mentioned—were coping in 1949–50 with the pressures of American deconcentration policy. Realizing that this policy did not aim at a highly decentralized organization of the market as envisaged by Eucken, but was designed to create larger production units as engines of economic growth in the oligopolistic tradition of the United States, Josten's model was quickly scuttled as unrealistic.[43] What also seems to have contributed to this halt was the impending founding of the Federal Republic. However, the debate that the Josten Circle had unleashed in the West German press facilitated the formation of a West German corporate front, spearheaded by the German Federation of Industries (BDI) that had been founded in the summer of 1949.[44] Fritz Berg, its president, was bitterly opposed to a ban of cartels and wanted to return to the rather toothless 1923 misuse principle of the Weimar days. At that time cartels were legitimate legal associations and could be dissolved only if courts convicted a particular cartel of having engaged in practices that had abused its position in the market. The weakness of this rule meant that cartels, as we have seen, continued to flourish in the 1920s and 1930s.[45]

Berg and a number of conservatives in the Ruhr region, with Hermann Reusch once more among them, succeeded in mobilizing parts of industry so effectively against Erhard that the Allies became quite alarmed and in 1950 thought of recommitting themselves to the issue to make certain that West Germany would have an anti-cartel clause. After all, this was what the Allies had decreed in 1945, modelled on the Sherman and Clayton Acts and now to be legislated in Bonn. Again much was made of the argument that these market innovations were for the benefit of the consumer who, thanks to competition, would enjoy lower prices.[46] Similarly, reference was again made to the need for West German employers to "re-educate" themselves and adapt to the new circumstances. Although several officers of the Erhard ministry continued to work on a draft and a delegation, led by Professor Franz Böhm, visited the United States in June 1950 to obtain more information on American anti-trust policies, it was not only the public debates but also the slow-moving work in the ministries and in parliamentary committees that badly delayed the presentation of an anti-cartel draft and this began to irritate the US high commission.

In anticipation of a West German government initiative, the BICO personnel had been reduced, but with progress in Bonn being so slow, this office, in a show of impatience, had worked on a draft of its own. In August 1950, even US president Harry Truman raised his voice to warn that the formation of international cartels presented a great danger to Europe. The Americans in a show of how serious they were began to prosecute the association of the grinding and polishing industry suspected of having formed a cartel.[47] Later Erhard, rattled by this move, sought an assurance from the high commission that the German effort had priority. In the meantime, the drafting of an anti-cartel law had been given to Roland Risse and Eberhard Günther, after Erhard had reached an understanding with the US high commission in October 1950 that they were satisfied with what he was doing. Yet it still was only many months later in early February 1952 that the seventh(!) draft was at last sent to the Federal president and the other Federal ministries. In June 1952, the Bundestag discussed a document that the Adenauer cabinet had meanwhile approved and now forwarded for discussion in the Bundesrat and Bundestag. The trouble was that the chancellor's coalition government had from the start in 1949 been working on shaky grounds, and by 1952, the parties were beginning to think of the next elections, to be held in September 1953. And so the bill was withdrawn with the promise that it would be reintroduced in 1954.

How closely the Americans continued to watch the cartel issue is reflected in the American press. Thus the *Wall Street Journal* (*WSJ*) published an article on March 25, 1953 that began with the unceremonious statement that German industrialists should be the last to favor cartels.[48] It continued:

> Hitler found it extraordinarily easy to bring German industry under his control. And the reason he found it so easy was that the machinery for control already had been built for him. It was not necessary for him to deal with individual plants. Most of the plants were already party to some cartel arrangement and Hitler had only to bring under his thumb the existing control points.

The article then added that many industrialists had "willingly or otherwise" cooperated with the Nazi regime: "As a result, many lost their properties, some lost their lives, and others spent some time in jails. It is a puzzling circumstance that the same generation takes the risk of building a similar booby trap for itself." Five months later, the *WSJ* was quite pessimistic about the possibility to effect change:[49] "Chalk up as a failure the attempt to sell American-style capitalism to German big business." In fact, "quietly and methodically trade and industry are returning to their traditional prewar patterns of cartels and trusts." The article concluded that there was "a fundamental difference in attitude. To a German, as to most Europeans, a cartel is not anti-social or iniquitous, as it is to most Americans" and "it is this attitude, perhaps more than anything else, that the U.S. has failed to change."

The *WSJ*, as soon became clear, was too pessimistic. To begin with, the victory of the CDU/CSU in September 1953 had put Adenauer's new government on a firmer political footing, However, it is true that Berg and his allies, themselves strengthened and now fully organized and well funded, had been sharpening their knives, and so the controversy resumed between Erhard and Berg. As happens so often in heated discussions, there were also various misunderstandings and hurt egos. This applied to Berg in particular who, as the owner of a relatively small steel spring factory in comparison to the big steel corporations, tried to compensate a nagging inferiority complex by using strong words and exaggerations. Anti-Erhard feelings ran so deep in the Berg family that his wife went so far as to remark at one point rather disdainfully that she could not bear seeing Erhard's face any longer.[50] However, by March 1954, Erhard's experts had composed another draft that contained a basic ban on cartels but left room for various exceptions to be granted by a future supervising cartel office. Erhard defended this draft in June 1954, asserting that this anti-cartel law was the Federal Republic's "economic basic law" that had to be put on the statute book, just as the political Basic Law had been ratified in 1949.[51]

With the Americans still in the background, the economic press, as in 1953, raised its voice again, this time with two telling articles by Gilbert Burck that appeared in the magazine *Fortune* in April and Mai 1954. The first piece, entitled "Can Germany Go Capitalist?" referred to Erhard's struggle who was quoted as being prepared to fight like a "madman" (Berserker) against those who were trying to kill his bill. But Burck also mentioned the "formidable opposition" Erhard faced: "It is nothing less than wrenching away from both private and state restrictions an economy that seems united to them by temperament and tradition." The second article entitled "The German Business Mind" mentioned the current "Draft Law against Restraints of Competition" directly with a mix of pessimism and hopefulness:[52] "Should the bill be rejected in toto, West Germany may well slip back into the economic authoritarianism of the old days, with repercussion that no man can yet foresee." At the same time "acceptance of the bill, even in a modified form, would mean a major victory, perhaps the greatest victory ever won in Europe, for the principles of dynamic American-style capitalism."

With the stakes so high, the spring and summer 1954 saw the formation of a group of industrialists who basically agreed that the country's economic constitution needed to be ratified to complement that parliamentary-democratic Basic Law. Above all, they were unhappy with the haggling between Berg and Erhard. In this context, rather a diverse group of executives of big and medium-sized enterprises began to meet in search of a compromise. They had met with Erhard at the hotel at the top of the Peterberg overlooking Bonn and Bad Godesberg on July 12. Subsequent discussions included Alexander Haffner of the Salamander shoe factory, but also of big players, such as Krupp, Mannesmann, Rheinstahl, Zellstoff Waldhof, and, significantly, once again Günter Henle.[53] From all we have learned about his attitudes to structural reforms, it is not surprising that he was among the opponents of Berg's hard line. As has been mentioned repeatedly, he also viewed these reforms against the backdrop of the catastrophic Nazi experiences. This time West German capitalism had to be organized and run differently from the pre-1945 years. In this sense, Henle's insights complemented well those that *WSJ* had articulated in March 1953.[54] The group authorized F. W. Ziervogel of the Ruhrgas Corp., rather than Henle, to write to the president of the BDI that they supported Erhard's straight ban of cartels and were critical of Berg's insistence on the ancient misuse clause.

Focusing on Henle attitudes, it seems that he later came to have a few reservations about the resolution of the conflict between Berg and Erhard. To be sure, he did not favor the restoration of the former cartel system but apparently worried about the threat of state intervention against corporations that had become too big. This distrust of the state was probably rooted in his experiences during the Nazi period. Several years later, in January 1959, he published an article in the liberal-conservative weekly *Die Zeit* in which he examined, with reference to the American example, questions of compulsion and the limits of concentration:[55] "A healthy market economy," he wrote, "will of course have to allow for competition. This means that market domination by an individual enterprise or a corporate group" had to be prevented. Excessive concentration of economic power was tantamount to centralization in just one hand and it invited the nationalization of the industrial branch in question. Unfortunately, Henle did not discuss his role as a member of this anti-Berg faction in his memoirs, except for a brief reference in which he tried to correct the "one-sided picture" of the dinner of "leading industrialists who were independent of industrial associations [i.e. the BDI]" and favored a ban of cartels.[56] Otherwise he merely cited the tensions that he had observed between Adenauer and Erhard, leading the latter to argue, rather sharply, that the chancellor had no understanding of the larger significance of his economics minister's fight for a competitive economy and that this ignorance made it so difficult to debate the issue with him.[57]

While the influential *Volkswirt* felt that the opposition to Berg indicated that the BDI front was "crumbling,"[58] the affair had also opened up opportunities for compromise. The BDI presidium felt obliged officially to strengthen Berg who had been reelected just a few weeks earlier. But his colleagues also nudged him to be more accommodating. A year later, it was clear that Erhard's ban on cartels would appear in the final version of the Law for Securing Competition but that exceptions could be made, especially in times of economic crisis. Having been scrutinized by both the Federal Council and the Bundestag, it was finally ratified at the end of 1957 after seven years of struggle.

As indicated at the beginning, this chapter was merely designed to map out some of the major topics that an account of Henle's life and professional work would have to cover more fully beyond these activities both before 1945 and his efforts in the early postwar years to help reorganize two key issues: labor relations and codetermination and West Germany's reintegration on into the Western community of nations and their industrial economies, culmination in the creation of the ECSC as a first step. It is to be hoped that other historians will research and write about the subsequent development of the Klöckner conglomerate from the late 1950s. What follows are therefore merely a few concluding remarks about Günter Henle and his work as the insider-outsider of German heavy industry.

Conclusion

As I tried to explain in the introduction and also in the last chapter of this book, my aim was not to write a comprehensive biography of Günter Henle and the history of the Klöckner conglomerate. Against the background of the family history and its fate both before 1933 and then under the Nazi dictatorship, I wanted to investigate what insights he and his colleagues gained after the end of the Second World War from their experiences and how they tried to apply these insights to the reconstruction of West German society, economy, politics, and culture during the first two decades after 1945.

Although Henle's memoirs are very sparse and do not mention at all aspects that must have deeply influenced him and his family, especially during the Nazi years, it is nevertheless possible to extrapolate from his decisions and activities after 1945 what these lessons of the past were and how Henle worked hard to put these insights into practice. After all, for him it was not just that the Hitler dictatorship must never happen again. Nor was it merely the rebuilding of the Klöckner trust, that had been badly damaged by the war and by subsequent Allied policies of dismantling and deconcentration. Nor is this the history of the G. Henle music publishing company, founded in 1948, however famous it continues to be to this day for the cultural world, not only of the Federal Republic but around the globe. Instead I was most interested in the contributions that Henle and his colleagues made to the shaping of postwar West Germany in the fields of domestic politics and economic reconstruction as well as international relations in the context of the postwar Pax Americana.

As far as domestic rebuilding of West Germany is concerned, the organization of labor relations was at the top of Henle's agenda both with respect to Klöckner but also more generally for the whole of industry. How this happened and what was Henle's role in putting more modern labor relations on the statute book took up considerable space in the first post-1945 chapters of this book. I could do this only in broad outline, and a more detailed evaluation of the archives of both the Klöckner Family Foundation and the collections of the Federal Archives at Koblenz will no doubt be undertaken at some point by other scholars. Henle's contribution to the introduction of parity codetermination in the coal and steel industry in 1951 and the Works Constitution Law of 1952 cannot be separated from Allied deconcentration policies and the compromises that were forged, at the end of which stood a "Social Market Economy" that prepared the Federal Republic better for its American-led reintegration into the world economy than the recipes that managers such as Hermann Reusch recommended with regard to the position of trade unions and workforces as well as a re-cartelized German and West European economy.

Henle also played a major role in reconciling West Germany's Western European neighbors among whom the memories of several years of Nazi occupation, mass murder, and looting were still powerful just a few years after the end of the Second World War. In this respect, Henle's skills as a former diplomat, his knowledge of foreign languages, including French and Spanish, were indispensable. I have traced in Chapter 5 the complex negotiations on the creation of the European Coal and Steel Community, the input of the Americans into the ultimate compromise, and how Henle, as during the debates concerning codetermination, insisted that this new legal framework had to be adopted. He fought for this also in light of the widely perceived threat of an invasion by the Soviet Bloc and fears of the Red Army that is also reflected in the expansion of NATO and the discussions on West German rearmament that ran in parallel to the efforts of integrating Western Europe economically.

The decades of Henle's life between 1900 and the late 1950s, with a focus on the years 1933–52, represented the time frame that I decided to cover in this study. The final chapter was merely designed to touch upon a number of issues that, together with others, will have to be covered in a full account of him as an industrialist, politician, patron of the arts, an insider-outsider up to his death in 1979. He lived through turbulent times of two world wars, a brutal Hitler dictatorship, and the chaos that the Nazis left behind and how he emerged from this period as a person who had a clear vision of the tasks that he began to tackle immediately at the end of the Nazi nightmare.

Notes

Introduction

1 Volker R. Berghahn and Paul J. Friedrich, *Otto A. Friedrich, ein politischer Unternehmer: Sein Leben und seine Zeit*, Frankfurt, 1993; Volker Berghahn, *Hans-Günther Sohl als Stahlunternehmer und Präsident des Bundesverbandes der Deutschen Industrie, 1906–1989*, Göttingen, 2020.

2 See the English-language website of Yad Vashem, Jerusalem, www.yadvashen.org/righteous/About the righteous/Database, Berthold Beitz and his wife Hilde.

3 See Joachim Käppner, *Berthold Beitz: die Biografie*, Berlin, 2010; Bernd Schmalhausen, *Berthold Beitz im Dritten Reich: Mensch in unmenschlicher Zeit*, Essen, 1991; Diana Marie Friz, *Alfried Krupp und Berthold Beitz: der Erbe und sein Statthalter*, Essen, 1991.

4 See Volker R. Berghahn and Paul Joachim Friedrich, *Otto A. Friedrich, ein politischer Unternehmer*; Volker Berghahn, *Hans-Günther Sohl*.

1 The First Decades from Hohenzollern Monarchy and Weimar Republic through the End of the Nazi Dictatorship

1 As mentioned in the introduction, the beginning of this chapter is based on Günter Henle, *Weggenosse des Jahrhunderts: Als Diplomat, Industrieller, Politiker und Freund der Musik*, Stuttgart, 1968, 9ff. There is also a shorter translation of his memoirs into English under the title *Three Spheres: A Life in Politics, Business and Music*, Chicago 1970. I was also given information by Peter Henle, Günter's son, and his wife Susanne Henle, as well as Felix and Clemens Henle, Günter's grandsons. The latter is the director of the Peter Klöckner Family Foundation and Archives (PKF) in Düsseldorf. As to Julius von Henle, the family archive contains an informative article that appeared in the *Main-Post* newspaper on May 23, 1964, on the occasion of Julius's one hundredth birthday (PKF, file V 1656) on which the following account of his career is based. As to Günter Henle's life, the denazification questionnaire that he, like most adult Germans had to complete, was particularly helpful. Henle had to certify the accuracy of his answers with his signature. Failure to do so or making false statements incurred tangible penalties by the Allied occupation authorities. As a result, this document can be considered a reliable

source that, like the memoirs, is not specifically footnoted in this chapter. See PKF, Henle Papers. The original is held by the Abteilung Rheinland of the Landesarchiv North-Rhine-Westphalia. Finally, Julius von Henle's statement published in the journal of the *Verein zur Abwehr des Antisemitismus* of May 1930, https://period ika.digitale-Sammlungen.de/Blatt bsb00000938,00058.html*FN* (accessed January 15, 2022).

2 Henle, *Weggenosse des Jahrhunderts*, 16–22. The diplomatic service files on Günter Henle are held in the Archives of the German Foreign Ministry in Berlin.

3 Ibid., 64–8. See also Erich Sperling, *Alles um Stahl: Wirtschaftsgeschichtliche Erzählung um die Klöckner-Georgsmarienhütte AG*, Osnabrück, Bremen-Horn, 1956, 21ff., with further details on the growth of the conglomerate.

4 See Protocol by Henle of the Meeting of the Stahlwerksverband in Düsseldorf on October 27, 1938, Bundesarchiv Koblenz (BAK), Henle Papers (GHNL) 384/000236. See also Henle to Maulick, June 5, 1939, ibid. At this time Henle was listed as "Direktor Dr., Klöckner-Werke A.G., Duisburg, Mitglied des Aufsichtsrats."

5 See Henle's file Note of his meeting with Schwede in Düsseldorf on December 20, 1939, December 21, 1939, ibid. Schwede was evasive though confirming that Klöckner's complaints were justified and that he sympathized with the situation of the smaller Klöckner A.G. in comparison to VSt. and other members of the association. Henle, on the other hand, remarked that he did not wish to take the matter to the Nazi authorities. After all, the private sector tried very hard not to be dominated by the regime or the RWHG. See also ibid. on the earlier tensions between the members especially in Wilhelm Zangen to Ernst Poensgen, December 13, 1938, with copies to Flick, Peter Klöckner, Löser, Lübsen, and Tgahrt. However, with the authorities in Berlin becoming ever more important once the war had started, Henle, after visiting Berlin on March 21 and 22, 1941, recommended that Klöckner, following the example of GHH, Krupp, Flick, Röchling, and Mannesmann, should also have its own representative in the capital, as the corporation would otherwise miss important information on what was going on. See Henle's file note on his trip for Florian Klöckner and the executive board, n.d., ibid.

6 Mauritz's protocol of the Stahlwerksverband meeting on July 9, 1940, relating to export quotas and prices for Denmark and Finland, ibid. See also Henle's file note on the main meeting of the Stahlwerksverband in Düsseldorf on April 11, 1940, with copies to Florian Klöckner, Baum, and the directors of the Works in Osnabrück, Düsseldorf, Troisdorf, as well as Klöckner & Co. in Duisburg, ibid.

7 See p. 63ff.

8 See Henle to Bochumer Verband (Knepper), May 11, 1940, and subsequent correspondence on this issue in BAK, GHNL 384/000229. Gustav Knepper was on the management board of Gelsenkirchener Bergwerks A.G. On the nominations

question, see, for example, Baum's file note, May 9, 1941, ibid., GHNL 384/000236, in which he discussed reservations relating to nominating Max C. Müller, who, in the 1929s, had been involved in the International Raw Steel Cartel as Maulick's successor. He was deemed to be even more "autocratic" than Maulick: "He is a man who always goes with the strongest faction and who has treated smaller members distinctly badly. Klöckner in particular had repeatedly experienced this." Moreover, he had been at loggerheads with the deputy National Group leader in Brussels. Nor the "attitude of the [Nazi] Party" was such that it would be "advantageous" to the Stahlwerk Association. The file note therefore offers a glimpse of what went on between industry and government behind the scenes of a system that was based on the Social Darwinist principle of the survival of the fittest.

9 See Baum's file note, June 12, 1941, ibid. On the larger context of German industrial exploitation in Western and Eastern Europe, see Volker Berghahn, *Hans-Günther Sohl als Stahlunternehmer und Präsident des Bundesverbandes der Deutschen Industrie, 1906–1989*, Göttingen, 2020, 57–66, 85–99.

10 In February 1939, Henle still gave Schwede as the Stahlwerksverband chair his apologies because he was about to take a vacation. In February 1941, he merely informed the Bochumer Verband that he was traveling at the time of its next meeting. On these telling changes, see, for example, Henle to Maulick, June 5, 1939, GHNL 384/000236, still signed with "Mit freundlichem Glückauf bin ich Ihr ergebener [Henle]."

11 See Henle an Knepper, May 17, 1941, ibid., 000229: "Glückauf und Heil Hitler!"

12 See Berghahn, *Hans-Günther Sohl als Stahlunternehmer*, 57–66, 106–11.

13 Ibid., 59–62. See also Gerhard Mollin, *Montankonzerne und "Drittes Reich" Der Gegensatz zwischen Monopolindustrie und Befehlswirtschaft in der deutschen Rüstung und Expansion, 1936–1944*, Göttingen, 1988, 52ff.

14 Henle, *Weggenosse des Jahrhunderts*, 68.

15 See Henry A. Turner, *General Motors and the Nazis: The Struggle for Control of Opel, Europe's Biggest Carmaker*, New Haven, 2003.

16 The following is based on several documents that the Familienstiftung kindly made available to me as well as on Henle, *Weggenosse des Jahrhundert*, 72–6 See also p. 30 and Sperling, *Alles um Stahl*, 248. The first document is a "Niederschrift" of a board meeting of the Peter-Klöckner-Familienstiftung on August 12, 1942, chaired by Jarres, according to which Henle had been forced, after negotiations with Terboven and Reich Commissar Hans Fischböck, to give up his positions in Klöckner Werke A.G. and the Familienstiftung-Kuratorium. Subsequently, Florian Klöckner also agreed to vacate the chair of the Klöckner Werke and KHD supervisory boards. The Niederschrift noted that "political reasons had without doubt been determining" factors. All compensation payments to Henle were to be stopped, though he remained executive partner in Klöckner & Co. It

was also a relief for him that a charge was dropped, alleging that he had known of breaches of price regulations committed by employees of Klöckner & Co.—a typical method to put pressure on people the regime wanted to oust from their positions. The accusation was very unsettling to Henle and his family. See ibid., Henle's correspondence with Karl Kimmich of Deutsche Bank, who, showing a "warme menschliche Anteilnahme," had supported him, together with Karl Jarres, in negotiating this outcome. The importance of such connections is also reflected in the helpful role that the SS-Obergruppenfuehrer Paul Koerner seems to have played in these negotiations. A secretary of state in the Four-Year Plan bureaucracy and close to Goering, his role deserves further investigation into the paradoxes of the Nazi regime. Another bonus seems to have been that Marotzke did not behave as a bully but stressed that he wished to have a cooperative relationship with the family, especially also as chair of the Klöckner & Co. advisory council. See also a similar exchange of words recorded in the "Niederschrift" of the board meeting of the Klöckner-Familienstiftung of October 3, 1942, at which Jarres reported that the new arrangements had been approved by all regional and central authorities involved in the matter. This included no lesser person than Reich economics minister Walther Funk who confirmed his approval of the settlement for the Klöckner Werke in a letter to Jarres of October 14, 1942. All this meant that the family had effectively been expropriated, except for Klöckner & Co. with Marotzke acting as watchdog.

17 See Volkmar Muthesius, *Peter Klöckner, und sein Werk*, published as Issue No. 1 in the "Ruhr and Rhein" series. I would like to thank Peter Soergel for drawing my attention to this booklet. Interesting enough it was republished in 1959, this time presumably with Henle's approval and with a postscript that referred to Klöckner's Lebenswerk as having been earmarked for "extinction, but, after undergoing various fateful developments," it could in the end be salvaged; even if it "did not resume its earlier shape," the corporation succeeded in regaining its former significance in the coal and steel industry.

18 See Clemens Henle's email to Jan Haas et al., July 22, 2021.

19 See the careful and comprehensive study by Beate Meyer, "*Jüdische Mischlinge*": *Rassenpolitik und Verfolgungserfahrung, 1933–1945*, Hamburg, 1999. She shows that around 1932 some 35,000 "mixed" couples lived in Germany, with around 8,000 progeny. As the regime stabilized, innumerable decrees and rules were introduced. Marriage bans were imposed and forced sterilization discussed. Yet, the contradictions between ostracizing this group and somehow integrating its members were never clarified. Meyer deals not only with official policies but also with the impact these policies had on the victims.

20 Gernot Jochheim, *Frauenprotest in der Rosenstrasse*: *"Gebt uns unsere Männer wieder,"* Berlin, 1993.

21 Wolf Gruner, *Widerstand in der Rosenstrasse*, Frankfurt, 2005; idem, *Gedenkort Rosenstrasse 2–4. Protest im NS-Staat*, Berlin 2013.

22 Nathan Stoltzfus, *Hitler's Compromises: Coercion and Consensus in Nazi Germany*, New Haven, 2016, esp. 244ff.

23 On Blumenfeld, see Frank Bajohr, Hanseat, und Grenzgänger, *Erik Blumenfeld, eine politische Biografie*, Göttingen, 2010. Blumenfeld was deported to Auschwitz where he was forced to remove the bodies from the gas chambers. His Danish mother happened to know Felix Kersten, Heinrich Himmler's physiotherapist. She asked him to ask Himmler to give her son another assignment. He was sent to Buchenwald concentration camp, but not before he had been forcibly sterilized. He survived to become a prominent businessman and politician in Hamburg.

24 See Maximilian Strnad, *Privileg Mischehe? Handlungsspielräume "jüdisch-versippter" Familien, 1933–1949*, Göttingen, 2021.

25 See Clemens Henle's email to the author, July 12, 2021, reporting that his grandfather once remarked that this kind of anti-Semitism might one day return.

26 Henle, *Weggenosse des Jahrhunderts*, 72.

27 Ibid.

28 See Berghahn, *Hans-Günther Sohl als Stahlunternehmer*, 115–20.

29 Ibid., 100.

30 Henle, *Weggenosse des Jahrhundert*, 73.

31 See Berghahn, *Hans-Günther Sohl als Stahlunternehmer*, 122.

32 Henle, *Weggenosse des Jahrhundert*, 75.

33 See, for example, Bernd Greiner, *Die Morgenthau-Legende*, Hamburg, 1995; Wilfried Mausbach, *Zwischen Morgenthau und Marshall*, Düsseldorf, 1996.

34 See Berghahn, *Hans-Günther Sohl als Stahlunternehmer*, 122–7.

35 See Klaus-Dietmar Henke, *Die amerikanische Besetzung Deutschlands*, Munich, 1995, 527ff.

36 See the File note that Henle wrote after the meeting on July 13, 1945, repr. in Gabriele Müller-List, ed., *Neubeginn bei Eisen und Stahl im Ruhrgebiet: Die Beziehungen zwischen Arbeitgebern und Arbeitnehmern in der nordrhein-westfälischen Eisen- und Stahlindustrie, 1945–1948*, Düsseldorf, 1990, 160–1. This volume is a most important collection of documents on which this and the next chapters rely quite heavily.

37 See the minutes of the meeting repr. in Müller-List, *Neubeginn bei Eisen und Stahl im Ruhrgebiet*, 167–75.

38 For details on Rohland's fate and postwar career, see Berghahn, *Hans-Günther Sohl als Stahlunternehmer*, 134–5.

39 File note signed by Kurz of the meeting on August 31, 1945, repr. in Müller-List, *Neubeginn bei Eisen und Stahl im Ruhrgebiet*, 175.

40 Henle and [executive secretary] Wilhelm Ahrend to Oberpräsident of
    Nordrheinprovinz, Economic Department, September 14, 1945, repr. in Müller-List,
    Neubeginn bei Eisen und Stahl im Ruhrgebiet, 175.

41 Lobeck/Maiweg/Wegmann to the director of the Labor Department,
    Oberpräsidium Nordrheinprovinz, November 10, 1945, repr. in Müller-List,
    Neubeginn bei Eisen und Stahl im Ruhrgebiet, 182–6.

42 Henle to Lehr, September 11, 1945, BAK, GHNL, 384/000482; Henle "Zur
    politischen Bereinigung der Wirtschaft," September 11, 1945.

43 Henle to Lehr, November 24, 1945, repr. in Müller-List, *Neubeginn bei Eisen und
    Stahl im Ruhrgebiet*, 188–9.

44 Henle, *Weggenosse des Jahrhundert*, 76.

2 British Occupation Policies, 1945–6

1 Günter Henle, *Weggenosse des Jahrhunderts*, Stuttgart 1988, 80–3, also for the
   following.

2 Heiner Wember, *Umerziehung im Lager. Internierung und Bestrtafung in der
   britischen Zone Deutschlands*, Essen 1991, esp. 96ff. For a complete list of the
   arrested managers, see "Verhaftungen in der Schwerindustrie," *Neue Rheinische
   Zeitung*, December 5, 1945.

3 Hans-Günther Sohl, *Notizen*, Bochum-Wattenscheid, 1985, 98–107.

4 Henle, *Weggenosse des Jahrhunderts*, 80. For the following account of Anne-Liese's
   attempts to find her husband, see Peter Klöckner Familienstiftung (PKF), file V
   1648, Annelis Sohl to Anne-Liese Henle, January 20, 1946. See also ibid., Michael
   Thomas to Anne-Liese Henle, September 20, 1946.

5 See the account in Volker Berghahn, *Hans-Günther Sohl als Stahlunternehmer und
   Präsident des Bundesverbandes der Deutschen Industrie, 1906–1989*, Göttingen 2020,
   130–5, also for the following.

6 See p. 18.

7 Henle, *Weggenosse des Jahrhunderts*, 81.

8 In his memoirs (ibid., 82) he wrote rather generously that he felt no resentment
   ("Groll") about his internment.

9 Ibid. See p. 19ff.

10 Henle to Lehr, 24 November 1945, repr. in Müller-List, *Neubeginn bei Eisen und
   Stahl im Ruhrgebiet*, 188–9. Their relationship was so close that they were on "Du"
   terms, but typically did not use their first names.

11 Quoted ibid., 48.

12 Fugmann's file note on the meeting 4 May 1945, repr. ibid., 158–9.

13 File note by Gerhard Schroeder of the meeting of the Nordwest Group's Social Committees, July 24, 1945, repr. ibid., 161–4.

14 On this "Preussenschlag," see, for example, Karl Dietrich Bracher, *Die Auflösung der Weimarer Republik: Eine Studie zum Problem des Machtverfalls in der Demokratie*, 3rd impression, Villingen, 1960, 635ff.

15 Jarres to Severing, December 4, 1945, repr. in Müller-List, ed., *Neubeginn bei Eisen und Stahl im Ruhrgebiet*, 189–90.

16 Severing to Jarres, December 12, 1945, repr. ibid., 190–1.

17 Jarres to Severing, January 2, 1946, repr. ibid., 194.

18 File note by Jarres on his meeting with three trade unionists, December 31, 1945, repr. ibid., 191–4.

19 File note by Jarres of the meeting with three works council representatives, January 9, 1946, repr. ibid., 196–9. See also the further details that Karl Strohmenger, a Klöckner accountant and Jarres "ear" with regard to labor relations learned about Harig and his associates, January 5, 1946, repr. ibid., 195–6.

20 File note by Jarres, January 12, 1946, dated January 15, repr. ibid., 200–1.

21 Excerpt from the minutes of the meeting of the Klöckner Werke Supervisory Board on January 17, 1946, dated January 19, repr. ibid., 205–6.

22 Excerpt from the minutes of the meeting of the WVESI Eisenkreis, January 18, 1946, repr. ibid., 206–9.

23 File note by Jarres of his meeting with Klöckner works council representatives, January 21, 1946, repr. ibid., 210–12.

24 Klöckner management board to Jarres, January 24, 1946, repr. ibid., 212–13.

25 Excerpt from the minutes of the joint session of employer and employee representatives, January 25, 1946, repr. ibid., 213–17.

26 Minutes of the meeting, January 31, 1946, repr. ibid., 217–19.

27 Excerpt from the minutes of the WVESI Eisenkreis meeting January 31, 1946, repr. ibid., 219–22.

28 File note by Jarres of his conversation with Reusch, February 4, 1945, repr. ibid., 222–3.

29 Excerpt from the minutes of the WVESI Eisenkreis meeting, February 16, 1946, repr. ibid., 223–5.

30 The following is based on a file note that Jarres made and signed after the meeting, February 19, 1945, repr. ibid., 229.

31 Jarres to Severing, February 20, 1945, repr. ibid., 229–32.

32 Strohmenger's note on Böckler's Troisdorf visit, April 10, 1946, repr. ibid., 232–3.

33 File note by Jarres relating to the merger of the employers of North-Rhine Westphalia, May 28, 1945, repr. ibid., 236–8.

34 Excerpt from Strohmenger's note on the meeting of representatives of the Klöckner Werke in Duisburg, April 24, 1946, repr. ibid., 234–5.

35 File note by Jarres relating to the merger of the employers of North-Rhine Westphalia, May 28, 1945, repr. ibid., 236–8.

36 Excerpt from minutes of the Second Conference of the Zonal Committee, Bielefeld, May 30, 1946, repr. ibid., 238–42.

37 File note by Ulitzka of the meeting between employer and employee representatives within the framework of the labor law committee, June 4, 1946, repr. ibid., 242–3.

38 Böckler to Jarres, July 6, 1945, repr. ibid., 245–6.

39 Harig to Jarres, July 24, 1946, repr. ibid., 249f. See also Strohmenger's letter to Harig, July 27, 1946 (repr. ibid., 250–2) in which he confirmed that Harig's letter would be helpful to the impending negotiations and that they would be examined at all levels.

40 Jarres to Harig, July 31, 1946, repr. ibid., 252.

41 Brisch to Strohmenger, July 31, 1946, repr. ibid., 253.

42 Reusch to Jarres, August 15, 1946, repr. ibid., 255–6.

43 Brisch to Strohmenger, July 31, 1946, repr. ibid., 253.

44 Dinkelbach and Linz to the VSt.-Vorstand, August 21, 1946, repr. ibid., 259–61.

45 Minutes of the meeting of the WVESI Eisenkreis, August 29, 1946, repr. ibid., 262–3.

46 Strohmenger to Klöckner-Vorstand, September 13, 1946, repr. ibid., 269. See also Strohmengers more detailed file note on his conversation with Harris-Burlanof September 11, dated September 12, repr. ibid., 269–72.

47 Excerpt from the report on the meeting of the WVESI Vorstand, September 19, 1946, repr. ibid., 272–3.

3 Decartelization, Dismantling, and Deconcentration

1 See, for example, Werner Plumpe, *Vom Plan zum Markt: Wirtschaftsverwaltung und Unternehmerverbände*, Düsseldorf, 1987; Horst Thum, *Mitbestimmung in der Montanindustrie: Der Mythos vom Sieg der Gewerkschaften*, Stuttgart 1982.

2 See p. 64 n2.

3 See p. 85ff.

4 See, for example, Hans Pohl, ed., *Kartelle und Kartellgesetzgebung in Praxis und Rechtsprechung vom 19: Jahrhundert bis zur Gegenwart*, Stuttgart, 1985; Volker Hentschel, *Wirtschaft und Wirtschaftspolitik im Wilhelminischen Deutschland*, Stuttgart, 1978; Jeffrey Fear, "German Capitalism," in Thomas K. McCraw, ed., *Creating Modern Capitalism*, Cambridge, MA, 1997, 135–219, with details on the Reich Court ruling, 149.

5 See, for example, Alfred Maizels, *Industrial Growth and World Trade: An Empirical Study of Trends in Production, Consumption and Trade in Manufactures from*

1899–1959, Cambridge, 1963; Glenn Porter, *The Rise of Big Business, 1860–1910*, New York, 1973.

6 See, for example, Theodore Kovaleff, ed., *The Anti-Trust Impulse*, Armonk, NY, 1994; Robert B. Heflebower, "Monopoly and Competition in the United States of America," in Edward H. Chamberlin, ed., *Monopoly and Competition and Their Regulation*, New York, 1954, 110–39; Robert F. Himmelberg, ed., *The Rise of Big Business and the Beginnings of Antitrust and Railroad Regulation, 1870–1900*, vol. 1, New York, 1994.

7 See, for example, Robert Lacey, *Ford: The Man and the Machine*, London, 1986, esp. 119ff.; Mary Nolan, *Visions of Modernity: American Business and the Modernization of Germany*, New York, 1994.

8 Moritz J. Bonn, *Das Schicksal des deutschen Kapitalismus*, Berlin, 1930, 44f.

9 See, for example, Hermann Levy, *Industrial Germany: A Study of Its Monopoly Organizations and Their Control by the State*, Cambridge, 1935.

10 See Klaus Hildebrand, *The Foreign Policy of the Third Reich*, London, 1973.

11 Quoted in Joel Davidow, "Seeking a World Competition Code," in Oscar Schachter and Robert Hellawell, eds., *Competition in International Business*, New York 1981, 361f.

12 Wolfgang Zapf, *Wandlungen der deutschen Elite: Ein Zirkulationsmodell deutscher Führungsgruppen, 1919–1961*, Munich, 1965, 91ff. There also developed disagreements within the OMGUS between officers who were keen vigorously to implement JCS1067 and William Draper, the OMGUS economic director and a businessman by background, who favored a moderate approach, especially on deconcentration. With the East-West conflict on the horizon, he was more interested in rebuilding West German industry.

13 See the experiences of Otto A. Friedrich when he met with his colleagues in the tire industry in the late 1940s in Volker Berghahn and Paul J. Friedrich, *Otto A. Friedrich, ein politischer Unternehmer: Sein Leben und seine Zeit*, Frankfurt 1993, 98ff. See also Dietrich von Menges, *Unternehmensentscheide*, Düsseldorf, 1976, 77, who comments on the puzzled looks of an older colleague "when I tried to explain to him how an unrestricted iron trade without syndicates might operate; with the dissolution of the syndicates a firmly built universal order had, in his conception of things, collapsed." Von Menges was with Ferrostaal at the time.

14 On "economic re-education" see Berghahn and Friedrich, *Otto A. Friedrich, ein politischer Unternehmer*, 99f. Very thoughtful also the remarks by the Harvard economist Edward Mason in his book *Controlling World Trade. Cartels and Commodity Agreements*, New York, 1946, 132:

> If any permanent anti-monopoly policy could be put into effect during the period of occupation, the disruption and disorder incident on this application would count for little. Of all the institutions and policies known

to history, however, those imposed by victors on a vanquished enemy are likely to be the most impermanent. The only lasting structural changes that can be made in the German economic and political system will have to be made, in the absence of continuous occupation, by the Germans themselves.

15 See p. 69, 152ff. for a detailed analysis.

16 See p. 130.

17 Henle, *Weggenosse des Jahrhunderts*, 64–8.

18 See p. 133.

19 See, for example, John Blum, *Roosevelt and Morgenthau*, Boston, 1972.

20 For an earlier account asserting that this very punitive strategy was in fact applied, see Hanns D. Ahrens, *Demontage*, Munich, 1982. For more recent scholarship, see Bernd Greiner, *Die Morgenthau-Legende*, Hamburg, 1995; Wilfried Mausbach, *Zwischen Morgenthau und Marshall*, Düsseldorf, 1996.

21 See, for example, Alan Kramer, *Die britische Demontagepolitik am Beispiel Hamburgs, 1945–1950*, Hamburg, 1991; most recently also in inter-Allied comparative perspective: Douglas M. O'Reagan, *Taking Nazi Technology: Allied Exploitation of German Science after the Second World War*, Baltimore, 2019.

22 See Erich Sperling, *Alles um Stahl: Wirtschaftsgeschichtliche Erzählung um die Klöckner-Georgsmarienwerks AG*, Osnabrück, Bremen-Horn, 1956, 251.

23 See, for example, Bernd Stöver, *Der Kalte Krieg*, Munich, 2007, 76ff.

24 See, for example, Volker Berghahn, *The Americanization of West German Industry, 1945–1973*, New York, 1986, 83f. British delegations of businessmen also came to the Rhineland and listened to a speech that Henle made in Düsseldorf on June 16, 1947. As he explained to the "English gentlemen," deconcentration was the "main problem." At the end, he added his opinion that "the democratic economic order" that was to be established should be implemented at the company level. Henle believed that a solution on the basis of parity, when entrepreneurs and unions would "sit together with equal rights," would contribute to the solution of all problems that were "so heavily preoccupying us." See the manuscript of his speech in BAK, GHNL, 384/000482.

25 See also Freda Utley, *The High Cost of Vengeance*, Chicago, 1949. On Crane see Volker Berghahn, *Hans-Günther Sohl als Stahlunternehmer und Präsident des Bundesverbandes der Deutschen Industrie, 1906–1989*, Göttingen, 2020, 154.

26 Henle, *Weggenosse des Jahrhunderts*, 90.

27 Ibid., 143.

28 Thus Harris-Burland quoted in Berghahn, *The Americanization of West German Industry, 1945–1973*, 96–7.

29 See p. 72.

30 Explanatory memorandum of the British zonal trade union committee to its resolution to participate in company governance, October 3–4, 1946, repr. in Müller-List, *Neubeginn bei Eisen und Stahl im Ruhrgebiet*, 275ff.

31 File note relating to the meeting of NGISC with trade union representatives, October 15, 1946, repr. in ibid., 279–83.

32 Notes on the meeting of NGISC with trade union representatives, December 14, 1946, repr. in ibid., 296–8. See also the presentations by Dinkelbach and Harris-Burland at this meeting, repr. in ibid., 298–302.

33 Notes of the TrHV meeting with Potthoff and Strohmenger, January 2, 1947, dated January 6, 1947, repr. in ibid., 303–4.

34 Jarres to Dinkelbach, December 14, 1946, repr. in ibid., 295.

35 Reusch's report on this meeting in Excerpt from the notes of the WVESI Eisenkreis meeting, January 9, 1947, repr. in ibid., 314–16.

36 Reusch to Oberpräsident Lehr, January 3, 1947, repr. in ibid., 305–6.

37 Dinkeldach to Reusch, January 8, 1947, repr. in ibid., 307–8.

38 Note by Werner Scholz (TrHV/NGISC), January 8, 1947, repr. in ibid., 308–14.

39 Reusch's report on this meeting in Excerpt from the notes of WVESI Eisenkreis meetingm January 9, 1947, repr. in ibid., 314–16.

40 Notes by Keller and Gentz, n.d., appended to repr. in Müller-List, *Neubeginn bei Eisen und Stahl im Ruhrgebiet*, 317–19.

41 See the Betriebsvereinbarung der Mannesmannröhren-Werke A.G., January 17, 1947, repr. in ibid., 319–22; excerpt from a file note of the meeting by the executive secretaries of the Employers' Federation of the Rhenisch-Westphalian Iron and Metal Industry, January 22, 1947, repr. in ibid., 322–4.

42 Note by Kuhnke for Henle, January 22, 1947, repr. in ibid., 324.

43 Ibid.

44 Ibid.

45 Excerpt from a file note on the WVESI board meeting on January 23, 1947, dated January 28, 1947, repr. in ibid., 325–7.

46 See p. 89ff.

47 Note by Werner Scholz of the meeting between TrHV and trade union representatives, January 29, 1947, repr. in: Müller-List, *Neubeginn bei Eisen und Stahl im Ruhrgebiet*, 327–9.

48 Dinkelbach to Reusch and Jarres, January 29, 1947, repr. in ibid., 329–30.

49 Henle to Adenauer, February 1, 1947, repr. in ibid., 333–5 See also the notes of a meeting of the preparatory employers' committee for the Province of Westphalia, January 31, 1947, repr. in ibid., 330–3.

50 Note on the meeting between NGISC/TrHV, steel managers, and trade unionists concerning deconcentration, February 6, 1947, repr. in ibid., 335–54.

51 See Henle's remarks at the first meeting of the supervisory Board of the "Hüttenwerk Haspe, Aktiengesellschaft" on February 12, 1947 in BAK, GHNL, 384/000482.

52 File note by Jarres on the deconcentration meeting, February 6, 1947, dated February 7, 1947, repr. in Müller-List, *Neubeginn bei Eisen und Stahl im Ruhrgebiet*, 354.

53 Excerpt from the circular of the trade union secretariat for the British zone of occupation, February 18, 1947, repr. in ibid., 355–6.

54 Quoted in excerpts from a note of the meeting of the WVESI Eisenkreis, March 13, 1947, repr. in ibid., 358–9.

55 On this context see Stöver, *Der Kalte Krieg*, 79ff.

56 Henle to Adenauer, April 16, 1947, repr. in Müller-List, *Neubeginn bei Eisen und Stahl im Ruhrgebiet*, 364–5.

57 Jarres to Böckler, June 18, 1947, repr. in ibid., 370–1.

58 Excerpt of Schroeder's letter to Henle, August 29, 1947, repr. in ibid., 373–5.

59 Works councils of the Klöckner Werke to Jarres, January 15, 1948, repr. in ibid., 388.

60 Jarres to Klöckner works councils, January 27, 1948, repr. in ibid., 389.

61 See John Farquharson, *The Western Allies and the Politics of Food*, Leamington Spa, 1985.

62 See also Werner Abelshauser, *Wirtschaftsgeschichte der Bundesrepublik (1945–1980)*, Frankfurt, 1983, 27.

63 Thus Hoffman before a subcommittee of the Senate Appropriations Committee. His remarks are taken from an article that appeared in the West German newspaper *Industriekurier*, March 9, 1950 (my translation, V.R. Berghahn).

64 See Bent Boel, "The European Productivity Agency: A Faithful Prophet of the American Model?," in Matthias Kipping and Ove Bjarnar, eds., *The Americanization of European Business, 1948–1969*, London, 1998, Ch. 3.

4 The United States and the Completion of the Reshaping of West German Industry

1 Quoted in Volker R. Berghahn, *Modern Germany: Society, Economy and Politics in the Twentieth Century*, Cambridge, 1987, 209.

2 See, for example, Wolfgang Benz, *Deutschland unter alliierter Besetzung, 1945–1949*, Stuttgart 2009, 183ff. also for the following.

3 Ibid., 166ff.

4 J. Davenport, "New Chance for Germany," in *Fortune*, October 1949, 72.

5 See p. 63ff., 111ff.

6 See p. 126ff.

7 Full text repr. in Elmar M. Hucko, ed., *The Democratic Tradition*, Leamington Spa, 1987, 194ff.

8 See Günter Henle, *Weggenosse des Jahrhunderts: Als Diplomat, Industrielle, Politik und Freund der Musik*, Stuttgart, 1968, 143.

9 See p. 126ff.

10 See p. 52ff.

11 Mitglieder der Treuhand-Vereinigung (TrV) see p. 178.

12 See p. 115ff.

13 Quoted in Gabriele Müller-List, ed., *Montanmitbestimmung: Das Gesetz über die Mitbestimmung der Arbeitnehmer in den Aufsichtsräten und Vorständen der Unternehmen des Bergbaus und der Eisen- und Stahlerzeugenden Industrie vom 21. Mai 1951*, Düsseldorf, 1984, 3n.

14 See the verbatim record of his speech on November 4, 1949, repr. ibid., 3.

15 See Richter's statement, repr. ibid., 4.

16 File note by Walter Raymond and Hans Bilstein of their conversation with Hans Böckler in Düsseldorf, 15 November 1949, repr. ibid., 6–7.

17 See p. 81ff.

18 See the notes on the negotiations between the social partners(!) on 9/10 January 1950, repr. in Müller-List, *Montanmitbestimmung*, 11–22.

19 Excerpt from the protocol of the first session of the DGB Federal Committee in Königswinter near Bonn on January 24–5, 1950, repr. ibid., 23–5.

20 Raymond to Bührig, March 3, 1950, repr. ibid., 28–30.

21 Adenauer to McCloy, March 29, 1950, repr. ibid., 31–2.

22 The handling of Law No. 27 and the various West German as well as American groups that involved themselves in this issue is another intriguing chapter of the deconcentration issue that will be discussed at the beginning of Chapter 5. See p. 116ff.

23 Notes on the negotiations of the social partners at Hattenheim, March 30–1, 1950, repr. in Müller-List, *Montanmitbestimmung*, 32–47.

24 Joint communiqué of employers and trade union representatives relating to the Hattenheim talks, March 31, 1959, repr. ibid., 50.

25 Raymond to Adenauer, April 4, 1950, repr. ibid., 51–2.

26 Notes on the negotiations between the social partners, May 24, 1950, repr. ibid., 63–76.

27 Notes on the negotiations between the social partners at Bonn, June 2, 1950, repr. ibid., 78–90.

28 Notes on the negotiations between the social partners at Bonn, June 9, 1950, repr. ibid., 93–104.

29 Notes on the negotiations of the social partners at Bonn, June 23, 1950, repr. ibid., 105–15.

30 Notes on the negotiations between the social partners at Maria Laach, July 5–6, 1950, repr. ibid., 115–30.

31 See the excerpt from the protocol of the 26th session of the DGB executive, July 15, 1950, repr. ibid., 134–5.

32 Brümmer to the DGB executive in Düsseldorf, August 2, 1950, repr. ibid., 142–6.

33 Raymond to Bührig, March 3, 1950, repr. ibid., 28ff.

34 See p. 70ff.

35 Excerpt from a file note by Theo Hieromini, managing director of the Mauritius Trading Company, August 1, 1950, repr. in Müller-List, *Montanmitbestimmung*, 140–1, following his private conversation with Bührig, vom Hoff, and Adalbert Stenzel of the DGB headquarters in Düsseldorf.

36 Joseph Viehöver to the DGB Executive, August 4, 1950, repr. ibid., 146. Viehöver was the director of the DGB press office. He added that he could not verify this information but that the journalist had a good reputation and was close to the SPD. Gabriele Müller-List later checked with the Federal Archives and received a reply on June 13, 1986, that Viehöver's text was largely identical with the protocol of the cabinet meeting on July 28, 1950. Ibid., 146n.

37 On this accusation see the next paragraph, quoting a speech by Otto Vogel.

38 Quoted in Werner Bührer, ed., *Die Adenauer-Ära: Die Bundesrepublik Deutschland 1949–1963*, Munich, 1993, 92ff.

39 Excerpt from the protocol of the eleventh session of the DGB executive, November 21, 1950, repr. in Müller List, *Montanmitbestimmung*, 165–9, esp. 167 and 167n, with remarks by Böckler that he had noticed an older pattern relating to entrepreneurial attitudes: "Behind the somewhat more liberal entrepreneurs that were delegated to the negotiations, stood the real gentlemen of the economy who had no intention of conceding anything to the trade unions." He felt that the conjuncture was nevertheless propitious. It was merely a matter of not retreating and of pursuing the struggle relentlessly. The opposition had exploited its advantage long enough. In the future it would be for them to carry the burden.

40 Repr. ibid., 166.

41 File note by Stenzel of a meeting of the Treuhand executive with the DGB executive, November 24, 1950, ibid., 172–4. For a more detailed discussion of the enlarged Treuhand and the Allied policies see p. 114f.

42 See p. 108ff.

43 Excerpt from a file note by Eberhard Böhmcke (senior counsellor in the economics ministry) on a meeting between Ludwig Erhard and the DGB executive in Bonn, November 20, 1950, repr. in Müller-List, *Montanmitbestimmung*, 161ff., cited 163.

44 Böckler to Adenauer, November 23, 1950, repr. ibid., 169–70.

45 See p. 126ff.

46 Adenauer to Böckler, November 27, 1950, repr. in Müller-List, *Montanmitbestimmung*, 176.

47 Böckler to Adenauer, December 11, 1950, repr. ibid., 185–6.

48 Excerpt from the protocol of the 44th session of the DGB executive, November 27, 1950, repr. ibid., 175.

49 Ibid.

50 On Arnold and his connections with Rhenish social Catholicism, see p. 168 n.2. Böckler and Arnold kept in touch in the New Year, and the latter also tried to arrange a meeting with Abraham Frowein, a prominent Rhenish businessman and president of the German economic council in the British zone of occupation. He was also one of the founding members of the Vereinigung der industriellen Wirtschaftsverbände, the precursor of the BDI, and since the Weimar days one of the elder statesmen in the Ruhr industry. On January 12, 1951, Arnold attended a meeting of the DGB executive (excerpt from the protocol of the 5th meeting on January 12, 1951, repr. ibid., 212) at which Böckler welcomed him as an "old and tested trade union friend."

51 See the note by Rudolf Petz, ministerial counsel in the chancellor's office, for Adenauer, December 15, 1950, quoted in Note 2 of Müller-List, *Montanmitbestimmung*, 191.

52 Sohl to Lehr, November 29, 1950, with copy to Henle, repr. ibid., 177–8.

53 Ibid., referring to Henle's very busy schedule.

54 Report by Harvey Brown, the director of labor affairs in the US High Commission for McCloy, December 6, 1950, repr. ibid., 178–80.

55 See p. 133ff.

56 See Berg's telegraph message to Adenauer, January 4, 1951, repr. in Müller-List, *Montanmitbestimmung*, 197, and Raymond's telegram to Adenauer, January 5, 1951, repr. ibid., 198.

57 Excerpt from the note on the meeting of the DIHT in Bonn, January 9, 1951, repr. ibid., 209–11.

58 See ibid., 194n. See also p. 101f.

59 File note by Winkhaus, January 8, 1951, repr. in Müller-List, *Montanmitbestimmung*, 201.

60 Winkhaus to Wilhelm Zangen, January 17, 1951, repr. ibid., 225–6.

61 Ibid. and Winkhaus to Böckler, January 9, 1951, repr. ibid., 204.

62 Kuhnke to Jarres and Schroeder, December 7, 1950, repr. ibid., 181.

63 DGB executive (excerpt from protocol of the 5th meeting on January 12, 1951), repr. ibid., 212.

64 File note by Henle on the meeting of coal and steel industrialists with Adenauer, January 17, 1951, repr. ibid., 227–8.

65 Ibid. According to Sohls, *Notizen* (133) Adenauer welcomed the group with the words: "Please take a seat, gentlemen. Time is money!" He continued: "I have just

told Herr Böckler and his colleagues that the strike he is threatening is illegal and unconstitutional; but I must tell you that my entire domestic and foreign policy will collapse, if there is a strike."

66 Protocol of the meeting between Adenauer and representatives of the DGB executive, January 18, 1951, repr. in Müller-List, *Montanmitbestimmung?*, 229–34.

67 Ibid., 233.

68 File notes by Henle and Hueck of the meeting between representatives of coal and steel with the trade unions, January 19, 1951, repr. ibid., 237–42.

69 Sohl, *Notizen*, 133.

70 File note by Henle on the meeting between coal and steel representatives and the DGB, January 22, 1951, dated January 25, 1951, repr. in Müller-List, *Montanmitbestimmung*, 245–6.

71 See the unsigned memorandum of the coal and steel delegation relating to an agreement on codetermination, January 22, 1951, repr. ibid., 246–7.

72 File note by Kurz on the meeting of the advisory council of the association of employers in the North-Rhine Westphalian metal industries on January 20, 1951, dated January 22, and also circulated to Wenzel, Sohl, Wolfgang Linz, and Walter Schwede (all of them VSt.), repr. ibid., 242–4. Kurz was a VSt. employee and the file note is another piece of evidence of how closely these negotiations were being followed.

73 Raymond to Adenauer, January 22, 1951, repr. ibid., 244–5.

74 See the letter of Friedrich Middelhauve, chair of the FDP Landtag caucus, to the FDP Bundestag faction, January 22, 1951, repr. ibid., 248, as well as the caucus's resolution, January 22, 1951, repr. ibid.

75 File note by Henle on a meeting of the coal and steel representatives with Adenauer, January 23, 1951, repr. ibid., 249; file note by Henle of a meeting between Adenauer (with his secretary of state Otto Lenz attending) Henle and Pferdmenges, January 24, 1951, repr. ibid., 252–3.

76 See p. 76ff.

77 It was not that the offer had been rejected but that the trade unions never replied, having lost patience and opted for an arrangement with Harris-Burland and Dinkelbach.

78 See the protocol of the special cabinet meeting on January 24, 1951, dated January, 24, repr. in Müller-List, *Montanmitbestimmung*, 255–8.

79 Protocol of the meeting between representatives of the coal and steel industry and the trade unions in Bonn, January 25, 1951, with two runs of hand-written corrections by Henle, repr. ibid., 259–67.

80 See the guidelines for codetermination in the coal and iron industries, January 26, 1951, repr. ibid., 268–71; file note by Henle relating to the work of the Redaktionsausschuss on January 26–7, dated January 27, repr. ibid. 271.

81 The Müller-List edition contains a number of additional documents mainly relating to exchanges between the two sides on small points that, given the speed with which the agreement was reached, still had to be ironed out, repr. ibid., 276–81. See also the note by Wolfgang Pohle for Wilhelm Zangen, January 27, 1951, repr. ibid., 272–4, with further details on the compromise whose outcome, he added, had left Wenzel "extraordinarily depressed." There was, inevitably, perhaps, an older generation whose conservatism could not imagine the compromise could ever be made to work. But as will be seen in Chapter 5, Henle and Sohl accepted codetermination in the coal and steel industries and made it work quite well to the advantage not only of their companies but also of relatively peaceful labor relations in West Germany, certainly if compared with Britain, France, Italy, and the United States.

82 Henle to Pferdmenges, January 31, 1951, repr. ibid., 305–6.

83 Protocol of the special session of the DGB Federal Committee, January 29, 1951, repr. ibid., 279–81.

84 See the documents repr. ibid., 311–17.

85 See the verbatim record of his remarks in the Bundestag on February 14, repr. ibid., 381–3.

86 See p. 50ff.

87 File note by Sohl about the telephone call from Pferdmenges, March 10, 1951, repr. in Müller-List, *Montanmitbestimmung*, 420–1.

88 Full text repr. ibid., 526–9.

89 See p. 133ff.

5 The Origins and Creation of the European Coal and Steel Community

1 See Berghahn, *The Americanization of West German Industry, 1945–1973*, 98.

2 See p. 74ff.

3 See the protocol of the meeting between Brian Robertson and representatives of the German political parties on October 18, 1947, n.d., signed by Henle, in BAK, GHNL, 384/000482. See also the brief mention in Helmut Uebbing, *Stahl schreibt Geschichte: 125 Jahre Wirtschaftsvereinigung Stahl*, Düsseldorf, 1999, 194.

4 See p. 63ff.

5 See, for example, Volker R. Berghahn, *American Big Business in Britain and Germany: A Comparative History of Two "Special Relationships" in the 20th Century*, Princeton, 2014, 339ff.

6 Uebbing, *Stahl schreibt Geschichte*, 214, listed the following new members: Karl Barich (president of WVESI and Hüttenwerk Geiswied), Heinrich Deist (economist

and member of the DGB executive), Gotthard Freiherr von Falkenhausen (banker in Essen), Willy Geldmacher (Lord Mayor of Bochum), Friedrich Harders (Hüttenwerk Hoerde), Heinrich Meier (Landesrat a.D.), Arthur Menge (Lord Mayor of Hannover), Herbert Monden (Fachstelle Stahl und Eisen), Erich Potthoff (DGB executive), and Alphons Wagner. See also the report in *Westdeutsche Allgemeine Zeitung*, June 2, 1949.

7 See p. 133ff.

8 See, for example, Edgar Wolfrum, *Die Bundesrepublik Deutschland, 1949–1990*, Stuttgart, 2005, 78ff.

9 See p. 112f.

10 See Werner Link, *Deutsche und amerikanische Gewerkschaften und Geschäftsleute, 1945–1975*, Düsseldorf, 1978, 44ff.

11 Ibid., 74ff.

12 Quoted ibid., 76.

13 See p. 97.

14 Karl Bunting to Heinrich Krekeler, January 31, 1951, repr. in Müller-List, *Montanmitbestimmung*, Düsseldorf, 1984, 309–10. See also the notes by Günter Große of a conversation between Andrew L. Gomory (vice-president of the Manufacturers Trust Bank) and Krekeler, April 10, 1951, repr. ibid., 503–5.

15 Brown's Report for McCloy, December 6, 1950, repr. ibid., 178–80.

16 File note by Heinrich Deist on McCloy's meeting with the DGB delegation, December 14, 1950, repr. ibid., 189–90.

17 It may be that McCloy's conversations with the DGB were not just born from political necessity at a critical moment, but were also related to his family background. His father, an upwardly mobile insurance clerk, died when his son was barely five years old. Two of his brothers had been killed by a diphtheria epidemic a few years earlier. Raised by his mother, he was fortunate to receive a good private education at the Peddie Institute and was subsequently accepted by the elite Amherst College in Massachusetts. This and his training at the Harvard Law School gave him an entry ticket to a prestigious New York law firm, before he joined the War Department. But however impressive his professional career, he probably remained conscious of the difficult years he had had in his youth. For details see, for example, Kai Bird, *The Chairman. John J. McCloy, The Making of the American Establishment*, New York, 1992, 23ff.

18 See Jean Monnet, *Memoirs*, New York, 1978, 148.

19 Quoted in Richard Kuisel, *Capitalism and the State in Modern France: Renovation and Economic Management in the Twentieth Century*, New York, 1981, 244.

20 Ibid., 219ff.

21 German translation of this article in Thyssen-Krupp Archiv (TKA) Duisburg, Sohl Papers, A32243.

22 See p. 89.

23 See, for example, Berghahn, *The Americanization of West German Industry, 1945–1973*, 108.

24 Among the extensive scholarly literature on the Schuman Plan, its origins, and completion, see, for example, William Diebold, *The Schuman Plan*, New York, 1959; Hans Dichgans, *Montanunion*, Düsseldorf 1980; John Gillingham, *Coal, Steel and the Rebirth of Europe, 1945–1955: Germans and French from Ruhr Conflict to Economic Community*, Cambridge, 1991, 228ff; Klaus Schwabe, *Die Anfänge des Schuman-Plans*, Baden-Baden, 1988.

25 See p. 121. See also Berghahn, *The Americanization of West German Industry, 1945–1973*.

26 See, for example, Oscar Schachter and Robert Hellawell, eds., *Competition in International Business*, New York, 1981.

27 For details on these contacts see, for example, Werner Bührer, *Ruhrstahl und Europa: Die Wirtschaftsvereinigung Eisen- und Stahlindustrie und die Anfänge der europäischen Integration, 1945–1952*, Munich, 1986, 117ff. Again, Henle became a major mediator of Franco-German relations, and it is intriguing how early older links between French and German industrialists were being reestablished. In September 1948, Henle had written a memorandum "Zur Frage der Möglichkeit einer internationalen industriellen Verständigung," September 18, 1948 (BAK, GHNL, 384/000299). By autumn 1949, these contacts had become quite warm. See also, for example, Vosgerau to Henle, October 10, 1949, ibid., transmitting greetings from the former director of Schneider-Creusot and now president of the Chambre Syndicale of the French iron and steel industry Aubrun who had met Henle during the war. On October 20, Henle wrote back to Vosgerau (ibid.) that he had been delighted to get these greetings and hoped that Franco-German economic relations could be intensified. See also Henle's undated file note, ibid., on a Franco-German meeting at Bernkastel on the Moselle on November 26–7, 1949 and ibid., an unsigned memo of the same month on "Deutsch-französische Industrieverständigung," with a number of attachments relating to topics for discussion and apparently assembled by Henle's office. There was however one point of friction: apparently the Lorraine steel industry was trying to tilt the power balance in its favor against the Ruhr which proved, not surprisingly, a no-no for the Germans. See Salewski to Henle, 20 January 1950, ibid. See also below p. 121.

28 Uebbing, *Stahl schreibt Geschichte*, 270.

29 Quoted in Berghahn, *The Americanization of West German Industry, 1945–1973*, 114.

30 Quoted ibid.

31 Quoted ibid., 115.

32 Ibid.

33 Quoted ibid., 118.

34 Quoted ibid., 129.

35 Ibid., 119.

36 Dichgans, *Montanunion*, 67.

37 Ludwig Kastl, *Kartelle in der Wirklichkeit*, Cologne 1963, 16ff.

38 Berghahn, *The Americanization of West German Industry, 1945–1973*, 121.

39 Quoted ibid.

40 See p. 142ff.

41 On Goergen and also his later career and demise, see Berghahn, *Hans-Günther Sohl als Stahlunternehmer*, Göttingen, 2020, 197ff.

42 Berghahn, *The Americanization of West German Industry, 1945–1973*, 125. More details on this and the following memoranda are to be found in the Federal Archives under B102.

43 Ibid., 125f.

44 Ibid., 126f.

45 Ibid., 128.

46 Ibid.

47 Ibid.

48 Ibid., 128f.

49 Ibid., 129.

50 Ibid., 129f.

51 Quoted in Dichgans, *Montanunion*, 69.

52 Ibid., 71.

53 Berghahn, *The Americanization of West German Industry, 1945–1973*, 132.

54 Quoted ibid., 133f.

55 Quoted ibid., 134.

56 Quoted ibid., 139.

57 Ibid., 142.

58 Quoted ibid., 144, 140.

59 See p. 105f.

60 Berghahn, *The Americanization of West German Industry, 1945–1973*, 138.

61 Ibid.

62 Ibid., 139.

63 Ibid.

64 See p. 108.

65 Berghahn, *The Americanization of West German Industry, 1945–1973*, 151f.

66 Ibid., 154.

67 Joseph Borkin, *The Crime and Punishment if IG Farben*, New York, 1978, pb. edition 1979.

68 Raymond G. Stokes, *Divide and Prosper: The Heirs of I.G. Farben under Allied Authority, 1945–1951*, Berkeley, 1988.

69 Wilfried Feldenkirchen, *Siemens, 1918–1945*, Columbus, OH, 1999; Clotilde Cadi, *Siemens. Du capitalism familial à la multinationale*, Strasbourg, 2010; Paul Erker, "Anpassung und Transformationsprozesse zwischen Wirtschaftsboom und Wirtschaftskrisen (1945–1989)," in Johannes Bähr and Paul Erker, *Bosch: Geschichte eines Weltunternehmens*, Munich, 2013, 255ff.

70 Werner Plumpe, Alexander Nützenadel, and Catherine R. Schenk, *Deutsche Bank: Die globale Hausbank, 1870–2020*, Berlin, 2020.

71 See the detailed analysis by Isabel Warner, *Steel and Sovereignty: The Deconcentration of the West German Steel Industry, 1949–1954*, Mainz, 1996, 22ff., 40ff., 96ff., 118ff.

72 See Werner Abelshauser, *Ruhrkohlenbergbau seit 1945: Wiederaufbau, Krise, Anpassung*, Munich, 1984.

73 Erich Sperling, *Alles um Stahl: Wirtschaftsgeschichtliche Erzählung um die Klöckner Georgsmarienhütte AG*, Osnabrück, Bremen-Horn 1956, 253ff.

74 See p. 70ff, 134.

75 Henle, *Weggenosse des Jahrhunderts*, Stuttgart, 1968, 141–2.

76 Ibid., 145.

77 Wilhelm Treue and Helmut Uebbing, *Die Feuer verlöschen nie*, Düsseldorf, 1969, 157ff.

78 Henle, *Weggenosse des Jahrhunderts*, 140–141.

79 Günter Henle, "Zur Frage der Möglichkeit einer internationalen industriellen Verständigung," September 18, 1948, copy in TKA Duisburg, Sohl Papers, A 32243.

80 Quoted in Bührer, *Ruhrstahl und Europa*, 179.

81 See also his retrospective remarks in Henle, "Zur Frage der Möglichkeit einer internationalen industriellen Verständigung," 274ff., stressing that the creation of the ECSC was very much in the interest of the West German coal and steel industry. But he also added a few critical comments on the community's subsequent development.

82 Quoted in Berghahn, *The Americanization of West German Industry, 1945–1973*, 152.

83 See p. 169f., note 14.

84 See Berghahn, *The Americanization of West German Industry, 1945–1973*, 147ff. See also Warner, *Steel and Sovereignty*, 30, who mentioned that Bowie called vertical integration a "German myth," to which Warner added that "old myths die hard."

85 See also p. 152, on the experiences that Otto A. Friedrich and Dietrich von Menges had with their colleagues in the rubber and steel trade industries.

6 Some Concluding Topics for Future Research

1 Henle, *Weggenosse des Jahrhunderts*, Stuttgart, 1968, 137.

2 Ibid., 143.

3 Ibid., 140–1.

4 Ibid.

5 Ibid., 191.

6 Ibid., 188ff. and Karl Lauschke, *Widerstand lohnt sich! Geschichte der Bremer Hütte – oder: Wieso wird heute noch Stahl in Bremen produziert* (unter Mitwirkung von Peter Sörgel und Eike Hemmer), Hamburg, 2017, 21ff., with important details on the history and expansion of Klöckner Werke A.G., starting in the late 1840s, and the construction program during the 1950s with the support of the government of the Hanseatic City of Bremen, an independent state of the Federal Republic.

7 See Lauschke, *Widerstand lohnt sich!*, 41ff.

8 Henle, *Weggenosse des Jahrhunderts*, 174.

9 Text of the agreement, February 9, 1950, repr. in Rudolf Judith et al., eds., *Montanmitbestimmung: Dokumente ihrer Entstehung*, with an introduction by Jürgen Peters, Cologne 1979, 117–22. See also p. 50.

10 For the full text, see Bundesgesetzblatt, Teil I, Nr. 43, published on October 14, 1952.

11 On codetermination at Klöckner, see p. 109f. and p. 108f., as well as the detailed accounts in Lauschke, *Widerstand lohnt sich!*, 61ff., 83ff., 110ff., 143ff., including the role of the works councils and worker directors as well as strike movements and their settlement in the 1970s. See also how Hans-Günther Sohl, the CEO of August-Thyssen-Hütte, handled labor issues and codetermination in Berghahn, *Hans-Günther Sohl als Stahlunternehmer*, 210–25.

12 Henle, *Weggenosse des Jahrhunderts*, 228–30.

13 Ibid., 114–17.

14 Ibid., 227.

15 On this intriguing chapter see Berghahn, *Hans-Günther Sohl als Stahlunternehmer*, 140–5.

16 In his memoirs (Henle, *Weggenosse des Jahrhunderts*), Henle said very little about these experiences, except for his general references to the Nazi period which now required a different approach to both labor relations and European integration.

17 See Berghahn and Friedrich, *Otto A. Friedrich, ein politischer Unternehmer*, Frankfurt, 1993, 229–32.

18 See Berghahn, *The Americanization of West German Industry, 1945–1973*, 255f. See also Wolfgang Benz, ed., *Ludwig Vaubel, Zusammenbruch und Wiederaufbau*, Munich, 1984.

19 See Berghahn, *The Americanization of West German Industry, 1945–1973*, 249ff.

20 See Richard Guserl, *Das Harzburger Modell*, Wiesbaden, 1973.

21 See Reinhard Höhn, *Die Armee als Erziehungsschule der Nation*, Bad Harzburg, 1963.

22 Discussions I had with Rolf Hermichen in Essen when I worked on the book cited in Note 18.

23 Henle, *Weggenosse des Jahrhunderts*, 178–9.

24 See p. 15ff.

25 These meetings were organized by the Deutsch-Britische Gesellschaft and continue to this day.

26 Henle, *Weggenosse des Jahrhunderts*, 149.

27 Ibid., 82. Like Hans-Günther Sohl and other German industrialists, he did not talk much about his internment. Nor did Henle mention in his memoirs anything about his Jewish family background.

28 Henle, *Weggenosse des Jahrhunderts*, 149.

29 Ibid., 275–7.

30 On British policy and de Gaulle's refusal see, for example, Hubert M. Gladwyn, *De Gaulle's Europe or Why the General Says no*, London, 1969.

31 Henle, *Weggenosse des Jahrhunderts*, 156.

32 Ibid., 205. See also Daniel Eisermann, *Aussenpolitik und Strategiediskussion: Die Deutsche Gesellschaft für Auswärtige Politik, 1955–1972*, Munich, 1999.

33 Henle, *Weggenosse des Jahrhunderts*, 162–8.

34 Ibid., 180–3.

35 Ibid., 236.

36 Ibid., 281.

37 Ibid., 269–72.

38 Ibid., 270.

39 See p. 63ff.

40 See *Industriekurier* November 17, 1948, with the news that Lucius D. Clay, the US Military Governor, wanted to pass this program on to the West German administration. On Erhard, his biography and postwar policies, see, for example, Berghahn and Friedrich, *Otto A. Friedrich, ein politischer Unternehmer*, 97–117, 134–51. See also Erhard's statements on his decartelization plans at the end of 1949 cited in *Hamburger Echo* November 30, 1949, and *Die Welt*, December 17, 1949. It was the *Handelsblatt* of December 5, 1949, that reiterated the underlying calculations: the aim was to recast both Germany's and also the industrial structures of the other European economies. *Hamburger Freie Presse* (December 8, 1949) pointed to the oligopolistic structures of the United States that were weak in comparison to the strong German cartels.

41 See p. 152. See also the reports in *Die Welt* (October 19, 1948) and the *Wirtschafts-Zeitung*, published in Stuttgart, of May 1, 1949. That summer *Die Welt* (June 16, 1949) and *Niederdeutsche Zeitung* (August 13, 1949) reported that BICO had

dissolved illegal cartels that had been formed. One of these was even prosecuted, although the trial was later suspended. See *Hamburger Echo*, July 18, 1950.

42 See Volker Berghahn, "Ordoliberalism, Social Catholicism, and the West German Social Market Economy," in Malte Dold and Tim Krieger, eds., *Ordoliberalism and European Economic Policy*, London, 2020, 74–90. See also *Handelsblatt*, April 1, 1949; *Wirtschafts- und Finanzzeitung* (Frankfurt), April 14, 1949; *Rheinischer Merkur*, April 23, 1949; *Hamburger Allgemeine Zeitung*, November 10, 1949, referring to the Freiburg roots of Josten's efforts.

43 See Berghahn, *The Americanization of West German Industry, 1945–1973*, 155ff. See also *Die Welt*, June 11, 1949.

44 See, for example, Gerald Braunthal, *The Federation of German Industry in Politics*, Ithaca, 1965.

45 See p. 122. See also *Die Welt*, July 29, 1949. That the Deutsche Industrie- und Handelstag (DIHT) was also opposed to a general ban indicates that it was medium-sized firms that had joined the big corporations. See *Die Welt*, April 21, 1951.

46 See, for example, Berghahn, *The Americanization of West German Industry, 1945–1973*, 30ff.

47 See the American-run *Neue Zeitung*, January 24, 1950; *Industriekurier*, January 24, 1950, mentioned that German tardiness might create problems to obtain American loans. However, there were also differences of opinion in Washington. According to *Die Welt* (June 11, 1949) there existed a Wall-Street faction and an antitrust faction, and the subsequent personnel changes at BICO may have been due to the latter, more hard-line group losing out. At least by the spring of 1950 more moderate officers, Grant Kelleher (of the Boston Anti-Trust Office) and Sidney Willner (hitherto a higher civil servant at the Securities and Exchange Commission), took charge of the anti-cartel section at the US high commission). For Willner's role in HIGOGs deconcentration policy in the creation of the ECSC see p. 131f. Truman's statement (see *Frankfurter Allgemeine Zeitung*, August 18, 1950) must be linked to the simultaneous discussions on the shape of the Schuman Plan. See p. 118ff. On the Allied consent to Erhard's procedure *see VWD* (Frankfurt), October 18 and 23, 1950.

48 *WSJ*, March 25, 1953.

49 Ibid., August 27, 1953.

50 See Berghahn and Friedrich, *Otto A. Friedrich, ein politischer Unternehmer*, 127.

51 Gilbert Burck, "Can Germany Go Capitalist?," in *Fortune*, April 1956, 118–20. It is interesting how Erhard handled both the Americans and his German critics. On the one hand and reassuring the high commission, he declared that the West German anti-cartel bill was being shaped "approximately" according to "its American model." See *VWD* (Frankfurt), March 14, 1950. Later at the height of

the controversy with Berg he denied that the bill was "a tender American plant" (ein amerikanisches Pflänzchen). See *Frankfurter Allgemeine Zeitung*, November 17, 1953.

52 Gilbert Burck "The German Business Mind" in *Fortune*, May 1954, 111–14. See also *WSJ*, October 5, 1954. The question of differences between European and American business mentalities had been raised at various earlier points on both sides. See *Neue Zeitung*, May 31, 1950. See also p. 131ff.

53 See, for example, Berghahn and Friedrich, *Otto A. Friedrich, ein politischer Unternehmer*, 128; Braunthal, *The Federation of German Industry in Politics*, 241. See also the list of names in *Hamburger Anzeiger*, July 20, 1954.

54 See notes 48–51.

55 See *Die Zeit*, January 23, 1959.

56 See Henle, *Weggenosse des Jahrhunderts*, 150–1.

57 Ibid., 123–4.

58 *Der Volkswirt*, July 31, 1954.

Select Bibliography

Bankier, David. *The German and the Final Solution.* Cambridge, MA, 1992.

Berghahn, Volker R. *The Americanization of West German Industry, 1945–1973.* New York, 1986.

Blumenthal, W. Michael. *Codetermination in the German Steel Industry.* Princeton, 1956.

Braunthal, Gerald. *The Federation of German Industry in Politics.* Ithaca, 1965.

Brenner, Michael. *In Hitler's Munich: Jews, the Revolution and the Rise of Nazism.* Princeton, 2022.

Cesarani, David. *Final Solution: The Fate of the Jews, 1933–1949.* London, 2016.

Dahrendorf, Ralf. *Democracy and Society in Germany.* London, 1968.

Dean, Martin. *Robbing the Jews: The Confiscation of Jewish Property during the Holocaust, 1933–1945.* New York, 2008.

Feldman, Gerald D. *Iron and Steel in the German Inflation, 1916–1923.* Princeton, 2015.

Gillingham, John. *Coal, Steel and the Rebirth of Europe, 1945–1955.* Cambridge, 1991.

Gimbel, John. *The American Occupation of Germany.* Stanford, 1968.

Hartmann, Heinz. *Authority and Organization in German Management.* Princeton, 1959.

James, Harold. *Krupp: A History of the Legendary German Firm.* Princeton, 2017.

Judt, Tony. *A History of Europe since 1945.* New York, 2005.

Knipping, Matthias, and Ove, Bjarnar, eds. *The Americanisation of European Business, 1948–1969.* London, 1998.

Kuisel, Richard. *Capitalism and the State in Modern France.* New York, 1981.

Lacey, Robert. *Ford: The Man and the Machine.* London, 1986.

Markovits, Andrei. *The Politics of West German Trade Unions.* Cambridge, 1986.

Mazower, Mark. *Hitler's Empire.* New York, 2008.

Monnet, Jean. *Memoirs.* London, 2015.

Nolan, Mary. *Visions of Modernity: American Business and the Modernization of Germany.* New York, 1994.

Roseman, Mark. *A Past in Hiding: Memory and Survival in Nazi Germany.* New York, 2000.

Schweitzer, Arthur. *Big Business in the Third Reich.* Bloomington, 1964.

Speer, Albert. *Inside the Third Reich.* New York, 1970.

Spiro, H. J. *The Politics of German Codetermination.* Cambridge, MA, 1958.

Stokes, Raymond. *Divide and Prosper: The Heirs of IG Farben under Allied Authority, 1945–1951.* Berkeley, 1988.

Stoltzfus, Nathan. *Hitler's Compromises: Coercion and Consensus in Nazi Germany.* New Haven, 2016.

Tooze, Adam. *The Wages of Destruction: The Making and Breaking of the Nazi Economy.* New York, 2007.

Turner, Henry. *General Motors and the Nazis.* New Haven, 2003.

Van Hook, James C. *Rebuilding Germany: The Creation of the Social Market Economy, 1945–1957.* Cambridge, 2004.

Wangenheim, V. von. *Industrial Relations in West Germany.* London, 1984.

Weitz, Eric. *Weimar Germany: Promise and Tragedy.* Princeton, 2007.

Wend, Henry Burke. *Recovery and Reconstruction: U.S. Foreign Policy and the Politics of Reconstruction of West Germany's Shipbuilding Industry, 1945–1955.* Westport, CT, 2001.

Index

Abs, Hermann Josef 42, 145
Acheson, Dean 127
Adenauer, Konrad 39, 44, 78, 91–5,
    97–104, 106–10, 113, 115–17, 123–4,
    126–7, 129–30, 148–50, 154, 156, 171–6
AFL viii, 115–18
Agar, John 52
Agartz, Viktor 77–8
Ahlen Program 103
AKU viii, 144, 146
Albert, Georgina 13
Albert, William 12, 25, 30, 35, 125, 147
Albingia, Insurance 146
Allianz Insurance 146
Alphand, Hervé 124
Americanization 170, 172, 177, 179–82,
    184, 187
Anti-Cartel law 64, 69, 153
Anti-Semitism 3, 9, 13, 18, 26, 148,
    162, 165
Antitrust 169, 184
Arnold, Karl 55, 64, 99, 103, 175
ATH viii, 133
Attlee, Clement 31
Auschwitz 27, 165

Bad Godesberg 31, 117, 149, 155
Bad Nenndorf 8, 41–4, 46, 72, 143,
    145, 149
Baden, Max von 14
Baden-Badener Unternehmer-Gespräche
    144, 179
BAK 162, 166, 170, 172, 177, 179
BASF viii, 132
Basic Law 89, 99, 115, 155
Bavaria 3, 9–11, 28, 97, 146
Bayer Corp. 132
BdA viii, 97, 106, 116, 144
BDI viii, 69, 90, 97, 101, 106, 153, 156, 175
Beethoven, Ludwig van 5, 15–16
Beitz, Berthold 6–7, 143, 161
Belgium 31, 120, 125

Benelux 120, 123, 131
Berg, Fritz 69, 90, 97, 101, 153–6, 175,
    185
Berlin Blockade 87–8
Berthier, Brigadier 34
Betriebsverfassungsgesetz viii, 110, 145
Bi-Zone 62, 72, 92, 111, 114, 163
BICO viii, 152–3, 183–4
Bilstein, Hans 93, 106–7, 173
Blücher, Franz 107
Bochum Works 74
Bochumer Verband 22, 162–3
Bock, Max 117
Böckler, Hans 50, 52–8, 62, 75–6, 78, 81,
    83–4, 91, 93–104, 106–9, 115–16, 143,
    167–8, 172–6
Böhm, Franz 153
Borkin, Joseph 132, 180
Bosch, Corp. 133, 145, 181
Bowie, Robert 136
Braun, Otto 46
Brentano, Lujo 13
Briand, Aristide 16
Brisch, Josef 59–60, 73, 168
Brown, Harvey 117
Brown, Boveri & Cie. 148
Brümmer, Hans 96, 99, 117, 174
Buchenwald concentration camp 165
Buenos Aires 5, 16
Bührer, Werner 136, 174, 179, 181
Bührig, Erich 94, 99, 173–4
Bülow, Niels, von 33, 38, 53
Bundesgesetzblatt 182
Bundesrat 108, 154
Bundestag 69, 92–3, 95–6, 98–100,
    107–10, 115–16, 124, 136, 143, 152, 154,
    156, 176–7
Bungeroth, Karl 77
Bunting, Karl 116–17, 178
Burck, Gilbert 155, 184–5
BVG viii, 110, 145
Byrnes, James 70

capitalism 65–8, 86, 90, 114, 119, 154–6, 168, 178, 181, 187
cartels viii, 22, 64–5, 68–9, 101, 121–2, 128–9, 131, 133, 146, 149, 152–6, 163, 184
cartelization 121, 142
Casella Corp. 132
Castorp 19, 135, 140
CDU viii, 78, 92–3, 96–8, 103, 109, 124, 143, 154
Churchill, Winston, Sir 31, 70, 114, 118
CIO viii, 116
Civil Service Law 18
Clay, Lucius, D. 31, 88–9, 111–13, 115–16, 183
Clayton Act 66, 130, 153
CNPF viii, 121, 124, 126
codetermination 5–6, 8, 51–3, 57–8, 62–3, 69, 74–8, 81, 83–5, 91–111, 115–18, 129–30, 142–3, 145, 147, 157, 160, 176–7, 182, 187
Combined Steel Group 92, 114, 131
Commerzbank 133
Commissariat du Plan 119, 124
Commonwealth 120, 142
Conseil de la République 119, 121
Control Council 57–8
coordinated capitalism 67
Corps Moenania 26
Corps Teutonia 26
Crane, Joan 71, 170
CSU viii, 143, 154
Cusworth, George E. 74

Daimler, Corp. 1, 148
Davenport, John 119, 172
De Gaulle, Charles 118, 150, 183
decartelization 62–4, 65, 67, 69, 71, 73, 75, 77, 79, 81, 83, 85–6, 118, 131, 136, 168, 183
decolonization 114, 129
deconcentration v, 8, 51, 62–5, 67, 69–73, 75, 77–86, 90–2, 95, 98, 101–2, 105, 109–14, 117–18, 124, 129, 131–6, 139, 142, 146, 152, 159–60, 168–73, 181, 184
Deist, Heinrich 104–5, 108, 117–18, 177–8
Demag Corp. 29, 43, 47
democratization 81
denazification 7, 11, 18, 44, 52, 82, 161

Denmark 24, 16
deportations 26–7, 147
Deutsche Bank 29, 145, 164, 181
Deutsche Jägerschaft 18
Deutsche Zeitung 131
Deutschmark 88
DGAP viii, 150
DGB viii, 93–108, 115–18, 124, 129–30, 143, 173–8
Dichgans, Hans 127, 179–80
Die Zeit 122, 156, 185
DIHT viii, 101, 175, 184
Dinkelbach, Heinrich 38, 44, 50, 54, 60–2, 64, 72–81, 83–5, 91–3, 98, 109, 111, 115, 134, 142, 168, 171, 176
dismantling v, 31, 42, 62–5, 67, 69–71, 73, 75, 77, 79, 81, 83–5, 88, 90, 112–14, 120, 129, 134, 142, 159, 168
DKBL viii, 108, 133
DKV viii, 133
DNVP viii, 37
Draper, Wiilliam 89, 111, 169
Dresdner Bank 133
Du Pond Corp. 38, 120, 132, 166, 181
Dulles, John F. 127
Dunkirk 118

ECSC viii, 8, 89–90, 98, 103–4, 110–11, 123, 126, 129–30, 132, 142–3, 146–7, 149–50, 157, 181, 184
Eden, Anthony 114
EEC viii, 150
EFTA viii, 150
Eisenhower, Dwight D. 114
Eisenhüttenwerke 74
Eisenkreis 167–8, 171–2
Emden 22
Empire and Commonwealth 17, 21, 114, 120, 149, 187
Erhard, Ludwig 64, 69, 88, 90, 95, 98, 107, 126, 152–6, 174, 183–4
Erler, Fritz 143
Eselheide 8, 28, 41–4, 46, 61, 72, 143, 149
Eucken, Walther 152
Eyrich, Erich 26

Falkenhausen, Gotthard von 98, 178
Farbwerke Hoechst 132
FDP viii, 107, 176

Ferry, Jacques 124
Flick, Friedrich 36, 143, 148, 162
Florian, Karl Friedrich 20, 25, 30, 162–3
Föcher, Matthias 117
Ford Motor Company 66–7, 169, 187
Fortune 89, 119, 155, 172, 184–5
Fragebogen 7
France 14, 24–5, 63, 90, 114, 118–20, 122, 125, 131, 135, 149, 177–8, 187
Franconia 3, 9, 12
Freitag, Walter 99, 104–5, 108, 117, 143
Freytag, Hermann 24
Friedlaender, Ernst 122
Friedrich, Otto A. 161, 169, 182–5
Fugmann, Bruno 46, 166

Gauleiter 4, 22–3, 27, 30
G. Henle Music Publishing 5, 159
Gentz, Ludwig 76, 171
GEORG viii, 24, 35, 52, 133
Georgsmarienhütte 1, 20, 30, 70, 134, 140, 162, 181
Gestapo 20, 26–7
GHH viii, 35, 74, 76–8, 82, 91, 109, 162
Gleitsmann, Georg 52
Goebbels, Joseph 27, 31, 70
Goergen, Fritz-Aurel 125, 180
Göring ix, 4, 22, 23–4, 28
Great Depression 12, 20, 121
Grosse, Franz 117
Gruner, Wolf 27, 165
Günther, Eberhard 153, 174

Haffner, Alexander 155
Hallstein, Walter 124–5, 127–8, 130, 136
Handelsblatt 184
Hansen, Werner 52, 73
Harig, Paul 48–51, 59, 167–8
Harriman, Averell 128
Harris-Burland, William 61–2, 64, 72–5, 78–8183–5, 91–6, 99, 109, 111–2, 134, 142, 170
Harvard Business School 144
Harzburg Academy 144, 183
Haspe 20, 59, 74–5, 79, 82, 84, 134, 140, 172
Hassouna, Abdel Kalek 150
Hattenheim Conferences 93–6, 99, 116, 173
Hauck, Jacobus von 13

Haus Hartenfels 29–30
Heinemann, Gustav 129
Henle, Günter, passim
Henle, Julius von 9–14
Henle, Otto 9
Hermichen, Rolf 144, 183
Herschbach 25, 28
Hesse 24–5, 92, 95, 115–16
Heydrich, Reinhard 27
HICOG viii, 117, 136, 184
High Authority 125–8, 130, 132, 142, 146, 149–50
High Commission viii, 69, 86, 92, 97–8, 101, 115, 117, 129, 131–3, 136, 153, 175, 184
Himmler, Heinrich 4, 27, 29, 165
Hirsch, Etienne 124
Hitler, Adolf vii, 3–4, 6, 12–13, 17–18, 20–3, 27–30, 33, 38, 44, 46–7, 57, 67, 97, 117–18, 134, 136, 143, 147, 154, 159–60, 163, 165, 187–8
Hoegner, Wilhelm 13
Hoelz, Max 15
Hoerder Verein 74, 78–9, 178
Hoesch, Leopold von 17–18
Hoffman, Paul 85–6, 89, 111, 122–3, 126, 172
Höhn, Reinhard 144, 183
Houdremont, Eduard 32, 35
Hueck, Heinrich 103–6, 176
Hugenberg, Alfred 37
Hull, Cordell 121
Hynd 76

ICI Corp. viii, 133
IG Farben 68–9, 86, 112–13, 132–3, 180, 187
IG Metall 118
Industriekurier 122, 172, 183–4
International Ruhr Authority viii, 120
IRA viii, 120
IRC viii, 121–2, 126, 130
IREC 121
Israel 6, 151
Italy 25, 68, 120, 123, 177

Japan 68, 133
Jarres, Karl 4, 24, 32, 44, 46–64, 72, 75, 77–84, 91, 93, 102, 109, 143, 147, 163–4, 167–8, 171–2, 175

JCS 1067 68
JCS ix, 31
Josten, Paul 152–3, 184

Kaiser, Jakob 14, 107
Kapp-Putsch 15
Karstadt Corp. 144
Kartellgesetzgebung 168
Kastl, Ludwig 124, 180
Keller, Paul 76, 171
Keynesianism 20, 90
KHD ix, 24, 38, 44, 69–70, 134, 139–42,
    145, 151, 163
Kimmich, Karl 28, 145, 164
Klasen, Karl. 145
Kleiber, Carlos 16
Kleiber, Erich 16
Klöckner & Co. vii, 4–5, 20–1, 26–31,
    44, 102, 139–40, 142, 145–6, 149,
    151, 162–4
Klöckner A.G. 5, 19–20, 24, 30, 34, 38,
    48, 63, 78, 84, 136, 139, 141–2, 145–6,
    149, 151
Klöckner, Anne-Liese 18–19, 26, 37,
    42, 150
Klöckner, Florian 24
Klöckner, Peter 3, 19–23, 37
Klöckner, Waldemar 21
Klotzbach, Arthur 148
Koch, Robert 9
Koerner, Paul 147, 164
Kohlenverkauf viii, 133
Königswinter Conferences 148–9
Korsch, Hans 108
Kost, Heinrich 51, 53, 103–6, 108, 133
Kransberg 36
Krekeler, Heinrich 116–17, 178
Krupp, Corp. 1, 7, 20, 32, 35–6, 46, 143,
    148, 155, 161–2, 178, 187
Kuhnke, Hans-Helmut 77, 102, 171, 175

Labour 31, 42, 44, 72, 74, 76, 90, 111, 114
Lamond, Frederick 15
Lampe, Walter 14–15, 25
Law No. 22, 57–9, 62
Law No. 27, 92, 95, 97, 99, 101, 105,
    110–11, 114–5, 129, 131–2, 173
Law No. 56, 111
Law No. 75, 85, 100, 111–12, 114

Le Monde 128
Lehr, Robert 18, 33, 37–8, 43–4, 51, 53–6,
    59, 76, 99–101, 109, 112–13, 129–30,
    143, 166, 171, 175
Lend-Lease 31, 118
Lenz, Franz 51, 176
Ley, Robert 97
Lloyd George, David 16
Lobeck, Max 77, 166
Locarno Treaty 16, 121
Lorraine 19–20, 120–1, 123, 179
Lotz, Kurt 148
Lübsen, Georg 35, 162
Ludendorff, Erich 12
Luther, Hans 16

Magirus Corp. 1, 20, 142
Malone, George W. 71
MAN 1, 39, 56, 73, 75, 80, 99, 110, 145,
    155, 163, 169, 187
Mannesmann Corp. 30, 38, 77, 101–2,
    147, 155, 162, 171
Maria Laach 95, 174
Marotzke, Wilhelm 25, 164
Marshall Plan viii, 85, 90, 107, 122, 135
Marshall, George F. 71, 111, 165, 170
Mason, Edward 136, 169
McCloy, John J. 6, 89, 92, 95, 99, 101,
    115–18, 127, 131, 133, 136, 173, 175, 178
Menges, Dietrich von 152, 169, 181
Merkle, Hans L. 145
Merton, Richard 148
Metallgesellschaft 148
Meyer, Beate 26, 164
Middelviefhaus, Clemens 125
Military Keynesianism 20
Mitbestimmung, *see* codetermination
    168, 173
Mitbestimmungsgesetz 111
Mixed marriages 4, 14, 27, 143
Monnet, Jean 114, 118–20, 122–4, 126–31,
    142, 146, 149–50, 178, 187
monopolies 65–8, 112–13, 128, 130, 152
Montanmitbestimmung, *see* parity
    codetermination
Morgenthau, Henry 5, 31, 70, 131,
    165, 170
Müller, Max C 125
Muthesius, Volkmar 25, 164

NAM ix, 116–18
Narvik 24
NATO ix, 129, 160
Nazi Party 18, 52
Nazism 3, 8, 43, 72, 97, 187
neoliberalism 90
Netherlands 3–4, 25, 120
Neurath, Konstantin von 17
New Deal 20, 90, 114
NGCC ix, 64, 72
NGISC ix, 61, 64, 72, 75–6, 78–9, 83, 85, 111, 171
Nipperdey, Hans-Carl 58
Nordwest Group 33–4, 34–7, 44, 54, 167
Norway 22, 88
NSBO ix, 33
Nuremberg laws 3, 13, 17
Nuremberg trials 143
NV Handelsmatschaappij 140
Nyerere, Julius 150

Oberpräsidium 33–4, 37, 53, 55, 166
Occupation Statute 91
oligopolies 68, 113, 121, 130, 132, 152, 183
OMGUS ix, 86, 111–12, 169
Opel Works 24–5, 163
Open Door 5, 69, 86, 91, 113, 119, 121, 131, 141
Ordoliberalism 152, 184
Osnabrück Steel Works 1, 20, 162

Panzer-Rohland 34–5
Papen, Franz von 17, 46
parity codetermination 6, 52–3, 62, 74, 76–7, 81, 84, 91–2, 96–8, 103, 108, 116, 129–30, 142, 160
Pax Americana 63, 114, 119, 159
Pferdmenges, Robert 25, 39, 46, 53, 103–4, 106–8, 110, 176–7
Piesberg Quarries 30, 84, 134
Pleiger, Paul 21, 147
Poensgen, Ernst 21, 24, 32, 147, 162
Pogrom, November 1938 14, 26, 33
Pohle, Wolfgang 30, 177
Poland 24, 26–8
Potsdam Agreements 48, 51, 68, 80, 111
Potthoff, Erich 75–6, 78, 171, 178
Productivity Councils 86

Quebec Conference 31, 70
Quint Works 20

Rathenau, Walther 16
Raymond, Walter 93–7, 101, 107, 132, 173–6, 181, 187
Reagan, Ronald 90, 170
Reich Court 65, 168
Reichsluftschutzbund 18
Reichsmark 76, 88
Reichssicherheitshauptamt 27
Reichswerke Hermann Göring ix, 4, 21
reparations 31, 71, 120
Reusch, Hermann 50–1, 54, 59–62, 64, 72, 76–83, 87, 91, 93, 97, 109, 129, 137, 153, 160, 167–8, 171
Reusch, Paul 30
Reuter, Hans vi, 29, 43
Reuther, Walther 115–16
Rheinstahl Corp. 155
Ribbentrop, Joachim von 3, 17–18
Richter, Willy 93, 173
Risse, Roland 153
Robertson, Brian, Sir 112, 177
Röchling, Hermann 36, 143, 162
Rohland, Walter 25, 32–6, 44, 147, 153, 165
Roosevelt, Franklin D. 20, 31, 67–8, 70, 90, 118, 170
Rosen, Friedrich 16
Rosenberg, Ludwig 143
Rosenstrasse 27, 148, 164–5
RWHG ix, 21, 24, 162

SA ix, 13
Scheuble, Julius 51
Schmid, Carlo 143
Schmidt, August vi, 99, 117
Schroeder, Gerhard 84, 102, 108, 167, 172, 175
Schumacher, Kurt 74
Schuman Plan 90, 98, 111, 118, 120, 123–32, 136, 179, 184
Schuman, Robert 120, 123, 125, 127, 179
Schwede, Walter 22, 42, 121, 162–3, 176
Second Industrial Revolution 65, 148
Severing 46–50, 54, 56, 167
Sherman Act 66–8, 130, 153
Siemens Corp. 70, 133–4, 141, 144–6, 181

SKF 146
Social Catholicism 175, 184
Sohl, Hans Günther vi, 6, 29–30, 34, 414,
    100–2, 104, 109–10, 136, 143, 147, 161,
    163, 165–6, 170, 175–8, 180–3
Soviet Union 21–2, 24, 26–7, 31, 42, 71,
    90, 135
SPD ix, 96–8, 174
Speer, Albert 25, 29, 34–5, 125, 147. 187
Sprenger, Jacob 24
SS ix, 4, 6, 27, 29, 41–2, 144, 164
Stahlwerke AG ix, 21, 42, 60, 64, 68–9, 72,
    74, 76, 86, 92, 133–4
Steel Works Association 21, 25. 162–3
Stokes, Raymond G. 132, 181, 187
Stoltzfus, Nathan 27, 165. 188
Storch, Anton 94–5, 97, 99
Stresemann, Gustav 16–17, 121
Strohmenger, Karl 51–2, 56–7, 59, 61,
    75–6, 78, 167–8, 171
Studebaker Corp. 66, 85
Studeny, Herma 14
Suez Crisis 114
Sweden 24, 141
syndicates 65–6, 68, 112, 121, 130,
    152, 169

Terboven, Josef 24–5, 82, 147, 163
Teutonia Club 13
Thant, U 150
Thomas, Georg 24, 75, 166, 168
Thomas, Michael 42
Thyssen Corp. viii, 1, 6, 24, 133, 178
Trade unions 4, 8, 15, 33, 36, 44, 47, 50–1,
    53–5, 57–64, 72, 84, 90–4, 98, 100–4,
    106–8, 111, 116–18, 124, 129, 142, 147,
    160, 174, 176, 187
Treuhand-Vereinigung ix, 92, 173
Treuhandverwaltung 64, 111
TrHV ix, 64, 72–4, 76–9, 81, 83–5, 92, 98,
    112, 114, 171, 174
Tri-Zone 114
Troisdorf Works 1, 20, 51, 56, 84, 135,
    162, 167
Truman, Harry 31, 153, 184

UK iv, 85, 92, 111, 114, 134
Usinor 119
Utley, Freda 71, 170

Van Tyll van Serooskerken, Baroness 16
Vaubel, Ludwig 144, 182
VDEh ix, 36
Verbundwirtschaft 19, 69, 72, 101, 110,
    115, 133, 140
Vereinigte Glanzstoff-Fabriken 144, 146
Viktor Mine 77, 134
Villiers, Georges 121
Vits, Hellmut 146
Vogel, Otto 97, 100, 116, 174
Vögler, Albert 147
Volkswirt 156, 185
Vom Hoff, Hans 97–9, 104, 108,
    168, 173–4
VSt ix, 21–2, 24–5, 29, 32–6, 38, 50, 60, 64,
    8, 77, 83, 98, 100, 103–4, 112–13, 121,
    147, 162, 168, 176
VWD 184

Wagner, Alfons 115, 178
Western Front 3, 14
Widmann, Eleonore, Edle von 9
Willner, Sidney 131–2, 184
Winkhaus, Hermann 101–2, 175
Witzleben, Wolf-Dietrich von 144
Wolff, Otto 74, 109, 147
Wolff von Amerongen, Otto 147
Works Council 46–51, 53–4, 57, 60, 75, 93,
    115, 142, 167
WSJ ix, 154, 156, 184–5
Württemberg 92, 95, 115–16, 141
Würzburg 3, 12–15, 26
Wuppertal Circle 144
WVESI ix, 33–5, 50, 53, 60, 62, 76–8, 83–
    4, 122, 125–6, 130, 167–8, 171–2, 177

Yad Vashem 6, 161

Zangen, Wilhelm 102, 147, 162, 175, 177
Zellstoff Waldhof 155
Ziervogel, F. W. 156